THE SHELL BOOK OF

BRITISH BUILDINGS

THE SHELL BOOK OF
BRITISH BUILDINGS

ANTHONY McINTYRE

DAVID & CHARLES
Newton Abbot   London   North Pomfret (Vt)

*Photographs by the author, except
where otherwise stated.*

Line illustrations by Emma Tovey

*Shell U.K. Limited, while sponsoring this book,
would point out that the author is expressing
his own views.*

British Library Cataloguing in Publication Data

McIntyre, Anthony
  British buildings
    1. Architecture — Great Britain — History
    I. Title
    720'.941   NA967

    ISBN 0-7153-8122-9

Typeset by ABM Typographics Limited, Hull
and printed in Great Britain
by Butler & Tanner Ltd, Frome and London
for David & Charles (Publishers) Limited
Brunel House Newton Abbot Devon

Published in the United States of America
by David & Charles Inc
North Pomfret Vermont 05053 USA

Contents

To my parents
and to
Barbara Wace

Introduction

A book on architecture can spend too long describing what people are perfectly capable of seeing with their own eyes. The only justifiable way to write about a visual art is to discuss its non-visual aspects. The ancient Chinese calculated that there were not five senses, but six: the five we know, and additionally the mind. The purpose of this book is to explore architecture with that sixth sense.

As a result I have written a series of nine chapters, the first five based on the history of buildings in Britain, and the final four based on specific themes that run unchanging through that history. The historical chapters are not in any sense an academic history of art. They present, rather, a more or less familiar pattern of history, and try to put that pattern into a broader context of social development. Obviously the whole history of British building could not have been presented here, but by focusing closely on several particular events in each period, it has at least been possible to illuminate certain important events and issues.

The final four chapters are designed to overcome the limitations to some extent inherent in the historical approach, and to help provide a method for readers to extend their own thoughts about buildings. Each is based on a theme — Technology, Power, Nature, and Cities — and follows its particular argument by looking in detail at several buildings from different ages. I hope that these chapters in particular will help to make many of the abstract issues of architecture, the issues of that sixth sense, accessible by illustration with concrete examples.

It may interest people to know how this book came to be called the *Shell Book of British Buildings*. Shell do not commission books, and this one was finished before it was sent to them for possible inclusion in their well-known series. So the work, although now part of that series, was written and remains as a rather personal view of the subject. Although the book of course provides the basic bones of historical fact, the Shell label should not mislead readers into thinking that it represents the 'official' word on the subject, or that Shell bear any responsibility for its contents.

As to the physical organization of the material, a few words only are needed. Buildings that illustrate the nine chapters of text are not necessarily accessible to the public, and a few no longer exist, but those that are will be found listed in the Gazetteer. The great majority of Gazetteer entries are buildings actually open to the public; there are some, however, that are not, but all are at least clearly visible from public property. Churches have not been included except where they illustrate a general architectural point particularly well. This was necessary if the whole Gazetteer was not to be taken over by churches. I hope that this part of the book will be used to encourage voyages of discovery as much as bee-line visits to the buildings mentioned. Britain is a country not vastly rich in palatial or grand architecture. Its architectural wealth tends to be widely distributed, so that almost every town and village can provide examples of buildings that show a standard of inventiveness and skill in the solution of particular building problems, far above what can be found in many other countries, even where these may be better able to show a good deal of palatial grandeur. The personal qualities of a designer or craftsman can be just as well reflected in a small and simple work as in one that is large and complex, perhaps better. But one's eyes must be open and looking. You may find the building you have sought to be quite different from what you expected, perhaps not of any special interest to you (though I have kept Doctor Johnson's comment in mind, 'Worth seeing, yes; but is it worth *going* to see?', and have tried to make sure that they are). But there will always be something on or near the way that is of interest. It was an hour with nothing in particular to fill it that led me to the Roman villa at East End, which in turn began thoughts of cities and empires, and ended as Chapter 9 of this book.

Sic monumentum requiris, circumspice is Wren's epitaph in St Paul's Cathedral: 'If you seek a monument, look about you'. It could stand alone as an introduction to architecture; the stress, of course, would be on *circumspice* — 'look about you'.

1
After Noah

> We carry with us the wonders we seek without us: there is all
> Africa and her prodigies in us; we are that bold and adventurous
> piece of Nature, which he that studies wisely learns in a com-
> pendium what others labour at in a divided piece and endless
> volume . . .
>
> Sir Thomas Browne, *Religio Medici,* 1635

This discussion of buildings in Britain starts with some very early examples
of monumental architecture. Before we can go on to look at the practical
aspects of buildings and their uses, we must be clear about the spiritual or
monumental aspects which cause these buildings to take on certain forms at
different times. These are the themes that provide continuity in the art of
architecture, and they remain ever accessible to those who seek them; they
are as much within as without us.

The quotation which heads this chapter tells an important truth: it
identifies man with the external world as a creation of nature. It is in this
light that we will look at the Neolithic monuments of Avebury, in Wiltshire.
We will be talking about the origins of architecture. Many theories have
been put forward about the possible use of these monuments, but before
looking at those, a brief description of the people who built them and their
culture will be helpful.

Neolithic culture began with an economic change from a nomadic existence of hunting and fishing, to a relatively settled life of mixed agriculture.
The people who brought these changes to Britain came between 5000 and
4000BC. The implements they worked with were mostly of bone, wood or
stone, and that stone was mainly flint, precisely the stone to be found in
chalklands, so their settlement on the Downs was not accidental. For two
thousand years or so their way of life continued, until first modified and
finally superseded by the arrival of the so-called Beaker People ('one of those
waves of which history is chiefly composed' as the authors of *1066 and All
That* would have it) who brought the first metals to these islands, and
eventually developed bronze.

In spite of the fact that their monuments were built using antlers for picks,

(left) All children are familiar with the act of picking up and treasuring stones. Here at Avebury, a number of people have acted together, chosen slabs of stone and mounted them in the earth, in one of the most simple of architectural gestures; *(right)* Inside West Kennet Long Barrow, there is a man-made cave, where ancestral bones were kept and occasionally visited, a notion not too distant from that of the Christian charnel house or family tomb

baskets to carry stone and ropes made of rawhide, Neolithic man should not necessarily be considered devoid of intellectual or imaginative power. At its lowest level there seems as much point in their activity, digging massive sarsens out of the chalk, as there is in ours, digging their broken pots out from under those stones. Neither were they naïve or innocent. Was it mere happy coincidence that, when human sacrifice was needed, a stranger made a much more satisfactory and propitious offering to the gods than a local man or woman? So, primitive as their architecture may be in refinement of expression, it should not be dismissed as simple-minded.

It would be pointless to dwell too long on the many theories concerning the supposed practical purposes of these stones, to graze in what Aubery Burl, in his book on stone circles, has called the 'lush, lunatic pastures' that surround the field of archaeology. Each age interprets monuments in its own image, and because it has been common for us to believe that science is the key which can unlock the mysteries of our universe, Stone Age monuments must be landing pads for flying saucers (a book was written about that one) or astronomical laboratories of the highest complexity. But apart from the fact that science is clearly not the key to the universe — even mathematicians like Whitehead insisted on this — there is no trace of evidence that such a highly developed mathematics existed. In cultures with refined geometrical knowledge, in Egypt and Greece, the geometry comes out clearly in buildings; it is not hidden away in obscure conjectural relations. And what was the supposed purpose of elaborate calculation and observation? Planting crops demands only the simplest of calendars. Beyond which, no one has proven that any of these circles actually works as a complex instrument. The geometrical gymnastics necessary to explain the dubious functions of stone rings reminds one of nothing so much as the pre-Copernican diagrams of planetary motion. These theories suffer not from an excess, but a paucity, of imagination; 'From a perception of only 3 senses or 3 elements, none could deduce a fourth or fifth', as William Blake observed.

The observations Neolithic man made were of a more subtle nature, and if we are talking about the determination of equinoxes, one is reminded again of Sir Thomas Browne: 'The number of the dead long exceedeth all that shall live. The night of time far surpasseth the day, and who knows when was the Aequinox? Every hour adds unto that current Arithmetique which scarce stands one moment.'

The point that is worth studying, since we are dealing with monumental architecture and not machinery, is the simple gesture of removing stones from the earth and standing them upright in it. The interpretation of this gesture as analogous to the placing of human bones in the earth will be discussed specifically in relation to the stone circles, but mention should be made here that there are two facts supporting what might be called a human view of stone. The first is the very name, sarsen, given to the large sandstone blocks that form these ancient rings, which is corrupted from Saracen: that is, infidel. The second is the legend current throughout the world about the origin of stone circles, that they were groups of brides or maidens, suddenly threatened by some evil, and turned to stone as they danced in their ring. They were not killed, but transformed.

West Kennet Long Barrow

Avebury's first monument was the West Kennet Long Barrow, built some 3250 years BC. To give some comparison, this is five centuries before the first Egyptian pyramids. Alas, the themes of primitive monuments are somewhat heavy, dividing as they do simply between life and death. At least as themes they are all-encompassing, as we know from the Russian novel. At any rate, West Kennet is a hill some 330 feet long, made of chalk and sarsens and

11

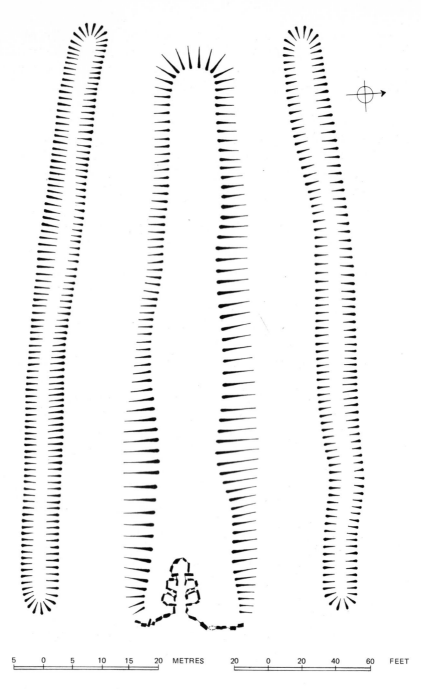

5   0   5   10   15   20   METRES   20   0   20   40   60   FEET

Plan of West Kennet Long Barrow, showing the relationship between the five chambers at its east end, and the long artificial hill that extends toward the west flanked by ditches. At its east end is a series of five chambers, to which bones were brought — bodies were not buried here — and taken away occasionally for ceremonial use. The chambers themselves are quite large, 7–8 feet high, and made from large limestone slabs. These were brought from a source 20 miles distant. The mound's beauty, architecturally, is that it is not, as one might suppose, symbolic. A symbolic cave can be constructed anywhere (provided it has an original) and they were constructed at Avebury. But a real cave is found in a hill or mountainside, and if you need a real cave in a flattish landscape the only answer is to build a hill to put one in. This then becomes a real cave, the master copy from which, perhaps, symbols were derived and used for the storage of real bones, themselves removed from time to time and used in symbolic rites. The necessity of reality as a source of inspiration is still apparent, and when Venice decided in the ninth century that it wanted to be a great republic, it recognized the need for such a source, stealing the bones of St Mark from Constantinople and building their splendid cave to house them.

Silbury Hill

Although Avebury's second building was a place now called the Sanctuary, nothing now remains apart from post holes. But third on the landscape was Silbury Hill, and here we are immediately in the presence of the largest man-made hill in Europe, begun around 2750BC, a time of known agricultural prosperity. The construction of Silbury Hill, which after five thousand years

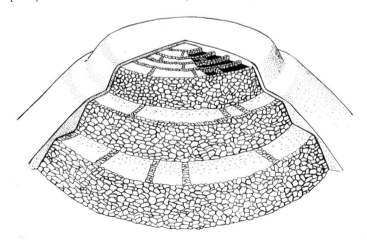

Schematic section of Silbury Hill. The radial and ring walls form structural cells, these are filled with rubble, and the whole covered with a layer of earth and turf

Silbury Hill sits in the landscape like an expression of its fertility, and obviously only made possible by agricultural success. In this respect it is the very essence of monumental architecture

shows almost no signs of weathering, is in itself an extraordinary technical achievement. To measure the hill's volume in Neolithic terms, in basket loads of chalk rubble, is almost painful: 35,000,000 loads, 'passed around the rising sides of the mound from person to person in a long spiralling chain'. This rubble was packed into the hollow cells of a primary supporting structure, consisting of a series of concentric rings built of chalk, connected and strengthened by radial walls. The finished whole was smoothed off and covered with turf, which helps explain the absence of erosion; but beyond that, there has been little if any settlement of the giant hill. This would perhaps seem more remarkable to our eyes if it were covered with roof tiles rather than grass. Construction time is estimated to have been in the order of 18,000,000 man hours. Discrepancies in carbon-dating methods make it unclear whether this represents a massive ten year effort, or a more realistic, though hardly leisurely, span of one hundred and fifty years.

The fact that several extensive excavations have uncovered no sign of burial in this mound, but at its centre located only a heap of rich fertile soil, and from the fact of its construction beside a natural spring, it appears that this monument's theme is birth, not death. We know from other sources that ceremonies of death had connotations of dryness, whereas here we find fertility and moisture. Bones were often burnt before burial to make sure they were quite dry (bone dry?), a pre-condition of the soul's escape from the body. The existence of two other artificial hills nearby, at Hatfield Barrow and Marlborough, though of nothing like the same size, implies an architectural purpose rather than a scientific or mystical one. Silbury Hill acts as a marker of local success and a demonstration of the land's fertility, made visible in stone. In size it is proportional to agricultural surplus. Or to put it another way, the mound itself grew out of the earth's fertility. The proof of this lies perhaps in the story of the hill's construction. To begin with, the base diameter was 50 yards less than its final 165 yards. Now had it been intended to use the construction for scientific purposes, its necessary size would have been predetermined. As it was, only when it became apparent that things were going rather better than expected did the monument follow the corollary of Parkinson's Law, expanding to consume the economic surplus available. Everyone knows, or should be told, that this is what architecture is for. The further representational uses of Silbury Hill will be discussed a little later.

Cows, stones and modern concrete obelisk. This little concrete marker shows the position where a stone once stood. Many of the sarsens were taken down and buried in the Middle Ages, put back into the earth from which they had been so hard won, because they were regarded as pagan beings

These rings were set up with much the same intentions that have in some ages inspired people to cover their buildings with statues, as at Wells Cathedral, or in others to fill buildings with images of their ancestors, like the National Portrait Gallery. These stones each have a number, but it would be safe to assume that each once had a name

The Stone Circles

Finally in this series comes Avebury proper, a vast stone circle that today encloses a town, and the two smaller rings within it from an earlier age. The rings were composed of giant sarsens, stones formed by the slow deposit of sandstone on an ocean bed and the subsequent breaking up of this layer when the ocean disappeared. These fragments were washed on to the Downs during the last ice age, where they lay embedded in chalk awaiting a use. Transporting these the 2 miles from where they lay to Avebury was again a miracle of effort. The ropes to haul them were made of plaited rawhide, and it is estimated that ropes sufficient for hauling an average 50-ton sarsen demanded the skins from a hundred cattle. Each stone's journey then lasted two or three days, a hundred men pulling at the ropes, and at last they were perched upright in prepared holes, packed tight with clay and small stones. These massive rocks were hauled off the hillsides and used as found, not dressed or altered in any way. And so they stand there today, vertical memories of a fluid existence; mobility transformed, as the brides were, into stone.

Whatever rituals were performed by Avebury's builders will certainly have been performed in circles, a shape that offers unity and is the most obvious gesture to mark off a place as being particular on a large surface. But a circle does not necessarily offer protection, and certainly these large stones, those of the smaller circles built long before the earthwork enclosure, offer none. The reason for their erection must be something different. Their architectural function is to represent the transformation of life into death, of dynamic matter into static. The stones are large statues, together forming a society of the dead, or 'transformed'. Dry bones of ancestors, though not all of them, were stored in West Kennet Long Barrow, as we have seen, taken out for some kinds of ceremony and usually replaced. The stones represent a different kind of death, but retain this quality of being very dry things that once were very wet. Because of the way they were formed, they still convey this watery nature. At Stoney Littleton in Somerset, a slab stone stands at the long barrow entrance, bearing the impression of a fossil ammonite that measures about 2 feet across. What better representation could there be of life rendered static, but also rendered permanent?

It is just at this point that man and architecture become inseparable in the mind. Having had the world forced upon him, its image necessarily his, man has forced his own image back on to the world and made the rocks themselves represent him around his places of ceremony. It is not so much harmony with nature as a hard won equality with it.

That image stamped mentally into the stones endures with the stones themselves. In medieval times these 'infidel Saracens' were thought of as objects too overtly pagan to be allowed to stand. They were not removed to distant fields, nor were they destroyed, but were buried like dead bodies. From this fate many have been recovered. But in a later age of science, puritanism and utility, at the same time that a Marlborough doctor was digging bones from the Sanctuary and grinding them into medicine, the locals were smashing up the old stones for use as building materials.

Those who searched Silbury Hill for bodies found nothing but soil. Those who dug in Avebury's circles for a central object, too, found a small pit of soil and nothing more. Signs of an obelisk were discovered, but not centrally. Why we should be so keen to look at the centre of a thing for some special object is not clear. A moment's thought tells us that the centre is a place not of things but of potential, not of the static object but of the spirit that gives it life. Again, Blake saw that: 'Man's desires are limited by his perceptions; none can desire what he has not perceived.'

17

A characteristic of sarsen stones is that they have a very pronounced back and front —
geologically top and bottom, but here turned upright. Without having to try to see faces in
the stones, which is a rather meaningless exercise, one can still see that this front and back
make the stones somehow intelligible as representatives of human presence. Judging from
the thousands of people who visit these monuments every year, they must be as accessible,
mysterious and provocative as people are. And what more could one expect from architecture
than that it should convey humanity?

Thirty spokes
Share one hub.
Adapt the nothing therein to the purpose in hand, and you will have the use of the cart. Knead clay in order to make a vessel. Adapt the nothing therein to the purpose in hand, and you will have the use of the vessel. Cut doors and windows in order to make a room. Adapt the nothing therein to the purpose in hand, and you will have the use of the room. Thus what we gain is Something, yet it is by virtue of Nothing that this can be put to use.   Lao Tzu

Churches are places of ritual, and are empty. The main square of a town is a square 'by virtue of its nothing', and is available for numerous uses precisely because its space has not been defined *a priori* in functional terms. Philosophically speaking most cultures believe that the world was created out of nothing. How else would you build an architectural image of that belief other than by constructing a large mound of impenetrable matter, at its centre only fertile earth, the condition of growth and not the thing that grows? Or by building a perimeter of history, and leaving the space it defines free for the spirit of creation made evident in ritual?

Here we have an architecture of statues, obelisks, a little wet soil; one can imagine it in use, the light of fires at night time illuminating the faceted statues and adding flickers of life to them, dancing shadows. And having been brought to life, they stand behind the living not so much to protect them as to witness their actions. The dead have not ceased to exist, the living are not growing more distant from their past. (This should be clear to us: we regard Neolithic culture as consisting of more or less the same people living over and over again for several thousand years, referring to 'Neolithic men' as though to a large family.) The dead stand in their ring, and like modern man in a room full of family portraits, the living feel the dispassionate pressure of watching eyes from a past that seems far from dead.

Or to take another modern example, there is Don Juan at the end of his escapades, shaking hands with a stone statue that had come to life, that had the power to drag him off to hell for his observed sins ('No, no, ch'io non mi pento . . .'; 'No, no I'll never repent') though presumably this lithic power would have been equally capable of less dismal actions if circumstances had been more agreeable.

The point of looking at these monuments has been that they show architecture in an early and unrefined state. It strikes me too that their size and frequency makes them of considerably greater importance than the fragmentary remains of Saxon door posts that usually illustrate the first chapter in a book concerned with architectural history. They have long lain like giant objects of modern art: we feel they are very important but can't quite sort out what they mean. Now that we know, we can jump over the Saxon door posts and land on the south coast with William the Conqueror.

2

Conquests, Castles
and Churches

As with many revolutionary events, the Norman Conquest may be said to
have been a beneficial event in the long run, but few people would relish the
idea of having lived in England at that time, when a parochial culture was
made subject to the imposition of fully developed feudalism. Yet it appears
that the feudal system itself was disintegrating within two centuries of its
introduction, while the political unity of England, in spite of regional
disputes, was gradually institutionalised. As the middle classes separated
themselves from the top and bottom of society, they made workers their
servants, but they made their apparent masters, the military rulers, their
servants too. And as the cathedral changed from being a type of palace to
become the communal expression of belief in order, partly disguised in the
stylistic change from Romanesque to Gothic, so during this medieval period
the castle gradually developed from being the fortified posts of an invading
army, turned inwards on the populace and located mainly inland, to being
the military equipment of that populace, sited along the nation's borders.

The architecture of the Middle Ages may be divided usefully into two
categories; one based upon manipulation of physical force, associated with
land, and another associated with money, gained and deployed by intellectual force. Castles in Normandy had proven so effective as weapons of war,
and William was so convinced of their military importance, that when he
sailed across the channel on 28 September 1066, he brought one with him,
prefabricated, dismantled and neatly packed. Sufficiently French to make his
first order on arrival the request for dinner, his second order was for the
erection of the timber castle, which was apparently complete by evening. So
the castle arrived quite literally with the Conquest.

The Private Fortress

The essence of a castle is its privateness, and it is this that mainly distin-
guishes it from Saxon fortifications. Those had been built of earth, timber or

The keep of Castle Hedingham was built around 1130, and is one of the most monumental of Norman castles. So eager were its builders to impress that they brought stone from Northamptonshire for the work, which is only rendered mildly less serious by the modern insertion of what looks like a pair of garages at ground level

stone, for the defence of a community under attack and were not places where people lived continuously. But the castle was a fortified house, and as he made his way through England, William consolidated his victories by erecting timber castles as he went, installing some relation or political ally to introduce and enforce feudal principles. These castles, such as that at Castle Acre, were of a type known as 'motte and bailey', from the fact that there was an artificial hill or motte on which stood a timber palisade, and at its foot an area enclosed by earthworks, called a bailey. The lord and his family lived at the top of the hill, his garrison in the bailey. William's success was a

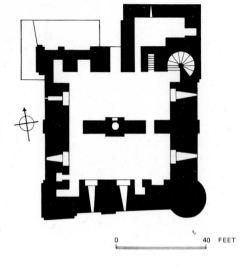

Rochester Castle, showing the rebuilt circular corner tower to the south east

function of the great number of castles he built — many hundreds in all — and the relentless methods he used practically to enslave the native population.

Since forced labour was used to build these castles, construction techniques were of necessity those familiar to the Saxon culture. It seems that stone was widely used and understood as a Saxon building material, as of course was wood, so it was not really a technical superiority that the Normans used to defeat the Anglo-Saxons. Their redefinition of a fortification as a private stronghold, replacing the native community defences: that was the novelty.

The sense of isolation produced by this social structure was obviously profound, and the lack of trust it induced was reflected in castle design. The custom in medieval castles was for the currently trusted man, like Macbeth's porter, more or less hasty, to scurry across the turf each night to the Lord's chamber, which was set apart, and place the key to the outer chamber under his master's pillow for safe keeping.

Rochester Castle was originally of the motte-and-bailey type, built just on the town's edge with one eye to domination, the other to escape. Of such importance was this site that in 1087 a new castle, of stone, was built on a

Time and light fingers have dispossessed the keep of Rochester Castle of its timber floors, but this has only left the building yet more impressive. The vastness of its interior now matches almost exactly that of its exterior. The most important floors and rooms can be identified by the richness or simplicity of carving around door openings, signs that have remained long after frailer marks of distinction have vanished

site adjacent to Boley (Bailey) Hill where the old wooden structure had stood. This new castle was properly engineered, its new bailey being levelled and the stone walls founded on a chalk base. At this stage Rochester still lacked its most famous structure, the great square keep, and the lord would have lived in a wooden building within the stone walls. Though built of wood, these keeps would not have been mere rickety sheds. As houses for the wealthiest men of the age, they were carefully and abundantly made, in some cases richly decorated. In fact as houses, the timber structures would almost certainly have been preferable to their subsequent stone replacements. Warmer, drier, quieter, they would have been more healthy and enjoyable in every way, but had the simple defect of flammability.

The great square keeps of the Norman period were with one or two exceptions built in the twelfth century. That at Rochester was begun around 1126. As structures they represent a curious and ultimately ill-advised confidence on the part of the invaders. Their earlier stone structures, known as shell keeps but with relatively low walls, built to replace timber palisades on the top of mottes, were circular in plan, like Launceston and Restormel in Cornwall. Though giving the highest ratio of floor area to perimeter walling, these circular walls did not really provide entirely useful or comfortable living areas. In special cases such as London, Colchester or Rochester, the Normans built square keeps, much more adapted to habitation.

After all, a powerful lord had to be seen to live in something rather better than a large barrel, if only to keep his dignity in the eyes of the populace. In many ways these keeps present the most powerful, moving monuments of their age just because of their rectangular form, so easy to understand as a house, yet vast beyond belief, void and ruined. This ruined quality was, of course, the fear rather than the aim of the Normans, and not entirely to their taste as far as their own castles were concerned. It was later discovered that the circle has structural advantages which give longer term comfort to a castle's inhabitants, because they are much harder to knock down.

Sapping was one of the medieval arts, and involved destroying part of a castle by undermining its walls. In a square structure, the corners form points of junction between flat planes, each of which is structurally isolated by being built at right angles to the others. If you dig under that angle, you have a good chance of bringing down the corner. The keep at Rochester provided a dramatic demonstration of this principle when its south-east corner was made to drop away in 1215. William of Albini had been deputed to take and hold Rochester against King John, whose castle it was, for John's failure to honour Magna Carta. Unfortunately when John arrived at the castle walls and discovered William in occupation, William found his

Rochester Castle. Looking at the keep from the south west, one sees the corner tower as reconstructed after the original square angle had been undermined in the siege of 1215

former supporters had deserted him and he was under siege. Having mined the outer wall, John proceeded to dig his way under the corner of the keep. The method for mining was to dig tunnels and use wooden props to prevent their immediate collapse. When a mine was judged complete, combustible material was used to fill it, including in this case 'forty of the fattest pigs of the sort least good for eating'. They clearly did the trick, for the tunnel collapsed and the keep was breached. The story continued, for the garrison isolated itself in the keep's northern section which contained the well, only surrendering when its supply of horseflesh ran out.

There was perhaps no rush to build round towers after this demonstration, because reasons of comfort and prestige continued to be as important

25

as structural reasons, or more so. But many were built, like Skenfrith, and the destroyed corner of Rochester itself was rebuilt not with a square, but a round corner.

From being instruments of subjection and then civil war, castles were developed as weapons of territorial expansion. Edward I had led the English on the eighth crusade, and returned with a wide practical knowledge of castles in terms of their design as well as their use. After this crusade and during a period of relative internal peace in the 1220s, he initiated two military campaigns against the Welsh, each overwhelmingly successful. To secure these victories, he constructed a series of castles, which have been described as the finest examples of military architecture from the Middle Ages in existence, though this does not mean to say they were never captured.

Harlech well represents the principles of this type of design. Standing high on a cliff edge once lapped by the sea, seeming to be the only stable object in a landscape of movement, the castle was wholly dependent on the sea for its provision. Supplying a castle was always a problem, because there is a basic contradiction between isolation and survival. But in being a national outpost, rather than an individual's house, Harlech was not entirely isolated. It was backed up by the power of England. To supply it, there was the navy, with its own gate at the shore. The castle may now be seen as part

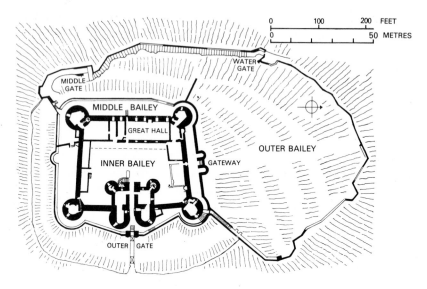

A plan of Harlech Castle

26

The hierarchy of defence at Beaumaris is clearly visible here, the bastions projecting upward to command a wall-walk, which in turn overlooks the moat. Behind this outer defence there is a higher wall still. Although appearing inoffensive today, being well inland, Beaumaris could once provide mooring for ships of 40 tons

of a military system of diverse elements, and as a military device it became more adaptable to the offensive as well as the defensive circumstances of war. To reduce the effectiveness of siege warfare, the number of gates and posterns in castles, formerly one of each, was increased to give better opportunity for making sorties, taking in supplies and perhaps escaping in emergencies. The keep, as the ultimate defensive position, disappeared from these buildings, replaced by immensely strong gatehouses which stood outside the curtain wall. This wall itself was powerfully built, each corner reinforced and defended by a round tower, raised well above the terrace of the middle bailey so that two lines of defence could be occupied at the same time. Only once did the Welsh manage to take Harlech, when Owen Glendower apparently bribed a half-starved, malign garrison. But thick walls have never provided much resistance to treachery.

Edward's castles all show this effort towards colonisation. Those such as Caernarvon, Conwy and Beaumaris, as well as sheltering troops, also gave protection to walled towns and at Beaumaris, begun in 1295 after the capture of the unfinished Caernarvon, 400 masons, 2,000 labourers, 30 smiths and

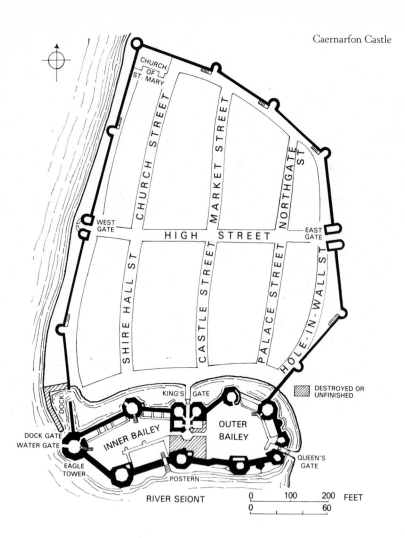

200 carters, in addition to 160 carts and 30 boats, were employed on the enterprise at a cost of £250 a week. These efforts in Wales are a first hint of future change to castle design in England itself. As has been suggested, the military became less the masters of society, and more its servants. The development of a money economy undermined the feudal system of service due to a lord, since it became possible to commute service with money payments with which the lord would hire agricultural labourers or mercenary soldiers as circumstances required. While this system had the advantage of providing professional soldiers in place of part-timers, its danger was that the professional soldier was quite prepared to fight his employer if the occasion arose.

28

Caernarfon — the most impressive of castles, with its exotic striping of different stonework and domination of the town and harbour which lie about it. Its appearance is in part due to Edward I's participation in the crusades. His travels gave him a wide experience of military architecture, and he was particularly struck by the Byzantine walls at Constantinople, which also have this coloured banding.

A castle is rather like an island, as difficult to leave as to enter, and troops could easily make the lord of a castle their prisoner. The result was that the strongest part of a castle became its gate rather than its central keep. Within this gate, the old physical separation of soldiery from command was maintained, as at Harlech, and later in England itself at Ashby de la Zouch.

It seems that as the town merchants became prosperous, paying for protection by commuting for service rather than fighting someone else's battles, living in relative comfort, and probably answering the lord's restlessness with a certain measure of amusement at his predicament, the lords themselves occupied an ever less-respected social position. For this reason, as well as for a further degree of personal safety, these lords often left their castles in charge of a Constable, to whom this ambivalent position passed, while they themselves moved into more comfortable and grander country houses, or into the towns. In this way, castles reverted to being merely forts, military machines to be used only at times of national emergency. The functions of castle and residence separated into distinct buildings, each type progressively less compromised by the other.

If the castle as fortified residence had arrived on these shores literally by ship, it left them literally as ships, with the foundation of an English Navy as a permanent institution by Henry VII. This was followed by the construction of artillery forts along the south coast, such as at Deal (built with stone salvaged from a local abbey). Before this period, ships from merchant fleets, chiefly from the Cinque Ports, had been used by the king, as required, for conveyance of land troops or war on the sea, when temporary wooden 'castles' would be built fore and aft. The word 'fo'c'sle' is of course a surviving indication of this. The armament of these ships was a number of archers,

At Deal we have a fort rather than a castle, so there are no pretensions to the appearance of an important dwelling. In fact this building is altogether unmonumental, in spite of being more strongly built than any medieval castle. Compare the rigid geometry of this plan to the domestic compromise of Rochester

MOAT

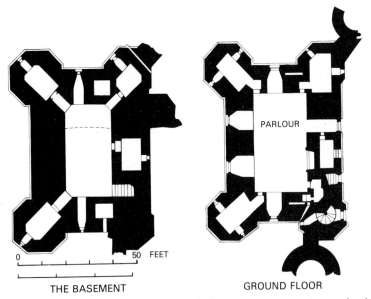

THE BASEMENT　　　　　　　　GROUND FLOOR

Tattershall Castle. The massive brick walls with their spacious interruptions can be clearly seen here, and occur even at basement level

who won, for example, the sea battle of Sluys against the French in 1340. Under Henry's authority ships were designed specifically for war, as castles had been houses so designed. Carrying cannon and providing living quarters for their captains and crew, they often imitated the internal niceties of plan and ornament of the finest town houses, at least in officers' quarters.

A writer in the 1430s had expressed his opinion of proper defence for England:

> Keepe then the sea, about in special,
> Which of Englande is the town wall;
> Keepe then the sea, that is the wall of Englande,
> And then is Englande kept by Goddes hand.

Here at last was the political unity of England, its walls defended by floating castles, the country itself a large defended bailey.

As residential and military functions separated, houses of the fourteenth and fifteenth centuries could use the imagery of fortification without needing to worry about its practical value. This romantic claim to prowess was in part a response to the lessening prestige of the aristocracy. Edward III had perceived the necessity of such a boost. His invention of the Order of the Garter and reintroduction of tournaments were both attempts to strengthen feudal powers against an increasingly merchant world. Tattershall Castle in Lincolnshire, for instance, was built in the 1430s and '40s, during chivalry's golden age. Its tower, though doubtless it would have been some defence against attack, has walls 14 feet thick punctured by windows 5 feet wide and 10 feet high. The effect is theatrical, of a castle but more so. A fortification in its imagery and solidity, it is a house in terms of physical comfort and internal space. Here the idea of a building was freed of its functional burden, and thus the story of castles comes to an end.

The Church in Stone

Religion to William the Conqueror was a political force above all, and although he did not carry a cathedral across in his convoy, he certainly brought with him the principles of Romanesque church architecture which formed such an important part of his occupation of England. Having procured the Church's support for his cause before the invasion, William was bound to further its search for increased temporal power.

Immediately following his victory over Harold, William founded Battle Abbey, an act of obeisance addressed not so much to God's attention as to the Pope's. While for military reasons dozens of castles were built throughout the land, only two stand out for grandeur and ostentation: the White Tower in London and Colchester Castle. The rest were generally of timber, meant to dominate physically. The job of psychological domination was on the whole left to church architecture. By taking an existing institution and reforming it rather than creating a new one, William provided a necessary continuity and could make it appear that an Anglo-Saxon institution, the church, was lending support to his regime. Of course the Church was given feudal estates and the income from these enabled the construction of immense buildings, which must have had a sobering, intimidating effect on the population. These massive stone monuments, at Canterbury, Winchester, Lincoln, St Albans, Ely and Worcester, like warships moored in an occupied harbour, are as much a show of strength as a display of piety. Physical models of the Church itself, vast beyond functional usefulness, they demonstrate that whatever the new king may have lacked, he certainly did not lack powerful friends.

A Romanesque architecture peculiar to the Normans had been developed during the time when they established themselves in Normandy and mainland Europe. Their frequent attacks in the Rheinland and the old

Durham Cathedral is one of the most assertively sited of churches, meant to inspire respect for the might of the Roman church as much as devotion in the hearts of God's children

Southwell remains a largely unchanged example of a Romanesque cathedral, and its imagery of the walled town can be clearly seen from a distance. There are its corner towers, palace rising up in the centre and 'town walls' with their abstract machicolations carved into them

Carolingian Empire did not escape reprisals, hence their desire to construct more important buildings like churches and palaces in such a way that they would not burn down with the crackling rapidity of timber. They developed a technique based on stone vaulting, and the impression it gives is certainly one of solidity above all. Constructional considerations play a part in this, of fire resistance on one hand and on the other a desire to build quickly of rubble work rather than ashlar, which made necessary an increase of mass to compensate for its structural inferiority.

The Romanesque developed in part from practical constraints of construction, and its appearance is a result of a piecing together of large architectural elements in formal groups, and the decoration of those elements. The pieces themselves were often quite crude constructionally.

It appears that Durham Cathedral was the first building to use a rib-vaulted roof, countering its outward thrust with equally original flying buttresses,

but these latter are concealed from view. Authority and domination in these churches was not to be compromised by niceties of structural expression.

The best idea of what a Norman cathedral would have looked like, from a distance as it were — since all have been greatly altered — is given by the cathedrals of Southwell and Durham. They were designed to symbolise the power of kingship in association with spiritual power, imitating small cities, the City of God. Immense towers mark each corner of the west end, and from the crossing point of transepts and nave rises another tower, of greater size. These three points immediately set out a procession and a goal at the end of it. Although both Durham and Southwell have lost their original west fronts, enough survives at Lincoln to indicate the idea of portals, of the principal gate to an important town. To stress the symbolic value of a gate, the portals have been topped by a band of blind arcading where on more ancient town gates had been galleries, specially reserved for ritual appearances of royalty. The ritual can be seen still both in religious and secular forms, at St Peter's in Rome, at Buckingham Palace and on the balconies of many a South American presidential palace. In England the primitive union of king and priest was regained by Henry VIII, the very unity that the Roman Church had so successfully broken during the Middle Ages.

Part of the west front of Selby Abbey, late Norman and Early English

Norman attitudes were slowly modified and native resistance overcome until in England, at any rate, there were the English. In twelfth-century Europe the Gothic conception of architecture, begun in the Isle de France, supplanted the heavy Romanesque, making it evident that authority was taking on a new sophistication and subtlety. The three distinguishing elements of Gothic architecture — pointed arch, rib vault and flying buttress — were each developed during the Romanesque period, and, as we have seen, were all used at Durham Cathedral in the early twelfth century. The fact is that these elements were selected from the vocabulary of that style by one Abbé Suger in the 1130s and became the axioms of a new architecture,

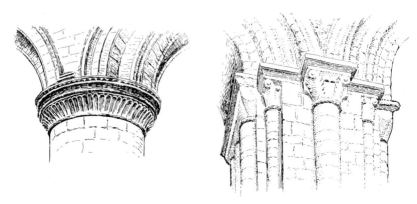

These two capitals from Selby Abbey were carved in the twelfth century, and make an interesting pair. They stand on adjacent columns, and indicate the simultaneous use of Romanesque and Gothic work, with no apparent worry or contradiction

the Gothic, its first essay being the rebuilding of Suger's own abbey of St Denis. What made his combination so convincing was his clarity of purpose and the fact that he wrote a book about the project. Suger was highly educated, a scholastic, whom the new learning gleaned on the crusades would not have passed by unnoticed. That authority could be founded on reason, rather than on physical intimidation (even though reason itself may ultimately rest on authority) is reflected in two aspects of this Gothic art. Firstly, in the invention itself which simply gave three axioms and allowed intellectual effort to do the rest, and secondly in the lightness and transparency of the resulting buildings. In France this national principle remained consistently powerful throughout the Gothic age, but as it reached Britain, first at Canterbury, it became the means for a national expression in art which had been more or less absent in the Romanesque period.

Lincoln is a very complete piece of Early English Gothic, a building which practically defines the period. The nave is of wide proportion, the triforium of low proportion and the resulting space relaxed. Spanning this nave is a rather strange roof without that strict correspondence of bays to columns found in French buildings; here the ceiling bays are shifted half a unit off the columns, giving to the space a vaporous, slightly giddy feeling. If this makes one giddy, the choir does nothing to calm one, with its odd stiff-legged clumping through space, and one senses there is more interest in experiments of decoration and emotional relationships than with the building's inner logic. The fact is that these are qualities that can be found again and again during the Gothic age, and many have seen this as a characteristic of the national culture.

What is also clear is that in English hands Gothic became a means to recover the possibilities of frame construction, in particular those of timber framing. When the block-like construction of Romanesque was replaced by a style whose basis was more intellectual than material, it became possible to replace decorated stonework with stonework that imitated other structures. In other words there was no longer a need to treat stone as a heavy intractable materials structurally, and only to decorate its surface as though it were wood, with carvings. It could also be treated structurally like wood, and you might say that Gothic architecture freed the conceptual properties of the material from its practical properties. Stone was used as a fire resisting plastic substance rather than remaining distinctly as stone, one of whose properties is to be fireproof.

Conceptually the building could be seen as a light frame with infill panels, just as houses had been and were continuing to be built. The pointed arch,

The west front of Lincoln Cathedral has an arrangement of architectural elements that echo those of the city gate and palace façade. The triumphal arch is a common form of gateway, and the arcaded front was traditionally given to palaces as places where kings made public appearances. Here the details are used symbolically, and in fact were soon dropped from English church architecture. Their meaning was closely related to certain forms of kingship that did not survive in England

distinguishing feature of the Gothic, is perhaps only another instance of the cruck frame, as may be clearly seen at Ripon and Ely cathedrals and in a more directly structural way, the flying buttresses of Lincoln. Though the idea of the pointed arch seems almost certain to have been brought from Syria to Europe during the crusades, English masons were equally certainly unaware of this. To them its logic would have been apparent for centuries, its reappearance in stone a curious irony rather than an innovation.

The move from Romanesque architecture and the development of Gothic reflects a move from religion dominated by dogma and ritual, a period of Church dictatorship, to one in which moral content was emphasised, where thought and inventiveness became important. The existence in society of an ever freer middle class, freed in fact by their money, made this change obvious. Romanesque building, inert and abstract, was superseded by an architecture which re-adopted principles of popular culture, in decoration and structure. Art left the realm in which authority was simply represented as absolute and entered another, where a population had to be shown how to behave, to be taught to govern their own actions.

Victor Hugo, in his *Notre Dame de Paris,* despairs of the death of architecture at the hands of literature, claiming that 'from the beginning of time' architecture had played this educational role. But really this was a Gothic development. Other epochs had built architectures of symbolism, but for carrying learning and precept they had employed literature: the Greek and Roman were both great literary cultures, but the same could never be said for medieval Europe, where reading itself was a forbidden skill. In that prohibition the power of literature was clearly recognised, and the development of architecture to speak in its stead was a specifically Gothic ideal.

Hall and Manor

In house design throughout the Middle Ages, the constant element is the hall. Around it the house was constructed, and around it too, was built rural society. The invading Norman population used the hall as the centre of their communities, as had the Anglo-Saxons, though usually they placed it behind thick walls, so that as the manor house developed into the chief economic institution of feudal Britain, its physical form was one identical in principle to that of earlier ages. It remained so well beyond the feudal era.

Manor houses built in the late thirteenth century were relatively small — about 20 by 30 feet — and like Boothby Pagnell had but one room apart from the hall itself. Needless to say those who were not land-owners con-

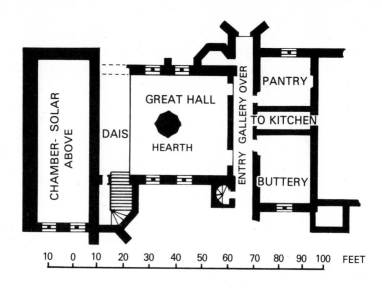

Penshurst Place

tinued to live more in their clothes than in their houses, which were still cramped, draughty and wet. In fact the great advance for cottages in this period was not one of size, but of height. As it became possible to build walls to a house, it became unnecessary to sink the floor below ground level. This, in a sense, is the story of all houses during the Middle Ages; there were no wrenching changes, no new forms invented, but an advance in constructional terms, an increase in numbers of rooms and a greater proportion of the population owning houses. The process illustrates Cicero's observation that quantitative change leads imperceptibly to qualitative change, for by the sixteenth century the proliferation of these buildings had obliterated the hall's original function as community space. Penshurst Place and Haddon Hall show the type of spaces used for community life, though it should be remembered that both were built for extremely wealthy men. Penshurst was, in fact, built by a retired merchant from London who wanted to cast himself in the role of lord of the manor. Each house shows two ranges of rooms of two storeys, with a double height hall between them. These ranges contain buttery and pantry at one end, sleeping chamber and solar or day room at the other. Kitchens were not brought into houses until rather later. The hall itself was a room for manorial business, or what might be called common action, including eating and, for many, sleeping. Early halls had a roughly square central area, with a raised dais at one end and screens passage at the other, each about ¼ of the central area's length. This produced an overall

40

proportion of about 2:3. Central to this space is an open hearth, still to be seen at Penshurst, an arrangement often scorned as second best, but with practical advantages over the later wall fireplaces. The wood burned in these hearths was charcoal, as many people forget, which is practically smokeless, and of course less heat is wasted in this system to the outside air. Apart from giving better ventilation to a room, which no doubt needed it, a central fire can warm twice the number of people. At a more emotional level, there is none of the melancholy that is associated with wall-fires. The central hearth is more primitive, partly in a technical sense but partly too, psychologically, as an imitation of the camp fire.

As the yeomen and smaller landholders became able to build their own houses, they copied their betters, often building for themselves in the fifteenth century houses the original size of Penshurst, which had itself expanded in every direction by that time. In this way they scooped themselves out of the social pudding, leaving it, little by little, all crust and no filling: the lord sat on his dais entertaining only the poor, which probably suited neither party, but certainly not the lord, who began taking his meals in private. Here begins the specialisation of rooms, for different functions and different people, which was eventually to provide such a formal problem for the great land-owners that they disguised the proliferation of specialised

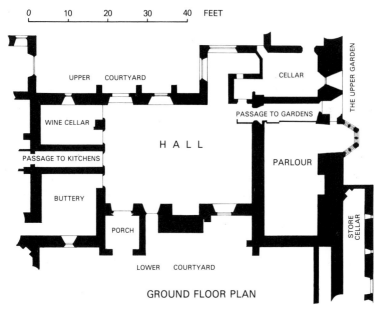

Haddon Hall as it was in the fourteenth century. A later gallery connects rooms to left and right of the hall at first-floor level

41

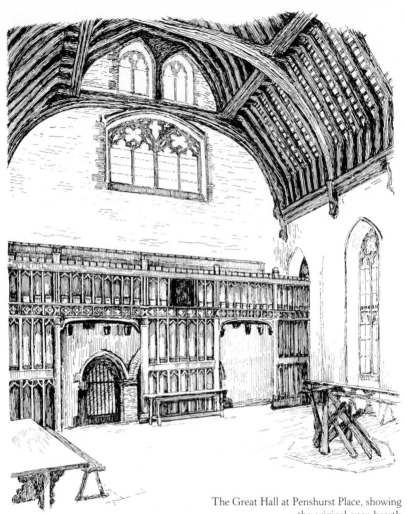

The Great Hall at Penshurst Place, showing
the original open hearth

spaces under the mask of a new 'style' of architecture, that of the classical
Renaissance.

Separate houses for families began to be constructed for many reasons, of
which a desire for greater privacy and comfort are often overemphasised.
The general adoption of money as an economic tool gave many people the
ability to measure and express their position in society. Especially for those
who had no title, against whom the chivalric code was built thick and high,
building was a clear path. Again, the untitled were the very people who had
as a group become wealthy.

Apart from this general improvement, medieval artistic expression in domestic buildings can best be seen in roof construction. Carpenters and not masons dominated the age in terms of constructive ability and inventiveness, and it is not surprising to find Gothic church architecture reflecting in stone so many woody qualities. Whatever walls were made of, they needed a timber roof (and this is true no less of cathedrals than of houses), and with the tendency in time for rooms to grow larger and spans greater, the carpenter was set most difficult problems. An early hall of large dimensions had a line of posts running its length, supporting the roof. The invention of tie beams turned these into

One of the hammer beams at Pilgrims' Hall, Winchester, said to be the earliest example of this type of roof construction

what are called king posts, confining them to a zone above wall level. The same principle was applied to roof an aisled hall, using two posts (queen posts) instead of columns. But the loveliest solution, one that produced the exceptionally fine roof at Westminster Hall, was the hammer-beam roof. For the very largest of spans it would have been impossible to obtain tie beams of sufficient length, and if it had, their own weight would have put excessive tension on the king post. On the other hand the hammer-beam roof behaves rather like a pair of girders tilted to the roof's pitch. Though they have the old fault of producing outward thrust on the walls, the rather clever practice evolved of moving the walls in slightly, or if you like, making the roof too big, so that loads acted vertically.

As self-expression implied a certain degree of privacy, a degree of separateness from the community, a new type of community developed in England during the Middle Ages that made a compromise between dependence and independence: the town. To specify the difference between town and village, it could be said that a village was a community that consumed its own produce but a town existed as an exchange point for surplus produce. As creations of the Middle Ages, they came to represent the freedom implied by the winding down of feudalism. In the case of a villein who could stay unclaimed in a town for a year and a day, it actually conferred freedom. But

43

These timber-framed houses at Church Street in Tewkesbury have recently been restored, and one is open to the public. They appear to have been built as a speculative development by the Church, and if this is so it represents an early example of such capital speculation in towns. The houses were by no means luxurious, and it may be that they were for some particular people of known quantity and quality, an investment rather than a speculation

as for architectural expression of this new identity, in houses, there was very little difference from what was happening in the country. House plans generally were simply turned sideways to fit narrow town sites.

Both at Spon Street in Coventry and in the lovely row of twenty-two houses in Church Street, Tewkesbury, one can clearly see this principle. Spon Street has become a gathering spot for Coventry's unwanted medieval buildings, and one of these, number 9, still has its open hall and open central hearth. The plan shows a shop facing the street with a passage to one side leading to the hall, from which a ladder leads to first-floor chambers. The Tewkesbury houses follow this same plan and were apparently built by the abbey as a speculative development sometime in the fifteenth century. Grander examples of medieval houses do exist, those of rich merchants for whom stone was the only acceptable material (though this had fire-resistance as well as ostentation to justify it). Grevel House in Chipping Camden is a late fourteenth-century example, and in Lincolnshire there is the restored but much altered Jew's House on Steep Hill, home of a twelfth-century merchant, whether Jew or not no one knows. Its plan follows normal practice in having all its living accommodation on the first floor, and puts storage vaults at street level.

Perhaps the most striking feature of town development is just this, that no new plan was needed for town houses because domestic life, urban or rural, was very much the same thing. What the towns do show is the development of new building types, dealing with the institutions associated with urban community life. So we find almshouses, hospitals, inns, schools, guild halls, moot halls and market halls, all developing as built expressions of urban conditions. While hospitals were founded by religious orders, these were often friary orders (as opposed to monastic) which themselves were always urban since they lived not by agriculture but by alms: by begging

The Jew's House, Lincoln, though much chopped about, remains a gem. Its most serious loss is undoubtedly the chimney stack which once rose from the arch that shelters the entrance and projected up above the roof line. The fireplace would of course have been on first-floor level, where the living accommodation was situated. The ground-floor level was given over to the storage of merchandise, as in rural houses it had been given over to animals or farm produce and implements

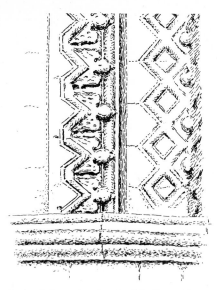

A detail from the chapel of St Cross Almshouses, Winchester. The new building types
developed during the Middle Ages were often
beautifully constructed and finely detailed

for agricultural surplus, rather than trading in it. Winchester School, as the first secular school in Britain, was founded in 1382, as a preparation for the also secular university, and in time guilds themselves began to sponsor grammar schools, where an education adapted to contemporary needs could be assured.

Freedom existed within the city, but not necessarily outside it; that is you were seldom free in another man's town. Trading was the right of a citizen but not of a 'foreigner'. (The word derives from the Latin *foris,* meaning outside.) And in this freedom of a city, there was submission to its customs and laws.

In every freedom can be seen an exploitation. Towns originated as communities adjusted to the exploitation of agricultural surplus, but obviously towns could not exist until there was this surplus, until there could be trade with money as its base. If the Gothic age seems to us a golden age, it is because in it was the growth of the modern era, to which people look back wistfully. Before it became possible to exploit the city, the city had to be made, with all its institutions, buildings, resourcefulness and diversity. It was not until the seventeenth century that the city became regarded as 'natural' in the same way that the landscape is considered 'natural', and this explicit statement came only after generations of men had treated the city as a device to serve the individual. To take an example, the guild was an institution much exploited for personal gain in the later Middle Ages, yet clearly this would not have been possible if the community had not first created the guild in such a way that all the community was involved.

All citizens were originally equal in any town, and were expected to exert their power as a community. In contrast to today's more gentle methods of protest, in some towns they would pull down the house of an irresponsible mayor. The good of the community was theoretically the reason for each collective action, and although building and sanitation bye-laws, anti-profiteering regulations and guilds were valuable conceptions, in practice

46

Chimney stack of the guildhall, shown in the following photograph. It was not only in timber construction that craft could take delight

Typical of the new building types developed to meet the needs of town culture, is the guildhall. This example at Lavenham in Essex shows how such buildings used standard techniques of construction, but simply carried them to unusually high levels of refinement

The Tribunal House in Glastonbury is, in a sense, the first terrace house in England, accepting its narrow deep plot and turning this new predicament into a civilized dwelling. It also stands politely next to its neighbours in the street, which is the essence of the English town house

48

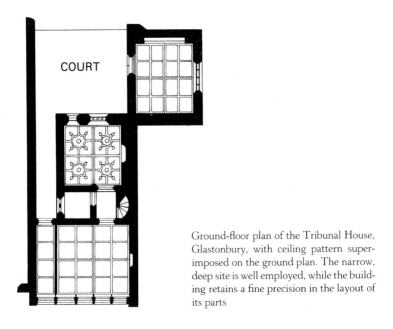

COURT

Ground-floor plan of the Tribunal House, Glastonbury, with ceiling pattern super-imposed on the ground plan. The narrow, deep site is well employed, while the building retains a fine precision in the layout of its parts

and over time they were open to abuse by the rich and used against the poor.

Technical advance was slow, for town and village differed in function more than form, and elaborate innovation was unnecessary. Towns even of the fifteenth century had strong agricultural connections, so that even in London the Law Courts ceased sitting during harvest time. A proportion of citizens were agricultural labourers, for large gardens and orchards were not uncommon. Special regulations were constantly needed to keep pigs from wandering the streets.

Water supply services were begun in the thirteenth century, adopted from developments within monastic houses, though their companion service, drainage, was ignored. As for fighting fires, the standard method was simply to pull down burning buildings and any near enough to catch alight, which gives some idea of the strength of these buildings, prone to demolition by a few grappling hooks. Bye-laws gradually came to control materials used for house building, but the more abstract regulations concerning heights, separation of dwellings and so on are products of a much later age. The medieval city was above all concerned with physical processes, with trade, and its institutions were run to help this trade along, to organise it. A town, whether Norwich, London, Chester or York, was a large device for handling merchandise. To think of the concentration of activity there was in medieval London, compared with today's acres of office blocks and

49

empty docks, makes sense of the medieval notion of a city embodying and symbolising the whole world.

What did this do to the countryside? By concentrating life in the city and leaving rural England in the hands of the aristocracy, it made way for the idealisation of the countryside as a place 'away from the world', a place where the rich merchant could take his wealth and retire, playing the role of a rural landlord which to him was completely foreign. Penshurst Place itself was built by Sir John de Pulteney, a wealthy London merchant. This vision of the countryside has persisted in England ever since, though it was a later age that gave it perfect expression.

3
From Goth to Gentleman

It is generally accepted that the material and intellectual establishment of a distinct English culture was a product of the Reformation. When the Bible became the chief source of divine wisdom and authority, its translation meant a widespread growth of literacy. Authority moved from the Roman Church's jealously defended mystery and dogma, to the words of a book. Whether the aim of making the irrational reasonable is a worthwhile one, or in itself reasonable, is another question. It was not a new approach: even the Egyptian priests had seen their power weaken beneath the weight of words. The point is that in sixteenth-century England the promotion of literacy for spiritual purposes had profound material results, providing as it did a ready tool for commercial and cultural communication at practically every level of society.

The secular nature of Renaissance architecture has frequently been explained by the observation that 'there were already enough churches'. This would be a reasonable statement if structures were built purely to satisfy need; but they are not. It is generally known, for example, that during the 1960s office space was being constructed in many English cities at a rate that far exceeded demand. In the end the government of the day was obliged to pass legislation permitting office construction only where a lease had previously been signed for its occupation. A more likely explanation appears to be that during the sixteenth century, power passed — was perhaps wrested — from ecclesiastical hands, and placed in the practical hands of worldly men.

In effect, the monasteries were not so much dissolved as redistributed, at least in terms of their latent commercial worth. They were in a sense nationalised, taken away from the English agents of a foreign ruler, the Church of Rome, and given or sold to men who could use the enormous capital potential of monastic lands to contribute to the development of an English empire. The buildings which were found on these lands were treated like the land itself, mere raw material for new enterprises. Some were turned into parish churches, some, like Malmesbury Abbey, were turned into factories, some into houses, as was Lacock Abbey in Wiltshire. Many others

51

Part of Fountains Abbey

Some eight hundred people are said to have lived and worked at Rievaulx Abbey at its height, but the Cistercian ideal of civilization that this type of community represented clearly did not please everyone. These monasteries were more or less carefully demolished, their materials used to build different dwellings, their lands taken to line different purses

Longleat, one of the first houses to abandon the introspective plan of a courtyard house and turn outwards to confront the open spaces. There is use of Renaissance detail, pilasters in particular, but otherwise little devotion to Italian architectural style. Undoubtedly anyone who had the confidence to build a house of these proportions would feel able to handle the aesthetics without trouble. Particularly well designed are the three-storey bay windows or towers — whichever one sees them as — detached from the main rectangle of the building by the insertion of narrow windows down their sides. It gives a light feel to an otherwise stolid rectangle

If the house of Audley End was, before its partial demolition, a 'prodigy house', it still possesses a prodigy hedge, requiring three different ladders for its maintenance

were carefully dismantled for the valuable materials they contained. This was not the iconoclasm of enthusiasts: that came in the seventeenth century with puritanism. The scene presented by the Dissolution is of a new manager in a commercial concern.

The curious fact is that having established an independence from Roman religion, the English within sixty years were dedicated to an architecture of the Italian Renaissance, itself based on Roman models. This reflects the opportunist and rather arbitrary nature of cultural development. This is not to decry such development, for after the English had sailed about the globe claiming as theirs whatever territory fell their way, there still remained the question of what to do with it, which is the major cultural issue. But the fact remains that the raw material one works with is somewhat a matter of fortuity, combined with an inventive eye.

Though it is often said that Renaissance architecture came late to England, there is some reason to believe that there would have been no need for it at an earlier time. Its first employment, in the sixteenth century, was for domestic architecture, being used as a decorative dressing on medieval architectural forms. The 'prodigy houses' of the Elizabethans, as Sir John Summerson has called such enormous buildings as Longleat, Burghley and

Audley End, were not homes in any previously accepted sense of the word. They were often built or greatly extended at short notice as pavilions for the entertainment of Queen Elizabeth, seldom being other than second homes for their owners. Their condition as virtually permanent building sites can have added little to their attractions as places to live.

At any rate, the only source immediately to hand for a language suitably grand for these enterprises was the large manor house or castle. But these buildings had an association of appearance and purpose so strongly traditional that the new buildings began to appear as a desecration of old values. The tension between these elements is at least half the pleasure of buildings like Layer Marney Towers and Oxburgh Hall. But at Bolsover Castle or Wollaton Hall, there seems to be an uneasiness in the formal aspects, as opposed to the more than festive decorative inventions. This uneasiness has something to do with a division, under one roof, into two separate buildings. It may be that the hotel-like nature of these grand Elizabethan houses had some influence here, where the served and the servants are increasingly an embarrassment to each other. The nature of this conflict, evident in the circulation patterns within a house, was only recognised in architectural terms by Inigo Jones, whose plans for Wilton and Coleshill are quite explicit in this.

To the new class of Elizabethan builders, mostly second or third generation aristocracy with political or trade wealth, imitating the forms of old houses soon lost its intended authority. The essential element of medieval 'halls' was indeed the internal splendour of the great hall. But now that these

Compton Wynyates, Warwickshire. Though giving the impression of a building pieced together over the centuries, with its irregular silhouette, it was in fact built in a span of some twenty years, in the early sixteenth century

stood empty, what message could they convey? The external ramblings of a Compton Wynyates was replaced with the regime of pure classicism, visible from afar to those no longer welcome beneath its roof. These new builders of the seventeenth century built to disassociate themselves from the traditional social and agricultural meanings of country estate architecture. They gave themselves classical authority for a break with native tradition, an authority older than that tradition itself.

As the planning of houses became more compact and assertive, and the type of house based on ranges of buildings disposed about one or more courtyards was abandoned, vertical movement through two storeys became increasingly important. There were practical problems connected with this. The traditional hall is a rather tall room, running the full height of a two-storey house. If it was between ranges of lower buildings, as was often the case, it effectively barred movement from one side of the house to the other at first-floor level. As time went by, this arrangement, where the hall was a point on every route, was found to be unacceptable. The fourteenth-century hall at Haddon was at a later date bridged by a gallery to overcome this awkwardness. But as each of a house's two floors took on its separate importance, one of its several staircases was usually made into a very elaborate recognition of this new relationship. It was this staircase that replaced the hall as the key item in the working of a house and eventually it took over the very place formerly occupied by that hall.

Stylistic Origins

One curious feature of early Renaissance architecture, which to a certain extent is a persistent characteristic in English building, is its use of the printed page as a source of information rather than buildings themselves. Because the educated in a literary culture began to collect books, and as books are more easily transported to men than men to buildings, Renaissance design first reached England as engravings. The books were generally Flemish interpretations of Italian work, with the result that by the time they reached this country they had become rather altered, to put it mildly.

The obvious fact about paper is that it is flat, and one can see in the chain of transferred images of a building from page to page, a decreasing interest in the architectural content and a corresponding increase of interest in the design as an elaborate figuration of a flat surface. It is this transparent image that the Elizabethan beheld as Renaissance architecture, and, as at Kirby, they engraved it as carefully on to their buildings as the artist had on to his copper plate.

57

Part of the ruined East Lodgings of Kirby Hall, Northamptonshire,
dating from the late sixteenth century

Inigo Jones, generally regarded as the initiator of Renaissance architecture in England, was one of the very few architects from this country who went to Italy to study the buildings at firsthand. The effect his trips had on him and on architectural development was profound and yet his example was rarely followed, English architects to this very day preferring a warm library to the rigours of foreign travel. They may like to read about travel, but that is another matter. Even Wren, for example, never visited Italy, although he did travel to Paris for eight or nine months. His authorities were French and Italian books and this literary tendency only increased. In the eighteenth century it became common for an architect to start his practice by publishing a book, and it certainly drew more attention to the designer than any building would have done.

A strong distinction between early and mature Renaissance architecture can be drawn between classical elements used as decoration and classicism as a formal discipline. Over the years a process took place of ordering and taming building façades, while internal arrangements were made dependent on this outer form. Earlier house plans, with their convenient proximity of kitchen to hall and hall to quarters, were basically medieval. Doddington Hall in Lincolnshire illustrates this point, and it makes an interesting comparison with, say, Castle Howard, where the kitchen is hundreds of feet from the dining-room in order to fill up building elements that were demanded by a symmetrical plan. But it would be wrong to laugh at these sacrifices made to formality. To that age it would have been intolerably inconvenient

The results of invention unrestrained by academic nicety is nowhere more evident than at Hardwick Hall. This is not the fussy elaborate 'invention' that complicates so much Elizabethan design, but the dramatic handling of space and material on an unusually large scale

to have to descend the stairs, cross a central hall and ascend another set of stairs simply to go between two first-floor rooms. Inconvenience is merely action made necessary by form, but deprived of its meaning; action without meaning is purposeless action.

When, in the seventeenth century, science was destroying the mystical foundations of classical and medieval intellectual life, expanding its inductive and pragmatic methods and abandoning the authority of the ancients, architecture was apparently moving in just the opposite direction. The chief concern of artists became a work's internal relations, as contrasted with earlier values of sensory or external relations; as it had been for medieval scholastic philosophers, so the validity or consistency of an argument was of far greater importance than its utility or correspondence with common sense. The whole point of reason had been to reach beyond the grasp of common sense, into a world of perfection, obviously and necessarily unlike the imperfect world that we could perceive through our senses.

Sir Christopher Wren, most famous of all English architects, is less well known to have been also a man of science, astronomer and mathematician, before taking up architecture. Did his art inherit an approach to understanding the world that his science could not contain? As a scientist Wren knew the value of inductive thought, but he also understood the usefulness of mathematics as a language to explore and describe the physical world. In architecture, classicism could be said to have had a parallel function in

A detail of Wren and Hawksmoor's Hall at Greenwich Hospital, 1698–1705

Detail of Castle Howard. Vanbrugh was called by Soane 'the Shakespeare of architecture' and his work is all of the highest dramatic quality

61

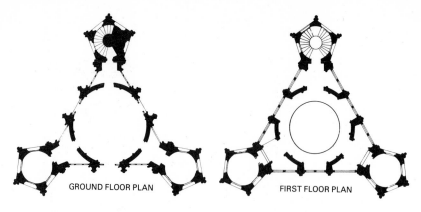

GROUND FLOOR PLAN

FIRST FLOOR PLAN

The Gothic Temple at Stowe, Buckinghamshire, of 1741. The delicacy of the plan contrasts with the rough texture and heavy forms of the exterior. Designed by James Gibbs

figurative terms. With the language of classicism Wren was able to experiment with space, and he did this in his fifty-three London churches. In many of these, he built miniature versions of spaces that he imagined for St Paul's Cathedral, which was under construction at the same time. These were elegant conversations in the language of architecture, not the radical searching for universal truth and laws that one might have expected from a man of science in a scientific age.

For the two great architects who followed Wren, Nicholas Hawksmoor and Sir John Vanbrugh, as well as to some degree the Scot, James Gibbs, details of architectural conversation became obscured by massive rhetorical figures: column and entablature were swamped by form. Their buildings leave the ideal plane of geometrical, proportional harmony and perform a curious dance with the force of gravity. This is the architecture of passion, finely expressed, paralleling David Hume's most carefully reasoned arguments for the prime importance of passion.

Base of the Cobham Monument, Stowe, by Gibbs and Valdre

A view of Stowe's Gothic Temple

The so-called English Palladian movement which followed was centred around the figure of Lord Burlington, though it might be more accurate to say that he centred it around himself. Burlington, with his designers such as William Kent, claimed to reject Vanbrugh's and Hawksmoor's ideas, but in fact they merely took the bite out of English Baroque — translated gusto into taste. The man whose ideas became the foundations of the movement was an obsequious and second-rate Scottish designer named Colen Campbell. His tastes seemed ideally suited to a self-satisfied Whig rulership that was horrified by any whiff of Catholicism such as wafted by the Baroque for example, then at its height in France and Italy. They wanted something English, and this they thought they had found in Campbell's works. His house at Wanstead in Essex was the exemplar of the style, though but a rough copy in brick of Vanbrugh's Castle Howard. It was claimed to be a return to the pure principles of Inigo Jones and of his source, Palladio, who himself had set up an almost puritanically severe classicism at the height of

In the age of taste, William Kent's Holkham Hall is the tasteful house *par excellence*. Beyond that, it is sometimes difficult to see what this English Palladian architecture has to offer. Though large, it is tame; though expensive, its materials are dull to look at; and though it is solid, it conveys an impression of flimsiness

the sixteenth-century Mannerism in Italy. But these movements of purification are generally more mannered than the decadence they oppose, and always less interesting. However that may be, English Palladianism was assured of success by its happy coincidence with a boom in country-house building in the 1700s, created by the many newly rich Whig merchants and politicians. (When the South Sea Bubble burst most of the richest were well out of earshot.)

The practical method of Campbell and Burlington's architecture, and perhaps even the conspicuous impracticability of its planning, was well suited to the Whig mind. Once a piece of property had been bought, one simply acquired a copy of Campbell's picture book of English houses, *Vitruvius Britannicus*, and chose the parts one wanted or which one could afford. The house of Stourhead in Wiltshire was built in this way by Henry Hoare, son of the great banker, who having purchased Stourton in 1720, as he said, 'immediately bought Mr. Campbell's books'. The result suffers from

Chiswick Villa, designed by Lord Burlington in the 1720s

Temple of the Four Winds, Castle Howard (1724–6), by Sir John Vanbrugh, and the Yorkshire landscape beyond

What the Palladians designed most successfully was the small monument, pavilion or bridge. This example at Wilton House is the earliest in England, built in 1737 by the ninth Earl of Pembroke. It was followed by others at Stowe, and Prior Park at Bath. But the traditions came to an ignominious end with the construction of uncrossable bridges, in fact mere timber scenery, as can still be seen at Kenwood House in London

all the faults one might associate with a house derived from looking at books and has few of the benefits. Where the Elizabethans had taken freely from books to aid their invention of decoration, these men took their planning too. One almost sees that in the distancing of this architecture from experience, there is a move towards designs which would look at their best when reproduced as copperplate designs. In this there is a return to Jones's principles, in which surface had been all important, although in this case it might be called an interest in the superficial.

In the end the purity and detachment of these buildings (though one wouldn't include Burlington's villa attached to Chiswick House) brought out their emotional counterpart of sentimentality. At first this produced romantic and free landscape gardens, and then a rather curious thing that can only be called a second version of English Baroque, the Gothic Revival, initiated, as it happens, by William Kent. The development of that movement belongs to the next chapter.

An eighteenth-century lodge in Kensington Gardens, London

Sophistication of the Town

As for the town, if the medieval age had created it, it was civilised and brought to perfection by the Renaissance. Towns now developed a house type of their own, based on the deep narrow plots that were a legacy of the medieval city. At Shrewsbury, Sherar's Mansion shows how a memory of the old separate plots remained even where four adjacent plots had been joined together and a single house built on them. Each old plot is expressed by a gable turned towards the street, showing the course to be followed in later town development, where houses were often spread out sideways to belie their façade treatment. To this extent the English town house has been a practical affair, less an instrument of fashion than the country house, which tended to focus men's dreams and aspirations. It remained relatively free of the cultural burdens which made such demands on the country house that the type both awes and bewilders us; we need constant guides and explanations as to how they worked and what they were for, whereas a town house is easily understood by everyone.

Many London houses showed this characteristic of being divided notionally into bays outside yet internally ranging from side to side. Bearing this in mind, two seventeenth-century London developments are of particular interest. The first of these was the building of Covent Garden in the early 1630s by the Earl of Bedford. The scheme was built in spite of the king's prohibitions which attempted to stop the growth of London. Apart from making a payment of £2,000 for a licence (which is, one imagines, sufficient explanation), it is not clear how the earl obtained his permission. What is known is that a condition attached to his licence obliged him to employ the Surveyor of the King's Works to supervise the design. At this time that position was occupied by Inigo Jones. His efforts produced not only a general plan type for later speculative housing development, but also a source for their appearance. With his deployment of the Tuscan order, a classical system sometimes described by antique and Renaissance authorities, he achieved a classical feel, as one might say, at a moderate price.

'The Tuscan being a plain rude order', said Palladio, 'is therefore very seldom used above ground . . . If simple colonnades are made of this order, the spaces or intercoluminations may be very wide, because the architraves are made of wood, which will therefore be very commodious for villas, because it admits of passage for carts and other country implements, besides being of little expense.' It was unthinkable to Palladio that any of the major orders should be made of wood, and any order made in stone was limited in

The famous St Paul's Chapel in Covent Garden brought respectability to the Tuscan order of classical architecture. The uncomplicated geometry is indeed slightly rustic, recalling Jones's reply to his client's expressed desire for a 'mere barn' for a chapel, that he should have the noblest barn in England

column spacing by the tensile strength of stone architraves. So this order, though rather despised as being vernacular classical and unworthy of important buildings, could appeal to Jones for possessing elasticity, cheapness and delight. Those practical problems confronting the Elizabethans could be met without sacrificing internal logic, and of course Jones's puritanism gave him a fondness for the simplicity and freshness — masculinity as he called it — of this style.

The idea of a 'piazza' for Covent Garden was borrowed from an earlier project by an unidentified architect at Leghorn in Italy, which included a cathedral where Covent Garden had a chapel. Whereas at Leghorn the cathedral is not orientated but faces south to Rome, Jones's chapel does face east, and its position on the west side of the piazza being made necessary by practical constraints, this gave him a new architectural problem. That was, to turn the normally dull east façade of a chapel into the architectural focus of the square. Again, the Tuscan order is perfectly suited to the purpose with its massive and simple projecting pediment, which sits well with the strangely bold quality of the façade. One notices only slowly that this quality is heightened by the absence of any door in what looks at first sight to be a building entrance — in fact this portico with the wall behind it forms a distinct building, open on three sides, like a classical theatre, and has always been used as such.

Yet more important of Jones's innovations was the continuation of this order through on to the houses, or 'piazzas' as they came to be called, that occupied the north and east sides of the square. Although none of the original buildings survives, Bedford Chambers on the north side was built in loose imitation of Jones's work and gives some idea of what the façades accomplished. Only a count of front doors, set behind a deep arcade, told the number of separate properties that made up a terrace. The whole series has its parts subordinated to a classical framework, even if at an abstract and rather minimal level, yet the houses behind the façade are not sacrificed functionally to this ordering process.

The houses in Covent Garden were planned with plots of equal frontage but narrow and deep. This later became standard for town houses, but at about the same date, 1640, one can see in Lindsey House, Lincoln's Inn Fields, classical architecture applied to the older, wide fronted house type. Built by a speculator named William Newton, it is said to have been designed by Jones as well, and a quick glance at the plan suggests that this might be true. The house plan appears as two interlocking squares, forming a rectangle of ratio $\sqrt{2}$ (a rectangle formed by using the diagonal of a square to give the length of its long side) and this ratio seems to be used to pro-

(right) Lindsey House in Lincoln's Inn Fields is one of the first houses (1641) to take classicism on to the streets as part of a continuous terrace. It is a risky business, depending so heavily on the neighbours joining in, and having joined, to stay in. This was possible later when a single developer took control of a whole street or square, but a look at Portland Place in London as it is reduced today will show what delicate instruments manners are; *(above)* The ground-floor plan showing the neat arrangement of rooms and access to them

portion the whole house. It is a wide house (it later was split into two), but the indications of this singularity are subtle and few. Of course the doorway gives it away, but that sits within a ground floor which is visually separated from the continuous upper storey by a device later common to the Georgian period, rustication. By treating it in this way, the architect has freed the ground floor from the ordered floors above. In a solid wall with no columns, it then became possible to offset windows and doors, which seldom do line up with openings above them, with scarcely anyone the wiser.

Just who promoted the building of London's squares is an interesting question. It seems to have been the speculators who pushed for the adoption of a consistent, continuous classical framework, while the aristocracy of west London, not primarily speculators, were content with the most random collection of structures. The Earl of Bedford obviously had his arm twisted to employ Jones, and is exceptional; William Newton is more typical. One

of London's first great developers was Nicholas Barbon who built Red Lion Square in the 1680s and who later covered many acres north of it. For Barbon, consistency was a function of mass production rather than urban idealism, and his houses were produced for a less ambitious (to be polite) or less successful (to be truthful) class of inhabitant than were the large squares. Even the balustrading remained identical in all the houses of a particular development, yet he took care to make the proportions fine, to make repetitions enrich rather than dull the street. Here again, 'implied classicism' is used to attract buyers to new areas in the age of taste.

Barbon's methods also show the primitive industrial techniques he applied to building. The artisan, creation and creator of the medieval city, was here dominated in such a way that his 'patron' was calling on him to perform identical tasks endlessly, an infinity of balustrading, numberless windows and doors, each exactly alike and interchangeable. The city was moving into a new phase; constructing it was becoming a profession, and an industry.

The age of Wren generally did not contribute much to the texture of towns. Odd buildings were erected — market halls and the like — but the Baroque theories of town planning developed in Italy and France and taken up by Wren were firmly resisted in England. Private developers continued to work their way through lanes and across fields. Jones, we have seen, became involved in Covent Garden *ex officio,* his role of surveyor, and later Wren's, being mostly concerned with royal or government buildings. The amateur who wished to build might consult one of the few architects of the day, or purchase books by foreign authors by means of which he could try to educate himself. On the other hand, he might choose to patronise some bright, promising artisan, give him the opportunity to study architecture, and in return apply his protégé's skills to his own projects. Precisely this happened to John Wood, born in 1704 and eventually patronised by Lord Bingley.

Having divided his early years between Yorkshire and London, Wood arrived at Bath in 1727 to begin a series of developments that were, together with the work of his son, to complete the architectural conception of English town planning. But as we stroll through these well-mannered, dignified urban pieces, we should reflect that they are mere shadows of the schemes that filled Wood's head. It is usually true in architecture that only the clearest and farthest fetched of ideas have the vitality to survive the muting effect that their embodiment in built form has upon them. Those who aim at the tasteful and graceful often fall far, far short. Wood's original proposals were, in his own words, the following:

In each design I propose to make a Grand Place of Assembly, to be called the Royal Forum of Bath; another Place, no less magnificent, for the Exhibition of Sports, to be called the Grand Circus; and a third Place, of equal state with either of the Former, for the practice of Medicinal Exercises, to be called the Imperial Gymnasium of the City, from a Work of that kind, taking its rise first in Bath, during the time of the Roman Emperors.

All this for gouty elders and geriatrics. But if the Palladians had a strength it was their complete disregard for historical accuracy. They used the past selectively (as Wood does in the passage above) to justify their predilections, rationalising the irrational and deceiving the general public into acceptance of buildings that could make large towns and cities function well and function beautifully.

Though Wood did not live to complete his schemes, his son John Wood the Younger was able to use the same empirical approach to create what is perhaps the most famous of all town-planning exercises in England, Bath's Royal Crescent. Built by Wood thirteen years after his father's death in 1754, this great half Colosseum completes the sequence of places begun by the elder Wood, an ordered progress from the town's core out into the parkland that surrounds it. Here, unlike the Circus, a giant order of pilasters has been used, that runs right through two storeys like that of a hundred and thirty years earlier at Lincoln's Inn Fields. And here we see the pilasters not simply tying floor to floor, but age to age, as the older London house type develops and spreads throughout the country.

Mention of both Lindsey House and Bath as types of the English town house, suggests the opportunity to glance forwards, and compare these works with that of the master of English house design, Robert Adam. Lindsey House is seen to be squarish, with central access into a large hall that proves to be the only room of consequence on the ground floor. The others were used as offices and small parlours. Beyond the hall, a stately staircase lit by a courtyard led to the first floor, or 'piano nobile', which contained the principal rooms. These were an ante-room, two drawing-rooms and a dining-room. There are no corridors in the house, and the skill with which it was planned is evident in the enforced symmetry, well-placed service stairs and proportioning of the rooms. But the generous width of this type of house, some 60 feet, was a disappearing luxury.

No 24 Queen Square, at Bath, was built in 1729 by John Wood the Elder, and admittedly the plan was not his chief interest. He really cared about the façade, and it was a condition of building leases that every house must continue the design, which added up to a palatial elevation. That can explain the horror of No 24's plan, but does it excuse it ? In a site one-third narrower

From certain angles it is possible to make The Circus at Bath
(*left*) look like a monumental space. In fact it is a smallish
three-storey development, in a form that implies a focus of
attention but doesn't have one. Yet perhaps this understated circus is just what is required as a preparation
for the surprise that lies around the corner . . . which is
the Royal Crescent. Here again we have, architecturally,
three storeys, but treated in an altogether grander
way. It is the perfect representation of English life:
half solid city, half rolling, manicured countryside

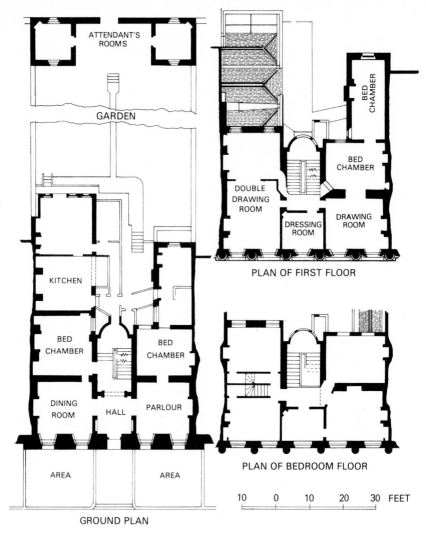

ATTENDANT'S
ROOMS

GARDEN

KITCHEN

BED
CHAMBER

BED
CHAMBER

DINING
ROOM

HALL

PARLOUR

AREA

AREA

GROUND PLAN

BED
CHAMBER

DOUBLE
DRAWING
ROOM

BED
CHAMBER

DRESSING
ROOM

DRAWING
ROOM

PLAN OF FIRST FLOOR

PLAN OF BEDROOM FLOOR

10   0   10   20   30   FEET

Plans of 24 Queen Square, Bath, by John Wood the Elder, c1729

than Lindsey House, an attempt has been made to construct the same plan.
Here is the same central hall and stair beyond — severely diminished — but
the dining-room has had to shift to the ground floor, with a bedroom opening off it, mixed up with parlour, bed chambers and kitchen. An enormous
garden is rendered almost invisible by two long wings which straggle out
from the house and leave only enough space to light the stairs. First floor
again confuses beds with drawing-rooms; again the garden is ignored. One

78

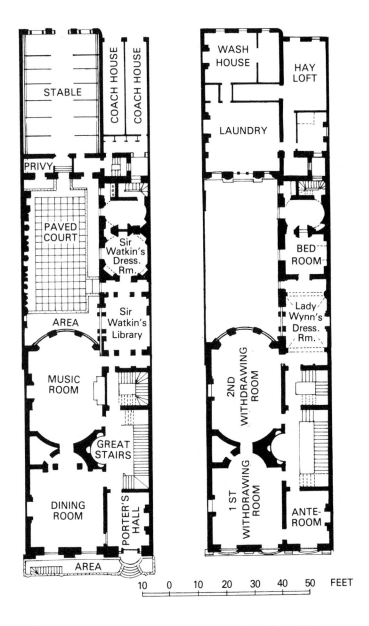

STABLE

COACH HOUSE

COACH HOUSE

PRIVY

PAVED COURT

Sir Watkin's Dress. Rm.

AREA

Sir Watkin's Library

MUSIC ROOM

GREAT STAIRS

DINING ROOM

PORTER'S HALL

AREA

WASH HOUSE

HAY LOFT

LAUNDRY

BED ROOM

Lady Wynn's Dress. Rm.

2ND WITHDRAWING ROOM

1ST WITHDRAWING ROOM

ANTE-ROOM

10   0   10   20   30   40   50   FEET

Plans of 20 St James's Square, London, by Robert Adam, 1772

79

needn't continue the list, for it is clear that Wood had his hands full with the elevations and couldn't or wouldn't come to terms with his plans.

Adam's work at No 20 (now No 15) St James's Square, London, is another story altogether. It was built in 1772 for Sir Watkyn and Lady Wynn. With the narrower frontage Adam immediately abandons central access as an unnecessary formality in terrace housing, where it is largely unnoticed. For it he substitutes a side to side progression of spaces through the house, thus making it seem much larger than it is, and has returned to proportional ratios to control the rooms. He has divided the width of the site into two strips, in ratio 3 to 5. The wider of these strips is then divided at right angles in ratio 3 to 6, so forming the principal rooms of squares and double squares.

The narrower of the 'width' strips serves the wider, and contains entrance hall, staircase, and service stairs. It then extends beyond the rear wall of the main house to form a series of private chambers in a lovely procession of rectangular and square pavilions. The first floor repeats this sequence in principle and each has a rear room looking out over a magnificent pilastered courtyard, making more of beauty from a few square feet of paving than Wood could squeeze out of an 80 foot garden. Again we have a plan without corridors, where the procession from room to room is a highly valued part of the architecture, and demonstrates that the plan need not be sacrificed under the economies of a narrow site. In Adam's hands, the plan becomes as beautiful a study as his elevations.

The period dealt with by this chapter has seen the city civilised and the country idealised. There was an unwillingness to allow the city to remain chaotic. The desire to order it was brought to its height, and there was no possibility of regarding it as other than man-made, as an artifact, while the country began to become abstracted into notions of paradise and the gentle life. In mentioning Adam we have come near to the age of neo-classicism and a point where the city, so carefully crafted over the centuries, came itself to be regarded as a 'natural' environment, out of control and as primitive as a forest.

4
Genius at Work

What is genius? . . . Where there is effectiveness, power, action, thought and feeling which cannot be learned or taught, there is genius, the most apparent and least describable thing, felt but unspoken, like love!

Johann Kaspar Lavater, 1775

If there is one gesture that signals the arrival of a new age after 1750, it is the abandonment of hard established rules and principles for the delights of genius and 'good taste'. Inspiration came to replace technical skill and craft as the artistic criterion, a fact that often becomes painfully obvious at the times when the inspiring muses were unavailable for a particular work. Only during the eighteenth century did the word 'genius' assume its present meaning of an artist inspired, and it is an essentially romantic meaning. The artist, freed from social and artistic constraint, now communed directly with the gods, an activity reflective rather than social. As Henry Fuseli said, in the 1780s, 'art, like love, excludes all competition and absorbs the man'.

Robert Adam, who presumably occupied the muses' time to the detriment of lesser architects, might be said to represent the developing type of artist, and his work at Osterley Park stands as an expression of his genius. Adam's position is a strange one. In the eighteenth century, the age of social pretension and ostentatious taste, he pinned all hopes of artistic, financial and social success on his ability to refine that taste to a nicety. As Adam first saw it, Osterley Park was a sixteenth-century house, built originally for Sir Thomas Gresham, founder of London's Royal Exchange and England's richest merchant. Adam's job was to turn this house into a modern palace in which to entertain and impress the clients of Robert Child, the banker. It has been suggested that Child's father, the first of English bankers, had bought Osterley for the great vaults that lie beneath its courtyard, ideal for storing cash.

So this was the new patronage in company with the new artist, conspiring to produce what for Walpole was, 'Oh, the palace of palaces!' Approving the new invisible methods of making money, by banking as opposed to the usual landed estate fortunes, he went on, '. . . such expense! such taste! such

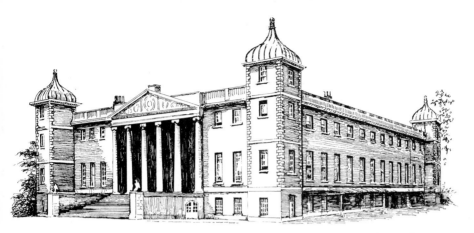

The entrance front of Osterley Park, Middlesex, as remodelled by Robert Adam, 1763

profusion! and yet half an acre produces all the rents that furnish such magnificence. It is a Jaghire [estate] without a crime. In short, a shop is the estate, and Osterley Park is the spot.' The sophisticated money market had obviously obscured social and economic relationships to the point where they are almost considered to be non-existent, and Child's money somehow a gift of the gods. Sir William Chambers, designer of Somerset House and Adam's chief professional rival, had begun to re-case the Elizabethan building in a new skin of brickwork, maintaining the turreted corner towers, and Adam continued this work. But his sense of 'movement' as he himself referred to it, his poetry, led him to contrast this solid container of squat brick with a spectacular open portico, sitting atop broad layers of steps. The courtyard of an Elizabethan house was its soul and nature. By being unroofed, but enclosed, it acted as a welcome at the end of a journey and the first room in the house. Because its walls were formed by the various rooms that made up the house, it was a domesticated space, rather like a town square. Here, that space is deliberately broken, against rules both ancient and modern, and Adam's genius lies in the fact that he can execute the project with delicacy, retaining the dignity and intentions of the older building. So the building is made at once pretentious with its giant classicism, traditional with its severe brick forms, and tense with visual and emotional pull from one to the other. It is this tension, in place of the repose aimed at by the older school of classical revival architects, that gives Adam his place

(opposite) At Osterley Park Robert Adam replaced the solid side of an Elizabethan house with this transparent portico, which invites the countryside into the house. The original courtyard had intended just the opposite, the exclusion of a hostile outside world

in the so-called neo-classical movement. His work is at heart romantic, playing the past against the future; the emotional struggle that results gives him the present.

The notions of movement and change began to dominate intellectual and social activity after the mid-eighteenth century, at first simply as discoveries but later considered and turned to cultural service. American, French and Industrial revolutions all manifested the astonishing forces that now lay in men's hands. First reactions to these forces included those of Edmund Burke, awed by their immense scale and apparently unintelligent action. What was the point of crafting a civilization, part by part, turning every thought to perfection, if its fragile structure were to be at the mercy of such ungovernable and aimless social forces?

But of course this had its attractions, as submission to overwhelming power often does. Even Dr Johnson had given into the exhilaration of speed as he pulled away from Adam's Kedleston Hall: 'If I had no duties, and no reference to futurity,' he said to Boswell, 'I would spend my life in driving briskly in a post-chaise with a pretty woman; but she should be one who could understand me and would add something to the conversation.' It would have been a lesson in various kinds of speed.

Burke did not invent, but popularised and gave emotional content to the concept of the sublime in art. Most importantly, he contrasted the sublime with classical canons of taste:

> . . . for as every thing new, extraordinary, grand, or passionate is well calculated to affect such a person [the unsophisticated judge of art], and that the faults do not affect him, his pleasure is more pure and unmixed; and as it is merely a pleasure of the imagination, it is much higher than any which is derived from a rectitude of the judgement; the judgement is for the greater part employed in throwing stumbling blocks in the way of the imagination, in dissipating the scene of its enchantment, and of tying us down to the disagreeable yoke of our reason . . .

It is this doubting of reason in the face of an unintelligent, unknowable universe that strikes such a pathetic but familiar note, signalling the true end of classicism. A glorious past, irrecoverable, a glorious future, unreachable, undermine the ideal of civilization. If primitive response is of equal value to refined judgement, why then bother with refinement? A sad passage from Burke's essay sums up this attitude:

> In the morning of our days, when the senses are unworn and tender, when the whole man is awake in every part, and the gloss of novelty fresh upon all the objects that surround us, how lively at that time are our sensations, but how false and inaccurate the judgements we form of things? I despair of ever receiving the

same degree of pleasure from the most excellent performances of genius which I felt at that age, from pieces which my present judgement regards as trifling and contemptible.

This conflict of emotion and intellect is typical of the period, apparent to some degree in Robert Adam's work and to a greater extent in the architecture and personality of John Soane. Men who wrote as beautifully as Burke, or whose works radiate the charm and erudition of Adam's, were by no means primitive. The voices raised in praise of the primitive and romantic were classically trained.

Soane himself was an odd figure, withdrawn, oscillating between extremes of tenderness and vicious paranoia. His architecture itself seems to represent the struggle of genius against itself which had become the critical feature of artistic endeavour, a conflict of rational and irrational elements which first destroyed classical architecture and ever since has sought its replacement. Together with neo-classical ideas of movement and change went an eighteenth-century obsession with archaeology, a minute study of dead cultures and with death itself. As the scientific method permeated historical research, a desire grew to dig deeper and deeper into the past in search of the true origins of our cultural existence. A rational search was begun for an irrational goal. Each man vied with his neighbour to unearth an architecture more ancient, more original, more primitive and more 'true' than any before. So it was with the British architect/archaeologists Stuart and Revett, whose famous *The Antiquities of Athens* was published between 1748 and 1762, Wood's *The Ruins of Palmyra* of 1753, *The Ruins of Baalbec* of 1757 and the many publications in Italy of Piranesi's engravings.

The process was complicated, but it could be said to have originated with René Descartes in the seventeenth century. His principal worry had been how one could know anything, and he tried to answer this by sitting in a stove and doubting everything that could be doubted. The only undoubtable to him was thought itself, a process entirely internal to the individual. If we jump now to the mid-eighteenth century, we can see a certain Abbé Laugier applying the same method to architecture. Rather than ask himself what could be done with existing architectural theory and practice, he asked himself whether it was necessary to have architecture at all. He doubted architecture to the point where he was left with the sparse logic of only a roof and a few columns to support it. This was, according to Laugier, the type of habitation built by earliest man, the primitive hut, and the fact that this hut would be functionally useless in the eighteenth century merely told against the century. The French have a wonderful confidence in this sort of theory.

Such extremes, needless to say, could not survive the channel crossing, but the archaeological character of neo-classical architecture is clear in Soane's work. He even went so far as to commission engravings of his Bank of England as a ruin, enjoying this dreamy idea as much as the thought of his lovely building being consigned to trade in stocks and bonds. (Not in his deepest nightmares can he have foreseen its true fate.) He seems to have spoken not to his own age but to one remote. A hundred years after Soane's imaginings, the romantic poet James Elroy Flecker wrote of the same feelings:

> We are dead, but our living was great: we are dumb,
> but a song of our State
> Will roam in the desert and wait, with its burden of
> long, long ago,
> Till a scholar from sea-bright lands unearth from the
> years and the sands
> Some image with beautiful hands, and know what we
> want him to know.

John Soane stands, not without occasionally overbalancing, on the line that divides romantic and classical ages. The silhouettes of his buildings are picturesque: the Dulwich Picture Gallery, his own house in Lincoln's Inn Fields; they are restless and full of movement, recession and projection of planes. He understood classicism, but used the orders — capitals, entablatures, shafts, bases — as picturesque elements concentrated in otherwise general designs. Although the Bank of England building in London has been mostly destroyed, the altered Tivoli Corner remains, at an acute angle in the plain curtain wall that surrounds the site. That angle demanded enrichment, and here Soane brought out the full power of classicism. Otherwise he tended to reduce the classical to abstraction in the form of incisions in stone and plaster, mannerisms difficult for many of his contemporaries to accept. In fact they were all he could justify on these otherwise primitive forms. Soane was caught in the trap of rationality. If decorative detail had no functional necessity or symbolic meaning, how could it be justified? Clearly, it had no primitive or fundamental necessity, because by definition it was elaboration. But Soane had been trained in and believed in classical architecture, and that meant all the paraphernalia that went with it. Although it may seem strange to suggest that reason and romanticism fed each other's fires, the Bank of England was the proof of it.

Sir John Soane had a difficult time obtaining permission to construct the façade of his house like this, because it projects beyond the building line and his neighbours objected. Altogether, Soane seems to have been on the point of bursting out of his three terrace houses, and it is hard to imagine that any more could be squeezed out of its particular rules and restrictions than he managed

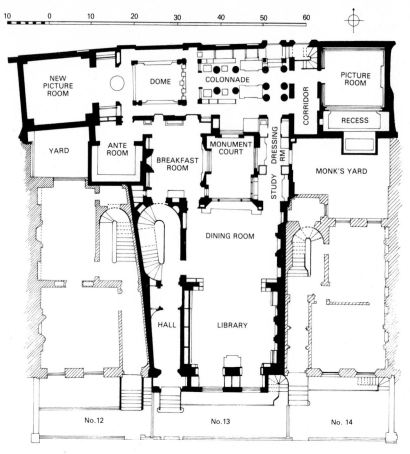

Plan of the ground floor of Nos 12, 13 & 14, Lincoln's Inn Fields

The houses Soane built for himself at Lincoln's Inn Fields between 1792 and 1824 illustrate the intellectual and aesthetic problems he faced. (Though practical matters weren't such a problem; to quote a passage about the building of No 13 in 1812:

The new house building proceeded very rapidly. Possession of No. 13 was obtained July 13, and pulling down began on the 17th, and was completed on August 1. On the 3rd they began to trench for the back front wall, and the next day at 9 a.m. began to lay bricks. The parlour floor was built in a week, 11–18th August. On October 6 the two statues on the facade were put up, and the upper part of the scaffold began to be removed. Slating began on October 9, and on the 13th the whole building was covered in.

Soane ate Christmas dinner in the house, too.) It is difficult to think what more could be done within the limits of the terrace house convention. He himself regretted having been unable to develop the site of his three houses all at once, rather than over a thirty-two year period, as leases fell in and land and money became available. Yet this is the rationalist, the neo-classical architect, regretting the unheroic achievement of piecemeal development; contribution to, rather than creation of, a city. Ever constrained by what surrounded him, he would rather have been free. These circumstances prevailed at the Bank of England as well, where for forty-five years he laboured to produce what was one of Europe's finest buildings. But all in the 'pragmatic' style! This pragmatic utility was precisely what classical architecture had been meant to offer, yet to Soane it was both welcome and resented. He must somehow have understood that our modern way would be no better, with architects and their clients, no longer able to perform delicate operations on the urban body, obliged to demolish on a large scale in order to modify things. For a neo-classical architect, the great achievement was the monument, isolated in a dreamy landscape, out of sight of all other buildings and people. So Soane balanced between these worlds not without trepida-

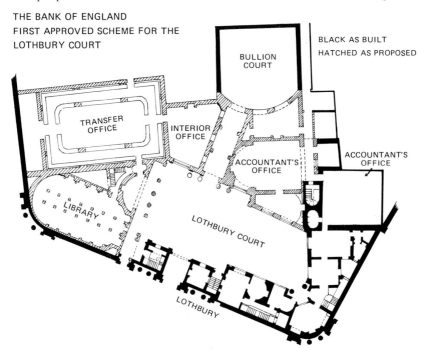

THE BANK OF ENGLAND
FIRST APPROVED SCHEME FOR THE
LOTHBURY COURT

BLACK AS BUILT
HATCHED AS PROPOSED

BULLION COURT

TRANSFER OFFICE

INTERIOR OFFICE

ACCOUNTANT'S OFFICE

ACCOUNTANT'S OFFICE

LIBRARY

LOTHBURY COURT

LOTHBURY

Part of a plan of the Bank of England, London, by John Soane, c1805. The so-called Tivoli Corner is at the lower right

89

The Tivoli Corner at the Bank of England

tion, but with skill that can only be wondered at, though the effort practically drove him mad. His subjective vision of architecture could not, by definition, be shared. For an introspective and paranoid man, this was a heavy responsibility. His spherical domes and top-lit spaces always suggest cave-like shelter, security. Above all, it would seem, Soane built for himself.

The fact that Soane's work was contemporary with that of John Nash is one of the wry ironies of architectural history: Soane the thorough professional, Nash the slightly shady; Soane the refined seeker after perfection, Nash the master of crude gesture and general effect. Yet Nash remains an architect to be reckoned with, for he gave picturesque architecture its greatest monuments, establishing his effects largely through the scale of his operations.

From the Palladian projects of the first half of the eighteenth century, formal houses set among sinuous parades of garden temples, the picturesque moved into architecture itself. Adam at Holkham gives this unstable, always-shifting quality to the building. Instead of the fragmented gardens of Capability Brown, such as Castle Ashby in Northamptonshire, these were now made with a sequence of framed views; man was taken out of the landscape, out of paradise, and asked to look in on it as the memory of a dream. Nash's close collaboration in the early nineteenth century with Humphrey Repton, the most impressive of the picturesque landscapers, produced works like Luscombe Castle in Devonshire, a picture within a picture. For Nash made the house itself become a collection of fragments, a kind of picturesque composition. It should be mentioned that a house at this time was still thought to be best served by an external appearance quite unrelated to its internal organization, its plan. It did not have to conform to the more strictly French neo-classical ideal of honesty, according to which a building should express externally its internal logic. Later the idea had some popularity in Britain, though curiously enough mainly as a Gothic revival precept, the architectural equivalent of phrenology. (That favourite Victorian preoccupation was, incidentally, the chief study of Johann Lavater, whose quotation heads this chapter.)

Building quaint cottages and lodges in large gardens was a well-established tradition. While Nash progressed in his career from cottages to houses, the principles that he had formed of the picturesque remained

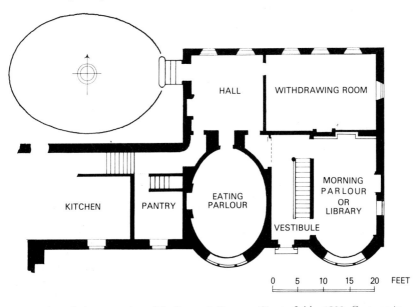

The simple and charming plan of Barlborough Rectory, Chesterfield, c1800. Gestures in room shapes affect the outside of such thin-walled buildings, and start to give a satisfactory correspondence between interior and exterior forms

Cronkhill, Shropshire by John Nash, 1802

constant. What in a former age would have been a small temple-like villa
with proper axial symmetry is now a jumble of rustic fragments. Is the round
tower of Cronkhill the stump of some giant column, part-buried, hollowed
out and inhabited? Its conical roof gives just that temporary and pathetic
feeling of ruined monuments when converted into barns or houses. The
Temple of Vesta in Rome, seen in Renaissance prints, could be a prototype.
Cronkhill is always concerned at an artistic level with sentiment, never with
intellect. His other houses, as Luscombe, were generally medievalized,
either Gothic or castellated, rambling about the landscape, presumably to

The Temple of Vesta
at Rome

John Nash had a more conventional understanding of classical architecture than Soane, but he put it to good use. At Regent's Park in London he surrounded green parkland with a number of terraces that resemble palaces, following Wood's example at Bath. It gives Sunday football a boost to have a permanent, if small, stand of spectators always present beyond the trees

establish an English version of the Poussin picturesque. Part of the value of this exercise, making a house into a cottage, must be that it allowed the architecture to become accessible to a wider range of people, who without the necessity of thinking would be able to understand a building directly through the channels of emotion. The house became a sentimental blur in a haze of greenery.

The picturesque was also an acceptable urban prototype, more so perhaps than a rural one because the piecemeal development and artificial nature of cities is more evident. (This notwithstanding the medieval monk for whom the existence of a river in all major towns was an indication of God's benevolence.) The 'constructedness' is more 'felt' in any case. The city's intellectual incompleteness is insuperable in terms other than picturesque, and the paratactic or random nature of cities, that is, the fact that they are jumbled together, makes them readily adaptable to such theories.

A pragmatic technique for the development of cities had perhaps begun with Christopher Wren scheming wonderful plans for the rebuilding of London after the fire, but being forced in the end to conform with existing land interests. It progressed with the Woods at Bath, and came back to London with Nash. How extraordinary his success was, wrapping aesthetic theory over the most hum-drum, thoroughly practical matters — canals, markets, houses — replacing the earlier hollow evocations of landscape paintings with an urban substance better than the originals. He created the jewel of garden cities, and none has since been built to equal it nor, perhaps, has been built so quickly. Nash was not interested in labouring his mind with details of composition and construction. On discovering the cornice of Gloucester Terrace (in Regent's Park) to be twice its intended size, Nash only observed that it had 'come out larger than he expected' and there it remains. His job was to create the image, literally the façade; he left to others the job of filling in the hidden workings of a building. He seems to have attached little importance to the quality of the object, a great deal to the quality of the idea. Regent's Park façades were each contracted for and built as separate objects, after which individual leaseholders were invited to line up rooms with windows as best they could. Nash seemed little concerned with what went on inside his buildings as a rule, and he concentrated on making urban space conform to his principles of movement, variety and romantic charm.

Consolidation of the Classical

The end of the Napoleonic Wars was practically a halting point for British architecture. European and domestic politics were nervous; and too, the middle classes were gradually assuming authority in place of the aristocracy, so circumstances tended to make respectability the safest refuge. Greek revival architecture was, of course, terribly respectable, and its main English protagonists, William Wilkins and Robert Smirke, were earnest about it to a fault. George Dance the Younger had helped Smirke design his first building, the Royal Opera House, in 1808, giving it a solid Greek portico. After that time practically every building Smirke designed had the same feature, sometimes more than once. His best-known building, the British Museum in London, has a portico that spills over into a peristyle and threatens to go on to infinity. Wilkins sponsored a rather more attenuated and anaemic Greek: the National Gallery and University College in London are well-known examples. Both men were very successful, building country houses, town halls and so on throughout the land.

Despite the emotional nature of Gothic revival rhetoric, that indicated another direction, Greek revival architecture, slowly transforming itself into Italian Renaissance, was being kept alive by men like C. R. Cockerell and Charles Barry well into the nineteenth century. Barry designed Manchester's

Oxford's Ashmolean and Taylorian Institution was built by C. R. Cockerell, last of the great classical architects, and a man whose classical learning is said to have been extensive and deep. This alone would set him apart from men like Robert Smirke and William Wilkins, and seems appropriate for the architect of one of the great collections of art and archaeology

St George's Hall is ever more isolated in the heart of Liverpool. But then, it stands on an island in any case, so the deteriorating quality of its surroundings gives a certain reinforcement to the building's dignity

The standard of architecture was perhaps not as high in Edinburgh's New Town as at Bath, but it may be that conventionality saved it from disaster. There is nothing new attempted, and principles developed elsewhere are practically applied. It seems to have worked out quite well in the end

Todmorden Town Hall, built in the 1870s, and demonstrating the continuing if sporadic use of neo-classicism late into the century

Royal Institution in 1824–34 and the new Houses of Parliament, 1837–67. On the last of these projects, of course, Gothic detailing was handled by A. W. N. Pugin. Further north things were more lively, in the towns where new wealth meant public commissions. Liverpool had the Custom House designed by John Foster in the late 1820s (destroyed in the last war), and it still has H. L. Elmes's St George's Hall. Elmes had the good fortune to have a commission for three buildings in one, and made the most of this in terms of formal expression. That empty and aloof quality so beloved of neo-classical architects is strongly felt, the result of an abundance of formal entrance fronts and an absence of windows. In this building English architecture approaches most closely to Continental neo-classical practice.

Scotland was more receptive to the Greek revival. Edinburgh's New Town was given a boost after 1815, with Archibald Elliot and William Playfair as its chief designers. Playfair perhaps more than anyone gives Edinburgh's 'Athens of the North' title its visual meaning, with his monumental National Gallery and Royal Institution. Yet the most successful of Greek revival buildings must be the Edinburgh High School, built in 1825 by Thomas Hamilton, splendidly sited on Calton Hill. Its inert forms seem to have walked casually through each other on fluted legs, finding at length a comfortable and picturesque position of unified repose.

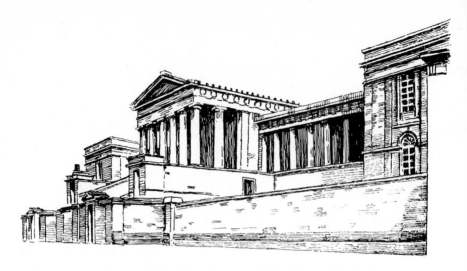

Edinburgh High School, begun in 1825 by Thomas Hamilton

Glasgow too shows a splendid range of building from the early and mid-nineteenth century, though much was lost during the last war as a result of bombing, and much subsequently sacrificed to what is now recognised as one of the less sensitive pieces of town planning. The work of David Hamilton, his Royal Exchange and his houses in particular, was followed by some very delicate work by John Brash and in turn by one of the most remarkable of British architects, Alexander 'Greek' Thomson. Apart from a number of well-known churches, Thomson built several terraces of houses and villas, which have no equal in Britain. While Philip Webb was refurbishing the Old English tradition, faintly medieval, and creating a style of warm and familiar domesticity, Thomson developed a more strongly intellectual approach. The fact that his houses were still called villas, long after the name had been dropped for serious buildings in England, is indicative of their severely classical nature. From the intractable stone he worked with, he made a very individual architecture, cool and expressive, from volume and form. The villa at 25 Mansionhouse Road, for example, built in 1856 and pressing on with the neo-classical experiment, separates the glazing plane of the bay window from the columns in front of it, which takes us right back to Laugier and his ideal architecture of columns and roofs only. As so often with the neo-classicists, Thomson innovates to reinforce the illusions he creates, here employing thin iron glazing bars for the first time domestically. A good deal of his work in speculative housing also survives, and it shows the extra lift that architecture can get from the use of stone.

25 Mansionhouse Road, Glasgow, built in 1856 by Alexander 'Greek' Thomson

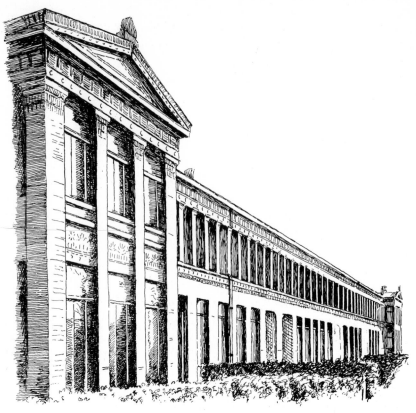

Thomson's Moray Place, Glasgow, of 1859

Queen's Park, Northpark and Great Western terraces and finally the superb
Moray Place of 1857–9, with their precise detailing, show the care with
which Thomson considered the building of a city.

   How different things were back in London, where Thomas Cubitt had
been learning how to industrialise the building industry, indeed the building
of London itself. Cubitt's role descended from that of Nicholas Barbon, who
was mentioned in the last chapter as the builder of parts of Holborn; but
whereas Barbon used plain brick and no architect, Cubitt stuccoed everything in Belgravia madly, under the direction of several architects, George
Basevi and Philip Hardwick among them. And it was Roman, too — no
sharp-edged Greek detail here, but luscious cream imperial style. The Upper
King's Road seems made for cheering hordes and imperial parades. With
growth in both private and public commissions, architect speculators were
increasingly regarded with suspicion. Though Cubitt was by no means considered socially outré — indeed he was a friend of Prince Albert — many

speculative builders were thought to be ethically unsound. The architect, too, sought respectability at this time; as he began the slow ascent to professional status, he gave over his speculative role, and with it any direct social control over his buildings. From this point architects only design buildings, they don't initiate them.

A new Morality

But other things were going on in London, too. A. W. N. Pugin, born in 1812, was in a sense the Romantic movement's first son. That he had detailed Barry's Houses of Parliament in 1830s has been mentioned, but it was as a writer and polemicist that he was most important. Whereas Walter Scott had dreamed of and written about the Gothic Age, he hadn't felt the desire that gripped Pugin, to dress up in cassocks or to take a moral stance towards the revival of medieval culture as a way of life. Pugin was in fact converted to the Roman Catholic faith through the emotional effect of ritual, the colour and the incense — its sensual trappings. His moralism has confusing similarities with principles expressed later in buildings like the Crystal Palace and the Palm Stove, Kew. Pugin believed in what he called 'truth' in architecture, a thoroughly neo-classical idea of undisguised structure, all elements of a building being expressed rather than hidden. Materials and function were to be treated 'honestly'. Why should a building's chimney look like a watch tower? Chimneys should look like chimneys, and so on. But from a logical viewpoint this is untenable. What does a chimney look like, essentially? Do we need them? Why has Pugin kept pitched roofs, and steeply pitched at that? He said it was for the better shedding of water and snow, but that has no scientific truth: it merely shifts our attention to the word 'better'. And steep roofs are expensive. Yet his method is justified, for all polemic is emotionally founded. By expressing and exaggerating the separate parts of a building, he was continuing the neo-Palladian tradition of movement, and the picturesque in composition. Like his church, St Augustine's at Ramsgate, his buildings tend to emerge as a series of pavilions. I mentioned earlier that this sort of composition had an unfortunate effect on a city's fabric because it destroyed the unity of streets, the great public rooms of the urban house. Pugin's sense of honesty demanded to be recognized as sincere, and his buildings similarly burst out in expressions of this sincerity, like Rousseau's *Confessions,* and embarrass their neighbours with their emotional outpourings.

As a first step into the shadowy land of truth in architecture, it would be prudent to say that architecture has many truths. There is the tautological

Leeds Town Hall, built in the 1850s by Cuthbert Brodrick, shows signs of trying to achieve the marriage of Gothic and classical that Barry and Pugin accomplished with London's Houses of Parliament. Here the effort is more openly classical, but the effects are distinctly Gothic

truth of a building's mere existence, but this is a truth perhaps not specifi-cally architectural. Bringing forward truth by reworking the constructional facts of a building may be more to the point. Fact may be truth, but truth is usually more than fact. What makes a poem stand apart from a simple list of facts is its effort of selection, suppression, exaggeration, which point in the end less at objective truth than at the value of subjective truth.

Pugin magnified Gothic architecture with the lens of neo-classicism. Structure became all important; the way a building supports itself should not only be honest, but like Caesar's wife must be unsuspected of deceit. That he was half French is a fact which may partly explain Pugin's passionate interest in neo-classicism. If one asks what Pugin was doing in a more general sense, he wanted to return to simpler and more direct ways of build-ing, a less pretentious architecture. Early nineteenth-century architecture *was* pretentious, with stuccoed villas littering the expanding suburbs and the humblest cottages aspiring to a nobility far beyond their means. If Nash had been sometimes feeble, he was the best of his kind, at a time when architec-ture was practically effete.

So far, Pugin's ideas seem reasonable. But making these ideas into moral dogma, turning artistic principle into moral principle, was a vastly egotistical act. Though partly empirical, his theories with their moral tone lead to a type of animism, an architecture with literal spiritual existence. Hence bad architecture (that is, architecture contrary to Pugin's ideas) was considered by him to be sinful.

Britain was, of course, submerged in religious debate during the middle years of the last century. Broadly speaking there were two currents that affected architectural matters. Those who were Tories, chiefly landowners, and suffering a progressive loss of control to the middle classes, sponsored the Evangelical Movement. This was the religion of silent suffering, stoical and paternalistic, imitating the traditional relationship between the land-owner and his dependants. As a movement it was involved in the practical alleviation, if not the elimination, of poverty. The Oxford Movement, on the other hand, concerned itself with spiritual salvation, considering this world best left to God's mercy or whim. The natural expression of such thinking is ritual, and to this the movement devoted itself wholeheartedly, and so stood opposed to the more Utilitarian-minded Evangelicals. To this Oxford theoretical position, Cambridge provided practical architectural advice. A society of undergraduates begun in 1839 and called the Ecclesiological Society from 1845, it began through its field researches and magazines to influence church design. Curiously, the resulting architecture tends toward a kind of expressionism, for while it does not abandon the Puginian egocen-

103

tric process of design, yet it has nothing to express beyond ritual, which is itself symbolic. Eventually this symbolism could not bear up under the philosophical load of function. Transepts, necessary for the formation of a symbolically cross-shaped ground plan, were found to be practically useless and too expensive to maintain. Even among the symbolists, there was a nagging desire for usefulness, and these expensive adjuncts were gradually omitted from building programmes.

A growing romantic belief in the perfection of some identifiable past age, combined in the nineteenth century with a loss of belief in the process of architecture. Even Joseph Paxton, who had built the wonderful Crystal Palace in 1851, built solid neo-Elizabethan when asked for Architecture with a capital 'A' — as Mentmore Towers bears witness. It is like an offering to the gods of gravity, who might have been offended by his earlier feather-light greenhouse. The Crystal Palace bears, practically is, a memory of its inception, construction and use. It well illustrates the idea that architecture can exist as a summation of processes. Mentmore is a lump, a symbol taken from the past, a vaster reworking of Wollaton Hall. It copies the processes of another age. As an object, the Crystal Palace was neither beautiful nor ugly and hardly commented on by contemporaries in aesthetic terms, remaining outside the province of their judgement. It would appear that the present, the 'now', scarcely interested the Victorians, who sought objective value in the past or the future, history or dreams. When they looked about them at what they produced, for the most part they beheld only ugliness; a sad but common condition.

Striking too are the parallel careers of so many nineteenth-century architects, the same men producing high art and a workaday style according to varying circumstances. It seems more than a simple case of manners in architecture, the appropriate style for the job. We are left to explain the great railway sheds and warehouses — King's Cross, York, St Enoch's in Glasgow, the Albert Docks and St Katharine's Docks in Liverpool and London, among many others. The truth is that primitivism had saturated the minds of these men, soaked into their bones. Just as many modern architects are 'closet classicists' with urges to bedeck their buildings with the pediments and capitals they have been taught to disdain, so these early Victorians were closet primitives, waiting for the moment when stripping of the orders was permitted. Decimus Burton was rather good at the classical game, but not exceptional. Yet there stands his Palm Stove at Kew, part building, part dinosaur, and part plant.

Burton built the Palm Stove in collaboration with Richard Turner between 1844 and 1848: 362ft x 100ft x 63ft high, it is one of the miracles

The interior of Lime Street Station, Liverpool. Outside, the station is almost unrecognizable, but this beautiful and delicate iron roof (only part of it is shown here) still survives. There is a general modern dictum that utility produces beauty, but a moment's reflection tells us that this is far from true. If it were, then structures with the beauty of this roof would not be the rarity that they are, nor would they cause so much astonished admiration

of architecture. It *is* sublime. Its first appeal is not to the intellect; most people feel slightly giddy when they first see it, unsure how far to trust senses that can be so stirred about. One cannot be struck by its pretentiousness because it doesn't speak that language; its rounded ends and mounting centrepiece are formal, but formal without occasion. Even the doors, items that often tempt architects beyond endurance to exercises in ostentatious elaboration, are here mere glass flaps recessed into the bubble. Nor is the project in any sense naïve. Both men had built similar structures before, had even worked together, though they produced nothing comparable to this. Though full of clever engineering, the highest aim of the Palm Stove is self-expression, which was sufficient to keep it from being anything more, to its contemporaries, than a wonderful toy. Our pleasures are twofold: we have the emotional pleasure, and we can follow it with an intellectual 'placing' of the building, a re-creation of the moment it was built. The decorative details charm us, too, their Grecian curves fixed beside the sensual turgid palms, from a more southern zone.

There followed a conscious movement towards vernacular or what might be called local expressionist architecture; art based on craft, a poetry of the everyday. The architect Philip Webb insisted that daily labour and activity could be used as a positive value. He therefore interested himself in the process of building, in the craft of creation. This was of course at the expense of ideal beauty, was in fact opposed to it, and his buildings were frequently described in his own time as being ugly. But John Ruskin, at about the same time Webb was building the Red House (1859–60), had written this:

> Now, in the make and nature of every man, however rude or simple, whom we employ in manual labour, there are some powers for better things . . . but they cannot be strengthened, unless we are content to take them in their feebleness, and unless we prize and honour them in their imperfections above the most perfect manual skill. And this is what we have to do with all our labourers: to look for the *thoughtful* part of them, and get that out of them, whatever we lose for it, whatever faults and errors we are obliged to take with it . . . Understand this clearly: you can teach a man to draw a straight line, and to cut one; to strike a curved line, and to carve it; and to copy and to carve any number of given lines or forms, with admirable speed and perfect precision; and you find his work perfect of its kind: but if you ask him to think about any of those forms, to consider if he cannot find any better in his own head, he stops; his execution becomes hesitating; he thinks, and ten to one he thinks wrong; ten to one he makes a mistake in the first touch he gives to his work as a thinking being. But you have made a man of him for all that. He was only a machine before, an animated tool.

Architecture like Webb's is based on circumstances, whose specific factors of location, use, client, artist, craftsman and time, are brought into relationship. The rules, then, are always changing, and comparison with the idealized eternal language of classical architecture reveals the radically original nature of this art. It was an attempt to found culture in the present.

John Ruskin was also responsible for turning the course of architecture from the strictly picturesque to the monumental. His books, *The Seven Lamps of Architecture* and *The Stones of Venice*, the second of which, written between 1851–3, provided the quotation used earlier, show an interest not only in architectural principles, but also in the emotional possibilities of the art. He revived that Byronic romanticism, the eighteenth-century love of vastness and repetition, depth in materials and their resistant nature. Sharp corners holding flat surfaces in tension, inlaid marble flush on shadowless planes; these techniques fascinated him. His vision of romanticism was not of something behind glass, a picture of another world; his romanticism would actively pace the streets, and struggle with passers-by.

Though the two are said never to have met, William Butterfield built the sort of thing Ruskin must have hoped for. All Saints' Church, Margaret

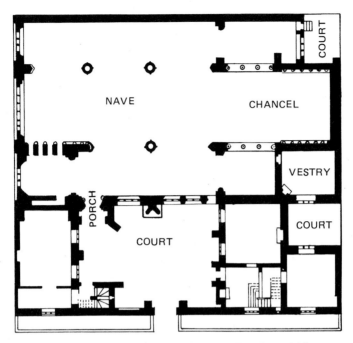

All Saints' Church, Margaret Street, London, by William Butterfield, 1849–59

Street, in London, is his best-known building, but considering that one of his aims and achievements was to astonish, it might be better to study the buildings he put up for Keble College in Oxford, red brick in a town proud of its stone. John Keble had roused the founders of the Oxford Movement with a sermon he gave in 1833; his death in 1866 roused them in turn to construct as his monument, Keble College.

Where Soane was moody and withdrawn, Butterfield was utterly reclusive. He never married, was an extraordinary moralist, and had few friends. He reached a point where all emotions issued from him as architecture, and it was just these emotions, this personal quality, that interested Ruskin so much. Both men would seem to have got on better with buildings than with people; rather than meet and chat in the public spaces of an ordered city, these Victorians shouted architecture at one another across the streets. If the neo-classical aim had been *architecture parlant*, the Victorians invented *architecture criant*. In a strange way, Butterfield's personal conduct, strict and private, seems to have allowed him adventures in the realms of architectural principle. He didn't balk, for example, at covering brickwork with render when it suited him, as it did in the church at Harrow Weald, and later he tacked half-timbering on to houses with no apparent misgivings. Pugin would have died before looking at such chicanery; and in fact, he did.

Keble is a very romantic building, set among trees, its asymmetrical façades raised on a formal plan. The traditional quad form is used effectively to set off the drama as one comes through the entrance gate, turns, following the low college buildings and then comes smack up against the mountainous chapel. Walls like these are not seen every day. Built mainly of red brick and Portland stone, their nature is at first peculiar, irrational and inexplicable. Yet there does seem to be a story to it. As they emerge from the ground these walls are quiet enough, but partly because wind and rain keep stone white, partly because of richer patterning, the top of Keble College Chapel resembles a blizzard of architectural materials. That is possibly the intended image: the first layers are held flat by gravity, while above them water forms wavy patterns of brick and still farther up the wind has shaken these pieces into fragments. Only the buttresses remain sedate throughout, to hold the display together.

These cottages at Baldersby St James, Yorkshire, were built in the 1850s by William Butterfield, architect of Keble College, Oxford. They show the growing interest and ability of architects in the simple forms and materials of everyday buildings, which was later to become a whole way of life for some designers — the Arts and Crafts movement. The artistic content of such buildings could be said to be no less than that of churches or palaces, with only this difference: everything depends upon the success of one or two gestures. In this case it is the way the dormer windows are tied into both roof and wall

The chapel of Keble College, Oxford, by William Butterfield. The eternal division between classical and Gothic revivals in the nineteenth century tends to obscure common artistic methods. This chapel, for all its vigorous patterning, could not be called exuberant. In its way it uses the same freedom that Cockerell employed in building his classical work, at the Ashmolean Museum, to take another Oxford example. Each depends more on the discipline of diverse elements for architectural effect than on any recipe or formula. Neither could be called eclectic in the rag-bag of loveable bits and pieces sense that men like Norman Shaw and Lutyens were later to employ to win the hearts of the public. They lack the sentimentality

Inside, the chapel's shape is plain, but as with the external composition this plainness acts as a ground for decoration, here in paint and mosaics. From the deep colours at floor level to the delicate painting on the vaulted ceiling, the feel of this space is like an indoor response to the external proposition of elements: earth, water and air, with fire (on a good day) blazing in at the windows. Here is a completely original interpretation, in symbolic terms, of the neo-classical ideal of correspondence between inside and outside of a building.

The simple fact that some 3,000 churches were built between the 1840s and 1860s would be reason enough for the falling off of church commissions in the late 1860s. Philip Webb's Red House of 1859–60, for William Morris,

The Red House, Bexleyheath, designed by Philip Webb in 1859–60 for William Morris

is regarded as a landmark in architecture from a twentieth-century view-point. That is possibly because it is a house rather than a church, and today we are interested not in churches but in houses. Webb himself apparently always regretted the fact that he could not concentrate exclusively on churches, and this would explain his attempt to transfer principles from the one type of architecture to the other. He was resisting, too, with a familiar sense of artistic pride, the distasteful notion that he was simply serving those who could afford to build.

The Red House can practically be interpreted as a visual and spatial representation of mid-century political belief, though perhaps one is more tempted to this view knowing that its owner was in later years a leader of British socialism. The house is formal only in a conceptual way; it is not simply a piecemeal, accidental composition, but pursues a strict policy of contingency, where elements are consciously encouraged in the expression of picturesque independence, within an abstract framework. No one ever went quite as far as Butterfield had with colour, and here the red brick and tile, local materials that actually give the house its name, glow alone among the greenery. In this kind of textural device, one see what it was that replaced classical formality. There was a belief among romantic socialists that a unified socialist culture, as had (supposedly) existed prior to capitalism, would by its nature produce harmonious relations among men. Hierarchy, order, class — these would either be superfluous or somehow acceptable in a pragmatic rather than an idealistic society.

From the late 1860s, until the end of the century, English architecture was centred on the work of Richard Norman Shaw, trained in the office of G. E. Street. One of the leading Gothic revivalists of his day, Street built London's Law Courts as well as countless churches. Shaw, though the same age as Philip Webb, developed a style altogether more polished and commercially acceptable. Both he and his close friend, W. E. Nesfield, took over the aesthetic principles of High Church architecture, but shed its accompanying moral doctrines in favour of a more practical, professional attitude towards their work. Shaw had none of Webb's regrets about the necessity of building houses; his belief was simply, that whatever you do ought to be done well. By and large he seems to have succeeded. Starting with his Leyswood House in Sussex of 1866–9 he built a number of country houses using a generalized 'Sussex Weald' style: red brick, tile hanging and nice white painted wooden windows. There was a practical, picturesque quality about this work, based on tradition and symbolism.

Undoubtedly Nesfield was a great influence on Shaw. His beautiful little lodge at Kew Gardens (themselves laid out, incidentally, by Nesfield's father), built in 1867, explores the first territory of the great Queen Anne style which dominated the 1870s. In this Queen Anne work — Lowther Lodge, 196 Queen's Gate, West House, the commercial New Zealand Chambers — Shaw had found a way of reaching into the middle-class traditions of native building and pushing them forward as a new architecture. Abstract in form and colour, free in proportion, these buildings seem

Detail of the decorated plaster coving beneath the eaves of Nesfield's lodge in Kew Gardens, 1867

111

to dwell on the middle ground between emotion and reason: it is common sense architecture.

After his Convent of Bethany in Bournemouth of 1878–80, where adventure in form was combined with his first exercise in the use of concrete, Shaw seems to have lost the ability to pursue the well-balanced architecture of his earlier years. New Scotland Yard is a fine building in its way, but already very solid chunks of pure English Renaissance stonework are planted in it, a first irruption of what was to become a stylistic plague, not only upon Shaw's work, but throughout English architecture.

A change had taken place in Victorian architects themselves, as in their work, and if Shaw can be said to have continued some of Butterfield's principles, the statement ought to be qualified. William Butterfield was a bachelor, dressed always in a black frock coat, who when he visited a building site would insist that it be cleaned and swept neat for his arrival, 'as if it was the king'. Norman Shaw called his wife, 'my duck o'diamonds pussy cat' and referred to her as his 'iddle wife'. What more can one add?

Architecture Reaches the Masses

William Morris, for whom Webb had built the Red House, tried hard to modify the social roles of art and artist in a practical way, by forming an atelier in 1861 with artists like Rosetti, Burne-Jones, Ford Maddox Brown and Webb. The hope was that such an association would be able to offer patrons a complete service of design, fabrics, furniture and buildings, and further would make good design available to a wider public. How far the aims of this group were met is difficult to judge, but clearly the necessity for a principal designer was soon felt, for in 1875 Morris set up a new atelier, completely under his own control. With C. R. Ashbee he founded the Society for the Protection of Ancient Buildings in 1877, as a political move against contemporary church restoration, specifically the project of Sir George Gilbert Scott for Tewkesbury Abbey.

Today Morris is known as much for his writing as for his designs: *News from Nowhere* contains the late Victorian Utopia, a world of communes in an age neither modern nor ancient, neither here nor far away; a society in which (unlike his ateliers) agreement can be reached co-operatively without domination; a society without problems, without drama, without power. If Nowhere was Morris's imagination of heaven on earth, the nowhere he was partly responsible for is the late Victorian suburb. Each could almost come from the description of the heavenly city in the *Book of Revelations*: a hand-crafted city without trouble or strife, though curiously lacking in craftsmen

The Tabard Inn, Bedford Park. Perhaps because of its size, this pub is the most successful of Bedford Park's buildings. Many of the local houses seem too small to contain all their architectural pretensions, but here, especially with the barn-like roof, Shaw manages a generosity of scale which makes it seem a spatial oasis. Perhaps this is really what medieval inns were for, who knows?

or anyone else, a place where nobody lives.

If that sounds a little unfair, one could look at the closest realization of his theories in practice, the development at Bedford Park, begun in 1876. Most of the early work for the scheme was designed by Norman Shaw. The houses and the layout fail to strike one with much force nowadays simply because so much that followed was of the same pattern throughout the country. The real achievement of Bedford Park's speculative developer, J. T. Carr, was the publicity he achieved. He succeeded in a suburb where the Adam brothers had failed in their Adelphi venture a century earlier, managing to attract relatively well-known artists and writers who in themselves attracted other residents. With its advertised cleanliness, and that virtue's neighbour housed in a plain brick church, with its trees and gardens, Bedford Park did in fact become a model that others followed. Perhaps it is telling, however, that the Adams' scheme failed because there were no tenants to be found for the Adelphi's industrial accommodation; at Bedford Park there was none.

Before continuing the story of garden cities, I want to turn back to the first half of the nineteenth century and look at another side of architecture and philosophy of that period, whose development often lends Victorian architecture its curiously paradoxical character. Philosophers of the Utilitarian school — Jeremy Bentham, James Mill and his son John Stuart and others — held, essentially, two beliefs: that environment was the forming tool of character, and that pleasure was the ultimate good. A rational analysis of society and men would lead, they thought, to a science of politics and economics as a replacement for the haphazard systems men used to govern their lives, laden as they were with superstition and, above all, emotion.

The dream of realizing a perfect society resulted from a recognition of the enormous power now in men's hands referred to earlier in the chapter. At last it seemed possible, through machine production and agricultural reform, to provide happiness for all. In architecture these theories appealed mostly to the Evangelicals, while a more romantic, heroic view of existence, in which will and spirituality played a great part, suited the Ecclesiologists. For the grand church buildings, then, a romantic medievalism was adopted, substituting Gothic for Greek as a romantic vehicle. Those architects working for Evangelical clients found themselves working on buildings of a different nature, buildings considered to be useful in a worldly way. Prisons, working-class housing, hospitals, schools: these were buildings with a new purpose, for a new society was to be engineered by their means. The coldness of much of the architecture reflects the deliberately anti-romantic stance taken by the Utilitarians. They thought of themselves as scientists, and perhaps took too many pains to appear detached, particularly when standing in company with the passionately romantic High Church movement, which had adopted as its own the brilliant colour and conscious symbolism of architecture.

The architecture of Utilitarianism has loose connections with the great railway sheds, bridges and other engineering works, since both types were considered as means to a greater end, parts in a mechanical system. In each case, there was a certain tendency to justify aesthetic brutality (ugliness) by reference to the higher purpose a building was to serve, and this was no doubt unfortunate.

While the Paxtons, Brunels and Telfords were gaining heroic fame, there were others in the strictly architectural field who are hardly known at all.

The Round House in Chalk Farm, London, was designed as an engine shed by George Stephenson's firm in 1847. Stephenson was a Northumbrian, and would undoubtedly have seen the practicality of round barns like the one illustrated. It is a common sight still on Northumberland farms.

Joshua Jeb, J. B. Brunning and Henry Roberts are three men who busied themselves constructing the houses and hospitals as models of a society that is still very much with us. The career of Roberts may not be typical, but it will provide a glimpse of the issues to be encountered in Victorian Britain.

Roberts had trained with Sir Charles Fowler, architect of Covent Garden Market, early winning a competition to rebuild Fishmongers' Hall beside London Bridge, which still stands. This was in the 1830s. During the late '30s and early '40s, Roberts built several country houses, churches and schools, in different styles according to clients' tastes, though his own leanings were always towards the classical. His patronage was mostly Tory Evangelical, and in these circumstances he naturally became aware of the appalling housing conditions of London's poor. Indeed most people became aware of them after the sudden cholera epidemic of 1837, the less charitable believing that the poor were poisoning them. In response to the findings of a Royal Commission on the subject, a group was founded in 1844 calling itself by the extensive name of The Society for Improving the Condition of the Labouring Classes. Lord Shaftesbury was its president, Roberts its honorary architect. A few years later Roberts was to marry a Russian aristocrat, giving him sufficient independent means to give up traditional architectural practice altogether and concentrate on his unpaid housing activities.

The Model Houses for Families, Streatham Street in London, was the society's second project and survives today as housing, one of the first buildings of its type in the world. The word 'Model' was to let people know that

The first and still one of the finest blocks of working-class flats in existence, the Streatham Street building by Henry Roberts. The access galleries were considered as streets for the purpose of window tax, which the building thus escaped. The handling of these galleries, in giant arches with intermediate levels supported on cast-iron beams, shows a consideration to detail and the quality of space seldom found again in such buildings until the end of the century. The date of this block is 1849

116

the scheme was only exemplary, a working experiment to encourage imitation by investors with building sense. Whatever their personal beliefs, the society's members thought they would attract no money from mere sympathy. They demonstrated that a 5 per cent return on capital could be achieved on housing even the quite poor. Unfortunately the fluctuating economic conditions during the 1860s and '70s damaged the economic base of this marginal activity. Throughout this period, too, standards fell in attempts to house the really poor and to sustain profits. Working-class housing was thus encumbered with a reputation for squalor and meanness that it has never entirely escaped.

Roberts thrived on making the most of an awkward site with little money, his approach to design remaining always rational and inventive, rather than emotional. The Streatham Street block is a good deal of housing on a little site, but the use of a major order of brick arches to support intermediate galleries, and the provision of a comparatively large and well-proportioned courtyard, make the effect surprisingly civilized. Constructionally, too, the building is innovative: each floor is an arched construction of hollow tiles, to give insulation against noise, less danger from germ-ridden floorboards and greater fire protection.

Roberts' approach to housing has been followed fairly closely by later designers, but notwithstanding its 'scientific' effectiveness, it seems to have ideological flaws. One of these is the apparent avoidance of ethical principles in design in an attempt to achieve ethical ends through mechanical means; for example, the idea that investment would follow the society's example as a mechanical necessity. The Victorian attachment to notions of progress is indicative of this desire to avoid ethical considerations in a complex, changing world by turning them into matters of science. It was thought that if progress were inevitable, then what would come tomorrow would necessarily be an improvement over today's world, and this pattern renders ethics a meaningless topic. Very neat, of course, for the Utilitarians: the pursuit of science would inevitably lead to a better life for all. Yet housing ideology since Roberts' day has tended to institutionalize rather than eliminate low-grade housing. The buildings themselves, clean, ordered and standardized with different rooms for different sexes, rooms for eating, rooms for cooking; these buildings have provided a means for imprisoning the poor in a model way of life, but a model of someone else's manufacture. Evangelism projected an alternative to revolution, so perhaps it is not surprising to find it also attempting to define the lives of those potential revolutionaries, the working classes. It has been said that society's problem prior to the Industrial Revolution had been production, after it, distribution. If human life were to be included in this scheme, you could say that it was the canals and roads, railways and ships that distributed goods; that the problems of distributing people in society were dealt with by housing, by hospitals and by prisons.

These institutions deserve further mention. Railways did in fact have a role in distributing the population of nineteenth-century Britain, as land speculation co-operated with railway development to build up vast suburbs, leaving city centres as workplaces. This had been a middle-class habit for some time, the proto-Pooters endlessly Coming and Going between the City and their Camberwells and Claphams. For the working class it was something new, a cheap version of the middle-class life that went hand in hand with their cheaper versions of middle-class houses, and the insupportable burden of their accompanying social values.

The progressive division of people's lives into the separate functions mentioned earlier — eating, sleeping, cooking, working, leisure, each with its separate and proper space — was noted by Ruskin: 'It is not, truly speaking, the labour that is divided: but the men:- divided into mere segments of men — broken into small fragments and crumbs of life . . .' When spaces, rooms, come to be given over to a single use, there seems to result both a loss of choice of activities and richness of cultural meaning. The loss of choice is obvious: if one cannot bathe in the dining-room nor cook in the living room, the implication is that if there is no specific space for an activity it cannot be carried out. Spaces have at times been more adaptable, and the church illustrates how specific use is attached to general space by ritual. A church must house birth, life and death, harvest festivals, marriages, ordination; and these things are all contained in one place. The many meanings of the space are in a sense always present, but specific activities have certain processions, prayers and hymns that mark them off from all others. The church is then not just an object but an idea that contains all the activities. Though it is less clear to us, houses once had a similar existence; the medieval hall comes readily to mind.

To us, all this may seem unnecessary. We can afford (perhaps) to build a special room wherever we perceive a new function, and do so. One of the early Victorian perceptions, and Henry Roberts bent his architectural abilities towards realizing it, was that separate sleeping accommodation for male and female members of a family ought to be provided to avoid incestuous habits. To accomplish this, one built more rooms: ritual and taboo were clearly seen as useless or moribund. When taboos against incest were demonstrably breaking down, for example, it was necessary to build physical walls to contain the imagination, as much as to segregate the sexes. For the only limits to the physical world are those of the imagination.

Second of these institutions, the prison, is in some ways the archetypal Utilitarian building. Bentham himself advocated the 'panopticon' principle, whereby a simple unobserved observer can supervise hundreds of prisoners, by occupying the hub position of a wheel, the radial spokes of which house the inmates. Several prisons of this type were built during the 1840s and 1850s, Pentonville being a good surviving example, Holloway a recently demolished one.

Some curious belief that an amoeba watched by God was thereby coaxed to a higher level of development, gave the paternalistic Bentham the idea that a watched transgressor would straighten his warped moral conduct. But the way that, as Marx said, people were being treated as 'a commodity, like every other article of commerce' becomes embarrassingly clear in a comparison of prisons with workers' housing.

Because the aims of each were similar, the types tended to develop along the same lines. Isolation was a common ideal. Poor families and criminals both needed attention because both were in a sense ill. Bentham's idea was never to punish criminals, but to help them learn good ways. (One recalls the Inquisition, where the heretic was put to death as soon as he recanted his heresy, on the principle that it was benevolent to send the soul of a proven backslider to heaven in a state of grace rather than allow the possibility of future mortal sin.) So too the workers, who were meant to pull themselves together and make themselves acceptable to a respectable world. The individual was of such great importance that he was to be isolated for his own good. 'Not only to make the dwellings fit for the poor, but, if possible, *to make the poor fit for the dwellings';* so said a correspondent to an architectural magazine in 1851.

It was this breaking up and isolation of men's lives that the socialists tried to combat, with dreams of a community in which work was performed for common well-being rather than for the worker's mere subsistence and another's private gain. This was the object of Ebenezer Howard's proposals of 1898 for a town he called Rurisville. In the sense that it was meant as a place to be in and not a system to move about in, his proposal was either two hundred years behind the times or a hundred years ahead of them. It came just before that absolute dedication to movement and change of the early 1900s, the culmination of ideas that had been stewing since the mid-eighteenth century.

To Howard the railway was a means of getting *to* a place and should, if possible, form no part in the life of the places it connected. He objected to the idea of commuting by train between home and work, thinking that the railway could serve us industrially while permitting more people to live an ideal village life. As Alexander Thomson used iron and Norman Shaw concrete, as hidden means to express ends, Howard wanted the railway to connect his Garden City to other places, but not to dominate it. His ideal was that workplace and house should be sufficiently close together so the journey between them could be made on foot. As often happens when one concentrates on one problem, he was overtaken by another unforeseen. Between railways and feet Howard saw no general form of transportation; yet the motor car soon disrupted this quiet duality.

Rurisville appeared in a book called *Tomorrow: A Peaceful Path to Real Reform,* which gave details of how such towns might be built. They were to be self-sufficient in agriculture and industry, co-operative ventures unhindered by private exploitation, though this did not exclude investment. They were based partly on a return to nature, partly on a return of 5 per cent on capital, and when Howard wanted to build a working community in conformity with his principles he founded the Garden Cities Association. Letchworth, the first of the towns built, was begun four years later in 1902, but a shortage of subscribed capital and the unenterprising architecture cooked up by Barry Parker and Raymond Unwin made the results disappointing. The plan itself falls far short of the grand principles set out as Rurisville.

Comparisons are sometimes drawn between Rurisville or Letchworth and the developments of Bournville, outside Birmingham, in 1879 and Port Sunlight, Cheshire, built by William Lever in 1888. Yet the former were abstract, general proposals for a way of living, while the latter were dedicated to specific known industries, where transportation and population in both number and class were known quantities at the outset. These towns were in no sense responsible for their own condition, and in no sense organic. Rurisville was a formal proposition, Bournville functional.

Alberti had said, 'a city, according to the Opinion of Philosophers, [is] no more than a great House, and, on the other Hand, a House [is] a little City . . .'. As a way of conceiving the city, even at an unconscious level, this analogy is very potent. Howard saw the community as self-sufficient, a social unit, but further than that as a place of shelter and refuge, as the house is to the family. Although there are undoubtedly romantic aspects to his plans, their source is Utilitarian thinking. Industry was necessary and accepted, where for Morris it had been rejected, but it was kept strictly portioned off from residential zones. Again, leisure becomes specific and useful, not simply a rest in a working, general environment; so that places are established, rooms in the city, where leisure is provided for. These are techniques familiar from early working-class housing, and contrast strongly with John

Nash's simple class divisions in the Regent's Park development.

In the building of Hampstead Garden Suburb, designed from 1907, the architects Parker and Unwin were joined by a third, Edwin Lutyens, who pulled the scheme up from mediocrity to a position of some authority. His North and South Squares, reviving Georgian formality in planning and appearance, give the suburb an identity and sense of place that both Letchworth and the later Welwyn Garden City lack. Lutyens is a central figure in late nineteenth- and early twentieth-century architecture, and deserves further mention. Norman Shaw had given him his start and he went on to train at a time when last attempts were being made to turn the philosophy of Arts and Crafts into practical success. But C. R. Ashbee's Guild and School of Handicraft, a rurally based organization on Morris's lines, folded in 1908, and Mackmurdo's Century Guild, founded in 1882, didn't see the new century in. Lutyens' early work, from the 1890s, demonstrates clearly his intention to continue to simplify the Arts and Crafts style, and that one of his simplifications was to abandon serious ethical commitment to craft production. Looking at a house like Tigbourne Court in Surrey of 1899, or at Deanery Gardens, Sonning, Berkshire of 1901, the architecture is being

Deanery Gardens, Berkshire, built in 1901 by Edwin Lutyens, with a garden by Gertrude Jekyll

reduced to formal, undecorated elements, and this makes him far more dependent on proportion than either Shaw or Webb. His walls become large planes of stone or brick; instead of oriel windows sprouting from these planes, the windows are discreet items, related to surrounding events geometrically rather than organically. Deanery Gardens' large bay window is a perfect example of this independence, as is its chimney. The move towards neo-Georgian architecture is such a general thing after 1900 that one would be hard put to say where it began. The most one can say in Lutyens' case is that his architecture always tended towards a dependence on certain classical principles, that is on rules of geometrical proportion.

The wonderful gardens of Gertrude Jekyll, for whom Lutyens built one of his first houses, give his buildings their perfect setting. The principles of their construction are, oddly enough, just those of Lutyens' houses: a formal layout presents zones of natural planting, where an infinity of colours and textures are perceived very much as they are in a wall of rough stone or hand-made brick.

Lutyens went classical quite suddenly, in the design for Heathcote in Yorkshire of 1906, and carried this classicism with him into the second phase of his career, involved as that was with public and commercial buildings. In this way, in his astonishing Viceroy's House at New Delhi and works like Britannic House, Finsbury Circus, in the City, he was able to sustain in his private style a position as the last great traditionalist. Contemporaries who shared his views lacked utterly his thoughtfulness and imagination: men like Reginald Blomfield and Herbert Baker, this latter who has the unhappy fame as the man who destroyed Soane's masterpiece, the Bank of England in London.

But the great (and inevitably neglected) end-of-century architect was C. F. A. Voysey. His career began only a little before that of Lutyens, and a parallel might be drawn between this pair and the earlier architects, Nesfield and Shaw. In each case the former was more original intellectually and aesthetically, yet neither achieved the commercial success of his contemporary. Whether it is a cause or effect of this failure is uncertain, but neither moved from his traditionalist position towards the classical revival. Nesfield's death in 1888 could excuse him for this, but Voysey, though living until 1941, paid the price of stylistic independence and had practically no work after 1910.

What is it that checked the progress of 'traditionalist' architecture in Britain at the turn of the century, so influential to contemporary theory on the Continent at the time, where it was considered the most advanced of European work? For it was not only Voysey, with the bare formality of Hog's

New Place, in Surrey, by C. F. A. Voysey, 1897

Back, Surrey, or the more elaborate Broadley's at Lake Windermere, who was isolated. Charles Rennie Mackintosh in Glasgow, after a short, brilliant career that had the Glasgow School of Art as its culmination, was more or less unemployed from 1904 until his death in 1928. In part, the British could be blasé about his work, at least comparatively, because it resulted from a long line of architectural and social development that had been wholly absent on the Continent. The work of Mackintosh, Voysey, Baillie Scott and others, came as a complete surprise when seen at exhibitions in Vienna and Turin.

Revolutions by definition are caused not by development but by change so sudden as to be indigestible, and aesthetic revolutions are no different. Superficially at least, it would seem that there could have been no aesthetic revolution in Britain in the early years of this century, but only a choice between two existing styles, techniques, beliefs — whatever you may call them. Successful architects like Shaw and Lutyens saw straws in the wind and immediately constructed wind-making machines. Britain's great commercial revival of the 1920s chose the safe style, the pretentiously academic style of Blomfield and Baker. The more essentially dramatic work

123

Many of the themes evident in English work at the turn of the century can be seen in Mackintosh's Glasgow School of Art, but here those themes are hardened and brought together in a very controlled way. It was designed a year after Smith and Brewer's winning competition entry for the Passmore Edwards Settlement in London. Both the offset doorway and projecting eaves are familiar elements. But working with stone instead of brick, enormous studio windows of metal instead of small wooden ones, Mackintosh makes the whole design much more assertive. He even turns the rainwater pipes into serious objects

of Voysey and Mackintosh was thundered off stage by their rhetorical bombast.

For a glimpse of what Britain possessed in this art, what she let slip away, and who picked it up, I offer a passage from the writings of Adolf Loos, an Austrian architect, about the work of a compatriot; this was written in 1898:

I am at odds with the faction that considers as particularly refined the fact that a building is designed by a single architect, down to the very coal scuttle. It seems to me that buildings of this sort are rather boring. All that might be characteristic is lost. But confronted by the genius of Otto Wagner, I must make an exception. Otto Wagner possesses a quality which until now I have seen only in a few English and American architects: he can step out of his architect's skin and enter that of a craftsman. He designs a glass — and he thinks like a glassblower, like

Staircase in Mackintosh's 1907 extension to his earlier Glasgow School of Art

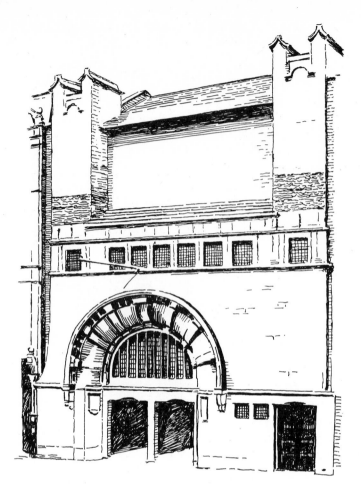

Harrison Townsend's Whitechapel Gallery in London, built in 1897–9

an engraver. He designs a brass bedstead — and he thinks, feels, like a brass-worker. All the rest, his profound architectural knowledge and skill, he has left in his old skin. One thing alone he takes with him: his artistic being.

Such was modern architecture as developed in England, and in that passage can be seen its influence as a revolutionary vision in Europe. Here, lacking such revolutionary content, these values were overcome by a growing desire by commercial and political institutions for the weighty safety of classical revival architecture. Perhaps we had returned to the conditions of 1750 — had, in fact, seen a kind of revolution.

5
The Twentieth Century

You are not to consider that every new and personal beauty in
art abrogates past achievement as an Act of Parliament does
preceding ones, or that it is hostile to the past. You are to
consider these beauties, these innovations, as enrichments, as
variations, as additions to an existing family. How barbarous you
would seem if you were unable to bestow your admiration and
affection on a fascinating child in the nursery without at once
finding yourselves compelled to rush downstairs and cut its
mother's throat, and stifle its grandmother! These ladies may
still have their uses.

Walter Sickert
The Spirit of the Hive, 1910.

So, Philip Webb had discovered a principle of architecture in a pragmatic
study of traditional design. This was taken up on the Continent, from about
1900 on, where social development was roughly equal to that of mid-
Victorian Britain. It was taken up, rightly, as a lesson in principle: each
country or region might discover a workable architectural language in its
native traditions. So in Vienna, for a time; so in France, where Le Corbusier
took his lessons, if rather hastily, from Mediterranean village architecture.
The principle of the thing was lost only when those visual solutions from
the Mediterranean were allowed to supersede local tradition elsewhere in
Europe.

This exclusive concentration on style detached from meaning, though
begun in the eighteenth century and still dwelt upon by today's architectural
journalists, has done the greatest damage to architecture. Its recurrence in
England in the first third of this century as an importation came just at the
time when the British appeared to be finding a way out of the nineteenth-
century fashion-fever, and so to clear the air, I quote a particular understanding of style, written in 1926 by the architect H. S. Goodhart Rendel:

> The only proper importance of style to architecture lies in its degree of aptness
> as a vehicle for the ideas of the artist who uses it. If it hamper him, or take control
> of his creative imagination unduly, it can do him harm; if it serve him as a ready
> and elastic means of expression, it can do him nothing but good. Some architects

The hall at Norney, one of C. F. A. Voysey's later houses, built in the late 1890s

there may be whose inventions are most easily conveyed to the world by means of a stylelessness which avoids all historic associations deliberately invoked. The difference between them is of no great moment if each work with sincerity and freedom. The apple of knowledge has been plucked and eaten; unconsciousness of style can never be regained. In almost everything which the modern architect has to do, he must choose one of many ways of doing it, each way having close positive or negative relation with styles of the past. However anomalous the way which he chooses may be on grounds other than those of art, to overestimate the importance of his choice on aesthetic grounds is to persevere in the Victorian error that style is the be-all of architecture.

And so if the style is only one issue, what can the others be? The concentration on style we have mentioned, and we should briefly describe its results. Voysey and Mackintosh were given practically no work after 1910 (though Voysey was awarded the RIBA Gold Medal in 1940 for his services to modern architecture, services he denied making to an architecture he found incomprehensible). Apart from that, who were some of the successful architects, and in active practice, who were thought highly of at the time? There were John Burnet, Charles Holden, Aston Webb (Admiralty Arch), Reginald Blomfield (Lincoln Library), Owen Williams, Giles Gilbert Scott,

Kodak House, in London, shows British architecture much closer to certain international ideals of modernism than is often imagined to have been the case. Adolf Loos in Vienna, for example, advocated the careful and plain use of high quality materials, and here we have just that: stone and bronze, not tortured into strange shapes, but simply 'presented' to the street. But then, hadn't Ruskin been saying the same thing years earlier? And hadn't Loos learned his craft from British exemplars? It is all a far cry from the flakey white paint of the International Style that soon followed

129

H. S. Goodhart Rendel, among others. Of these, Webb and Blomfield, though now enjoying a certain revived popularity in some quarters, produced exotically dull work. John Burnet did some really lovely work, from his brick and tile, almost oriental, Drumsheugh Baths in Edinburgh of 1900, and the British Museum extension of 1904-14, with its Cyclopean scale and severe classical interiors, to his Kodak House in Kingsway, 1910–11, which is in a sense one of the first modern office buildings in London. All his work shows fine detailing and is well built.

Charles Holden had a rather strange career, another man who was free of any religious dedication to style. He did a lot of work for London Transport, including its headquarters in 1927, and stations on the north and western extensions of the Piccadilly Line in the 1930s. With Frank Pick, his patron from the Underground Electric Railways Co, he travelled to the Continent in 1930 to study architectural solutions to similar problems, and took a particular interest in contemporary Dutch work. Holden was not alone in his admiration for this architecture. It is characterized by the use of brick, and its aim was to re-establish architecture from first principles in terms of space, surface and volume, but with no great interest in mass. As distinct from what is called International Style architecture, the nature of surfaces, whether walls, windows, pavements or floors, was not suppressed or hidden. The best-known Dutch originator of this movement was W. M. Dudock. Traditions of brickwork are as strong in Holland as they are in England, and part of their appeal for Dudock was undoubtedly romantic, recalling those far-off days of noble simplicity in building, those days that never existed; Dudock apparently admired the 'simplicity' of many old buildings whose decoration had simply dropped off long ago. This only proves that a misconception is not necessarily a poor conception.

The first noticeable feature of Holden's stations is their formal unity; the second is their construction of concrete and brick. But while you see a lot of exposed concrete, the feeling of the buildings is softened, in fact dominated, by the brickwork. It can be seen as an industrially produced finish applied to the cruder form of concrete, for although concrete has unlimited plastic possibilities in theory, in practice it is poured into wooden moulds and forms a negative image of heavy crude carpentry. So generally it requires a finish of some sort applied to it, in this case brick, used in large planes and allowing occasional glimpses of the concrete structure. And at Arnos Grove, said to be Holden's favourite station, both the massive central supporting column and the ceiling are left as they were when the shuttering was removed, which seems right for the inside of the building; as if one has passed through the brick skin and is inside the beast.

Owen Williams's Boots Factory, at Beeston: the finished product

Owen Williams, in fact an engineer, was one of the men who continued the 'Utilitarian' or 'scientific' attitude to architecture, in which forms were thought to have been derived solely from the internal necessities of the building programme. His Boots Factory at Nottingham was one of the most impressive achievements of British architecture between the wars. Yet few architects could understand that they admired engineering not so much for its intrinsic value, but for its ability to proceed without preoccupations of style being paramount.

The semi-scientific rationale of the Boots Factory is undoubtedly its main appeal. This is rational architecture, planned around production routes like a huge organism, taking raw material into itself at one end, delivering the finished product at the other. Uniform lighting is used as a requirement for the general form of the building, while the use of concrete as a structural material for economic reasons makes the use of mushroom-headed columns and cantilevered floor slabs an equally rational choice. Of course, the

The Boots Factory under construction. The simple rationale of the building is clearly evident here; concrete frame spiked into the earth and being wrapped up in the lightest of skins

131

rationalism is not as immutable as is often believed, because matters like uniform lighting and economics are abstract things; they have no meaning apart from reality. It may be questioned whether uniform lighting is the ideal type; whether the production line ought to be planned the way it is. Williams was indeed a fine architect, but the scientific method of building that the Boots Factory represents should be understood for what it is: a rationalization of circumstances, not an absolute answer to them.

He has made astonishing use of glass in the building. Walls, both internal and external, are glass, the external glazing being a very early use of curtain walling, where light metal frames are fastened back to the building's main structure. So we have not only a conceptual separation of support (one set of calculations, one material) from supported (different calculations, different material), but also the achievement of a completely new type of wall. It could, as the Crystal Palace had done, escape the label of brutal modernism because it hadn't stripped ornament from window surrounds, or left off cornices — for what is the meaning of these words in such a building? They have none. The rules have changed to accord with the economics and production techniques of an industrial society. In traditional terms it is not only desolate, but sterile.

Inside the Boots Factory, like a town square on market day

Everything in this building is used as far as possible as it was manufactured: window mullions are long extruded sections, glass is used in standard-size flat sheet, and even the concrete floors were designed to keep the bending of steel reinforcement to an absolute minimum. Here is a return to that primitive character of building so much longed for by the moderns. Just as the farmer would choose to build according to availability of water, farmland, roads and local materials, and 'cut his coat' to fit the conditions, so here, decisions are based on industrial availability and hardly at all (apparently) on aesthetic grounds. Our admiration for this factory is similar to our admiration for a Cotswold barn: it pleases because of its rightness, the apparent inevitability of its outcome which goes unchallenged.

The Finsbury Health Centre in London, designed in 1938 by Berthold Lubetkin with the Tecton Partnership. The idea of this clinic was modelled on the Peckham Health Centre

Williams also acted as architect for a project of key importance in the 1930s, a paradigm of what modern architecture was hoped to have been: the Pioneer Health Centre at Peckham. It is an example of architectural skill applied to bring about social change; what was known as social engineering.

The idea for a clinic to study the state of the healthy as well as of the ill came from two doctors who began in 1926 in a large existing house. Families in the area paid a shilling a week, and were obliged to have periodic health checks, in return for which they had use of a crèche, ante-natal clinics, a club-room and so on. There was no treatment given at the centre. After five years of study, the doctors felt that some action was required to remedy what they discovered to be an appalling state of general health in the community. For this they required a new building, because they wanted to increase the club

Hay's Wharf, Head Offices. The mannerisms of modern architecture are here — windows
following the staircase, stone cladding erected grid-like rather than bonded — but they don't
get out of hand. The Portland stone has weathered into a lovely texture of black and white

facilities to include a gymnasium, swimming pool, theatre, playground and bar, and to create a community centre. The modern word is leisure, but in the 1930s it was recreation. According to the doctors, the building's facilities were 'instruments for the development of the potentialities of member families, while at the same time being the means of assessing the growing capacities of individuals and families alike'.

Of course there was no necessity to build the new health centre of concrete and glass. The same facilities could have nested together in a more conventional building. Yet clearly the idea of a new building type to serve a new social aim, and the vision of openness and light that went with it, was felt to require a new sort of architecture. And here we have the other side of the style-free architecture theme: the building is ill-proportioned and awkwardly mechanical. The sad postscript to this story is that before it had a chance to establish itself, the centre was forced to close as a result of the 1939 evacuation of London. Today it is an adult education centre.

A Strident Reasonableness

If Williams designed in a fairly easy way, untroubled by the 'problem' of design, he was rare. Most had the problem and few solved it at all well. One who did was H. S. Goodhart Rendel, a rather neglected designer and teacher of the period. It seems remarkable that those who cried loudest for rational modern architecture did so with an irrational zeal. So we have Wells Coates, a Canadian but one of the most able designers in Britain in the 1930s: '. . . we are concerned with a future which must be planned, rather than a past which must be patched up at all costs. And, more often than not, we find that the past is not all behind us: but out there in front blocking the way to the kind of future we can picture but not yet achieve. And blocking the way, moreover, in the most alarmingly durable materials.'

Anthony Bertram, an architectural writer, in 1935, argued for tubular steel chairs: 'The old dining-chair was a relentless object by the end of a long dinner; and when you pushed back for the port and stories, it did not sympathise with your replete wish for ease: nor does the tired worker, enjoy-ing shrimps with his tea and evening paper, find a rigid wooden chair harmonises with his slippers and shirtsleeves. The steel upright chair is comfortable, light, easily cleaned, lasting, unbreakable and beautiful. Those whom its austere sweeping lines do not please are probably people who confuse design with ornament, who cannot appreciate the pure beauty of form, which is the only true basis of design, whether of the Parthenon, an aeroplane, a greyhound or a human being.' And the man who gave us the

135

Parthenon and the aeroplane as modern images, Le Corbusier himself: 'Our architectural studio at 35 rue de Sèvres is fifty metres long. It is almost wholly occupied by the architects. The administrative staff have been relegated to rather poorer quarters. I myself am installed in a windowless air-conditioned office, a kind of cell; my visitors are conscious of this fact, which makes them speak concisely and to the point.'

This kind of language succeeds less for its reasonableness than for its revolutionary tone; it is polemical. It is a good way, but self-contradictory, to sell rationality. Goodhart Rendel on the other hand was a man of patience and level discussion, working slowly and carefully through architectural problems. Any search for art based on uninhibited passion he found too earnest, too subjective and unreasoned. The typical Englishman, perhaps. And I imagine that many found him reasonable to the point of frustration.

Hay's Wharf, on the south bank of the Thames, is an example of his work from the 1930s. When asked what style it was in, Goodhart Rendel replied that it was 'Early French Gothic'. A nice comment, if rather enigmatic. One presumes he felt that, like those architects of twelfth-century France, he had thought out the problems of integrating structural logic with aesthetic order, not within a known tradition, but to establish a tradition. Take his treatment of the columns. They thread their way through the façade, emphasised top and bottom, while the horizontal window bands flutter across them. The building's constructional and aesthetic logics are open, apparent; without this logical strength the central decorative panel surrounding the double-height boardroom and directors' common room below it, would be more difficult to accept. As it is, the decoration is seen to be as much a part of the architecture as the structure, an enrichment, a twisting of the rules. At a more subtle level, the stonework, a thin cladding over a steel frame, is arranged with continuous horizontal and vertical joints, not imitating the bonding arrangement of structural stone (this has proved technically dubious). And then the windows that climb up the stairs on the street façade . . . the building is undoubtedly 'honest', but that is a mere starting point: its ambitions are architectural. Of Modern Architecture, the architect once said, 'Nobody much practises it here but everybody talks about it and the young and the serious believe in it. My advice to them is to put off indulging in it until they have ceased to believe in it and begun to enjoy it. Treated as a style and not as a religion it has great capabilities.'

Wells Coates designed these flats in Lawn Road which were mainly used as minimal dwellings by the artistic avant garde. Were these the descendants of Bedford Park's first fashionable inhabitants, leaving the Middle Ages to confront the modern world?

And so, what about the 'white box' moderns, Lubetkin, Conell Ward & Lucas, Wells Coates, Max Fry, the people everyone takes great pleasure today in deriding, since now *their* thirty-year period is up? The trouble is that in Britain they did so little, and only one or two buildings of absolutely top quality. The best work was done not by Englishmen in any case, but by immigrants from Europe and the colonies. The major part was based more on the ill-digested stylistic forms of French and German architecture than on any understanding of artistic principles. Possibly this is why, although there was much discussion, there was relatively little building. It has been said, with some truth, that there was no modern architecture in Britain before the 1950s. Yet now that the death of modern architecture is gleefully proclaimed throughout the world, England wants to be in the forefront, rejecting principles they never really held, condemning a generation that didn't exist for the work it never built. All this for what reason? Intellectual orthodoxy? The real failure of modern architecture in Britain has been its failure to convince. Inasmuch as what is of this century is necessarily 'modern', much of it is indeed very unpleasant. Yet most of the large office buildings, housing estates and city centre redevelopments owe nothing to theories of modern architecture, and a great deal to the post-war economic boom in which the most stripped-down building could double as both modern and cheap. Since everything was new and the rules were unknown, who could even tell whether the emperor was wearing clothes or not?

After the last war, the architectural profession grew enormously in size, as patronage shifted from the private to the public sector and local governments developed large architects' departments of their own. This meant a concentration on the construction of housing and schools, both of which were urgently required to provide an increase and replacement of stock.

It was a promising situation, but in the end ideology ran away with itself,

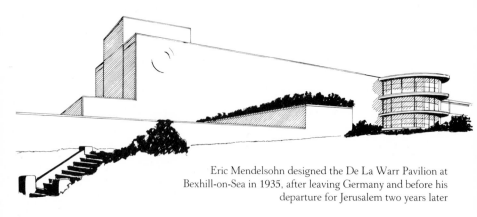

Eric Mendelsohn designed the De La Warr Pavilion at Bexhill-on-Sea in 1935, after leaving Germany and before his departure for Jerusalem two years later

while the ideologues — the architects — remained unaware of what political use was being made of them. With the social base of schools and public housing, and the large scale of operations foreseen, architects saw their opportunity to inject virile modernism straight into the veins of the working-class, a type of industrialized social reform. Unfortunately many politicians, being usually cynical and rarely ideologically inspired, exploited this visionary attitude to further their own short-term aims of getting and keeping power. So frequently architects' naïve visions were subverted.

The post-war plan to get industry and housing out of London was not the vision of architects, but their enthusiastic acceptance of the programme gave ideological authority to a plan of economic and political convenience. Ideas which had clear and immediate utility were transformed into visions for the future.

Yet there was one project, for an industrialized school system, that met with success. Immediately after the war, with problems of an increased school leaving age as well as a large school age population, Hertfordshire County Council developed a prefabricated building system for its schools, known as CLASP. Not only did the buildings it produced cost less than conventional schools, but they were quickly constructed. Within two years of the first prototype appearing in 1946, thirty schools had been completed. Unlike the many ideas and experiments with prefab houses during and after the war, the CLASP scheme did not propose a factory-finished object, did not propose an ideal or fixed type of school. The concentration was on a rationalized building process using industrialized components. Each school had still to be designed according to requirements of site and users. The point was that it could be done more quickly, more cheaply, and attractively. Those who looked to prefabrication as an easy way out of complex problems, and who searched for the button in factory production which, once pushed, would never stop turning out the answer to their problems; these people were disappointed. Architectural answers somehow avoid that simplicity.

It should be remembered that each model of a car, as each design of an aircraft, goes through the most elaborate prototype testing. Two or three models are built in wood to get the planning right, and then two or three in metal, and tested to destruction to assess performance. So that when production starts, things will work. One might ask why it is that in architecture, when building an estate of say 1,000 houses, no prototype is made and tested, even with conventional building techniques? How much time and cost this scientific method would save. And how much freer it would leave architects to think about what they were doing in a wider context.

In housing, prefabrication developed only slowly, and was perhaps held up by this notion of houses jumping off the end of a production line like so many cars. Eventually this somewhat naïve belief has given way to concepts of standardized components and servicing systems. Drainage and water come to mind as two examples of the latter, ready-made factory units replacing much complicated and expensive work on site. But repetition of on-site work continued on into the skies, as tower blocks, augmented by 'system buildings'. These were patented designs for limited run prefabrication of dwellings, lots of bits of concrete hoisted into place by tower cranes (themselves an innovation of the 1950s). Yet somehow these systems never rose out of the mud with much conviction. The joints are too big, perhaps, between components, giving the whole a 'constructed' but scarcely architectural character.

As an alternative to designing new building systems or merely choosing from existing ones, some architects began to see their role as being the selection and assembly of a number of component systems. The American designer Charles Eames built a house for himself in 1949 using only components ordered from catalogues: floors, structure, walls, windows, doors, etc. This had a great appeal for British architects, partly because the technique was similar to that used in Victorian times. There was no need to reinvent the whole of building construction for each new project, only to specify what item was required and where. The difference was in machine production, but the belief remained that art could be produced — or at least assembled — with industrial products. A great many people felt this to be untrue, and the notion that beauty and mass production are mutually exclusive remains widespread and potent today. The point about design from catalogues is that it depends on the quality of the catalogue, something well out of the architect's control, and his inventiveness, his artistry. Catalogues of standard parts tend to be richest when they are competing in a field where there are many manufacturers of one-off special designs. As catalogues become used more and more, the specialist manufacturer disappears; along with him goes the necessity to produce a wide range of catalogue parts . . . and the rot has set in. In Britain the process took about twenty years. Nowadays, you can only get about three different door handles and two window sizes. The catalogues are empty.

Mature Modernism

The interest in using systems and objects 'as found' led to one of the richest veins of post-war architectural thought, and a style, or perhaps 'method' would be a better word, called New Brutalism. The name was meant to

140

shock, aimed as it was at a rather conservative group of designers, and originated as an assertion of True Architectural Principles against a contemporary movement that made similar claims. This second movement was led by the *Architectural Review*. It tried in the 1950s to stir up interest in what it called 'townscape' or the New Empiricism. Essentially they called for a picturesque, make-the-best-of-it approach to architecture. They liked creating little scenic problems and then solving them with old world charm. Except that the London County Council, the stronghold of the New Empiricism, could usually only afford the problems, seldom the charming solutions. The New Towns were almost without exception designed in this way, dumping grounds as they were for London's surplus population. In a way there is nothing wrong with this attitude, yet one always feels that one is missing out on the possibilities contained in the unknown for the sake of a world already too clearly understood. (The method of design, according to John Outram who worked for a time at the LCC, was this: 'They would build a little model of the scheme, with pitched roofs and everything, all quite regular. Then they gave the model a kick, and that was the design. We called it "modelling along".')

Brutalism, on the contrary, accepted the ugly and ordinary into the scheme of things because that's the way the world was and to pretend otherwise was to avoid the possibilities inherent in reality. Alison and Peter Smithson are generally regarded as the initiators of the movement and its title, though their first building, the Hunstanton School in Norfolk of 1954, is only partly of this style; or perhaps is its idealization, if such a paradoxical thing is possible. Hunstanton (known as the Smithdon Secondary School, incidentally) is surprising in its formalism, its steel frame and symmetry deriving from the work of Mies van der Rohe in America. All the materials used are left as they were made, and beyond what Mies had done, service pipes and electrical ducts were left exposed as part of the building's open and frank quality. If it seems a bit like Owen Williams' Nottingham factory in this, it had the difference that the Smithsons added ideology to this method and saw social possibilities in their architecture. It stands positively *for* something, where Williams' designs were content to stand aloof. Hunstanton rejects certain attitudes as much as it adopts new ones, throwing over the coy friendliness of the Festival of Britain buildings, where almost without exception designers had chosen to be over jolly in the hope of pleasing. The wavy pattern decorations everywhere, pale colours and spotty patterns: these were distracting images to disguise an architecture that had skill, but was unable to direct that skill in any positive way. It became an architecture of mere entertainment. T. S. Eliot once referred to the plot of a novel as

The Park Hill housing estate in Sheffield acts as a hard edge to the city, and a civilizing one. The complexity of the façades is a result not of decoration, but of the way the building has been conceived and carried into execution

being the meat thrown to a dog while the author burgles the house. The Festival of Britain was the meat, but the poor thieves, having entered the house, couldn't distinguish silver from Sheffield plate. The Smithsons felt that the problems of modernism, both social and aesthetic, should and could be dealt with in a forceful way, even if, or perhaps just because, the logical consequences were difficult to accept.

Speaking of Sheffield, an attempt was made there to put Brutalist principles to work, in a housing scheme at Park Hill in 1961. The overtly formal nature of the movement was dropped, and remained only in the logic of the design method. Forms were now derived from a study of how people in the area had traditionally lived, or at least that was the intention. For it was flawed by a certain architectural myopia, and it is hard to understand how anyone can have believed that the famous 'streets in the air', access decks 12 feet wide on which the scheme was based, would have borne much resemblance to ordinary streets on the ground. They were after all a third the width, had one side precipitously open, and most obviously were covered

(opposite) Hunstanton School, Norfolk. The quality of construction in this building is very high, but this no doubt has something to do with the care given to the design of the elements. There are those who feel that steel is too unsympathetic for a children's school, but possibly it is the only material the sensitive little creatures would find difficulty in destroying

with a solid roof, the underside of the 'street' above. The comparison is not promising. Coleridge's definition of art as the willing suspension of disbelief depends for its truth on that word 'willing'. Clearly the *architects* were willing . . . Nonetheless, in its use of the sloping site, and the generosity of its common spaces, the Sheffield scheme is one of the most successful of post-war efforts, and has some conviction as urban housing.

The Brutalists' search was a search for the necessary components of architecture, and the rigorous questioning this involved did produce astonishing results. In spite of its many mistakes in thinking, mainly derived from over-zealousness, the method was sound. It forced architects to consider anew those questions that architecture can deal with, rather than those it cannot. While appearing to many as a revolutionary attitude, it was in fact an affirmation of belief in the traditional principles of architecture.

At about the same time as Park Hill, a building was going up at Leicester University that combines most of the issues central to modernism. Designed and built between 1959 and 1963, Leicester Engineering Laboratories gives a first impression of being a functionalist building. The way its functions are separated from each other and each given its independence in the scheme of things, reminds one strongly of British motorcycles of the same date: gearbox, engine, oil tank, exhaust pipe, each was made separately and hung on to the frame. (Who was it who said that much modern sculpture looks like machines, but that unlike machines, it doesn't do anything?) Beyond that, Brutalist ideals present themselves, and there seems to be a moral necessity about this building, standing among its dull neighbours, to declare itself as the true architecture, and challenge anyone to deny it. The architects were James Stirling and James Gowan, and it should be pointed out that the earlier buildings they put up did not use this same aesthetic. Indeed, each building brief was considered in its own terms, so that their flats at Ham Common and their housing in Preston are quite different from each other and from Leicester.

Most critics, seeing something here that appeals to them, are content to let the matter rest there, believing, as it were, what the architects have told them. It is clear enough these days, I think, that 'functional' architecture is not the reduction of buildings to their practical minimums, but applies rather to the employment of functional requirements as a basis for the

(opposite) The aesthetic of the Leicester building is not a result of functional demands, but rather shows, if not a disregard, then a degree of scepticism towards them. People still have to be told in writing how to open a door

Rooflights at the Leicester Engineering building: more akin to medieval carpentry than to modern machine production

generation of a building and its architectural expression. In this sense it is possible to imagine that a common form of architecture, a common language, could be developed with this as its main idea. It is curious that the Leicester building, though producing a few weak imitations, has not done anything to develop a concern in Britain for functional architecture. One of its architects (the two split up after this project, possibly indicating the intensely individualistic nature of this design), himself imitated it as long as he could, but soon had no more work, while the other immediately abandoned the style. We are left with a building which stands outside or above architectural discussion, an architectural masterpiece that provokes no discussion, only praise.

But I think the point is that the functional elements of the building have been exaggerated. The famous 45 degree roof-light orientation, said to be a functional necessity to achieve true north-light, is a bit of a sham: all the glazing is packed with fibreglass to diffuse light. And the joints at the edges of this roof are in a certain sense undefinable. Each was handcrafted on site, without a drawing, because the thing could not be drawn. That, surely, is pragmatic. The patent glazing, too, cheats, because you can't use these systems upside down as it is apparently used here: in fact the system of glazing changes with no concession to the visual nature of the exercise. Then there is the internal circulation, and it seems rather strange to divide the accommodation into two towers connected only at ground level. It makes their use fairly fixed. This architecture is not meant to respond to function so much as to create it.

These points may seem trivial, and in a way they are. But perhaps one can say that the building is so obviously not the product of its brief that you don't notice the intellectual sleight of hand. It so overpowers with romance, a picturesque tribute to function with enormous intellectual and visual appeal.

One could almost sum up British architecture since the mid-1960s with the careers of these two men, Gowan the intellectual artist, Stirling the romantic. As I said, Stirling continued using the Leicester aesthetic, though it became ever thinner until his work became more a diagram of architectural ideas than architecture itself, for example in the Florey Building at Oxford. He now makes occasional stylistic leaps and has won enormous international fame. He went through the 1970s with hardly any work in Britain.

Gowan immediately felt the architectural language of Leicester had been pushed to its limit, and continued to develop forms and expression adapted to each commission, less dramatic but more insistently logical and wilful.

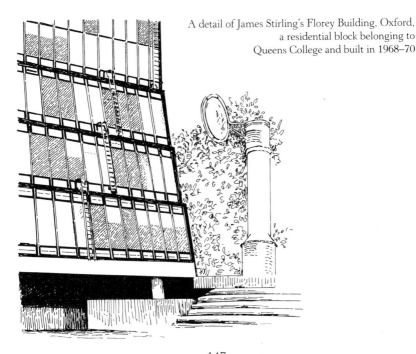

A detail of James Stirling's Florey Building, Oxford, a residential block belonging to Queens College and built in 1968–70

His interest has been more in the social field of architecture than the monumental. The public housing he built in 1968 at Trafalgar Road in Greenwich is often passed by without notice, but is a good example of his later work. He, too, has had little to do since the mid-1960s.

Remaining both rational and romantic, Leicester is a difficult knot to untie. Conventional critical access seems to be somehow denied, but James Gowan himself supplied a criticism of it, indirectly, when asked to comment on the Millbank housing competition in 1977. His comments appeared as a series of sketches, showing a tatty dog and the Leicester building in juxtaposition — in a sort of dialogue — on and in the Thames. The dog protests, howling as he sees admiration for the mechanical drawing attention away from him. The industrial product is turned into a religious totem, much admired by architects and critics. But the flea-ridden (I suspect) dog raising his voice in protest, is sure to attract the attention of the general public in the end, as a more lovable creation altogether.

Recent Skirmishes

Since the passionate 1960s, architectural discussion and practice has seen an abandonment of strident moral posturing. Men like Stirling and Smithson follow the example of Brer Fox and Tar Baby: 'Tar Baby ain't sayin' nuthin' an Brer Fox he lay low.' There has been a tendency for architects to leave specialized subjects like sociology, mathematics and biology, to specialists. One hopes this is because they have been busy sharpening their architectural skills, and does not show a decline in interest in the wider issues. What we have now is called pluralism in architecture: less trench warfare between two patriotic forces, than apparent peace with an undercurrent of guerilla warfare, with the many splinter groups that this necessarily involves. Yet the main duality of functionalist/formalist remains.

Among formalist guerilla groups (and at present this side, the right-wing of architecture, is making considerable gains) is the High Technology unit, with Norman Foster and Richard Rogers at its head. Clearly they are extremists, attempting to pre-empt all discussion with arguments of technical inevitability. A beautiful disguise: the very uniform of functionalism! The origins of their discontent were clearly explained some years ago in a lecture by Richard Rogers. While building a house in Cornwall with Foster and others in 1965, using traditional methods of on-site construction, Rogers found himself being constantly wrong-footed by the builders. For example, in place of proper bitumen damp-proof courses, they were substituting copies of the *Daily Telegraph,* painted black. Wry builders, you may think; but it was not a pleasant experience for Rogers, who from that day has been committed to factory production of buildings, so that a number of specially made components is simply assembled on site. This is quite distinct from 'as found' building with catalogue components: in factories you control people easily, and their mistakes are not the architect's responsibility; on a building site things are more difficult, people have to be dealt with, confronted. So the technologist operates from a well-barricaded position.

Part of their armouring is 'flexibility': a building's capacity to be infinitely changeable, extendable, adaptable, etc. In the para-language of Foster: 'The technology which enables them [the users] to work at present also provides the flexibility for them to reflex into quite different patterns.' Another subtle trick. While allowing for, indeed foreseeing change, they deny its essential quality, which is personal expression or marking of one's environment. Everything changes in the way they foresaw. You alter a technologist's building and . . . it all looks just the same, somehow. But if you start hacking away at the steelwork to put in some timber windows (as happened at a factory in Wiltshire by Rogers), they get very upset indeed, and scurry off to plan the next flexibility campaign. Change is *their* territory and they have mined its perimeter; if the users can find a way to change things outside their parameters, this is regarded as defeat.

Another group, under the leadership of a former Tecton partner, Denys Lasdun, has formalized modern movement architecture into a heavy, serious style. His designs for the University of East Anglia had many good points, but his National Theatre raises more essential problems. There was a time when exposed concrete was used as an element in Brutalist construction, others when it was used to shock and appear Very Modern. What is its point here, used exclusively on a major state building? I suppose it could be said to reflect the National Theatre as an organization, a very wealthy, rather complacent state theatre trying to act the part of an anti-establishment fringe theatre. That might seem too unfair but it is part of a tendency seen in other places — Covent Garden — where civilized behaviour is isolated in a particular 'zone'.

Denys Lasdun's University of East Anglia in Norwich. Certainly one of Lasdun's finest buildings, or series of buildings, UEA also has an impressive site over-looking lovely river meadows. Perhaps only in the handling of the service and access road that runs like a high street between teaching buildings, on the left, and residential buildings, on the right, could he have been more attentive. There is nothing wrong with a building having one formal face and one informal face, but things here seem less informal than simply out of control round at the back

It is difficult trying to photograph a building that is trying not to be there. Modern technology, so called, is here being asked to make architecture a transparent servant of our needs. Personally I prefer my servants substantial. Two points are raised by Norman Foster's Wills Faber building in Ipswich. First, if one argues that the glass reflects the other buildings, and therefore accepts the aesthetic of its surroundings, then there is no future in this architecture: all buildings will eventually simply reflect one another . . . a nightmare. Second, as this photograph does show, the visible parts of reality that one is left with are the grubby signposts, delivery doors and ventilators. It is like having transparent flesh and exposing one's inner workings to the public gaze; an unpleasant thought

The National Theatre was conceived in the mid-1960s and could be seen as an attempt to defend the formalist salient against the most astonishing attack it received this century, from a group that called itself Archigram, led eventually by Peter Cook. Things had been stewing in the architectural schools for some time in the late fifties before the publication of Archigram One in 1961. This was simply a printed broadsheet containing various student projects, each of which was concerned with the process of architecture as a kind of biological analogue. Most buildings illustrated had no conventional form. Rather they were skeletons covered with skin, and circulation areas took on tubular forms; they were conceived as growing organically according to their internal requirements and those of their environment. In short, Archigram amounted to the manifesto of a new generation of functionalists. As such, this was welcome: a modern architecture was possible whose meanings were not limited in advance by convention. It rejected no possibility, and all meanings were potentially available. But soon Archigram itself became exclusively concerned with the imagery of a consumerist Utopia, a sort of Coca-Cola fun-life architecture either without intellectual aspiration or without intellectual ability, depending on circumstances.

A consequence of this little bomb was that for many it exploded the idea of buildings altogether. Early functionalists had claimed theirs to be the best method of creating good buildings. Now, some people wondered how, if we began merely from a stated problem, we knew from the start that we were going to end up with a building at all. The question was, is architecture buildings or is architecture a form of environmental servicing? Electricity, water, heat and light — all of these things can be made available without the necessity of making buildings. Although Archigram contained more con-sumer imagery than thought, Cedric Price, an architect loosely associated with the group, is undoubtedly the movement's intellectual force. His ideas often appear so contrary to common sense as to leave people speechless, and if he sometimes overstates his case, it is to disturb what he regards as general ignorance and apathy. Characteristically, Price called his educational servicing project of 1966 not a university but a Thinkbelt. His proposition was to treat education as an industry rather than a gentlemanly exercise, and he chose to think of it as a network set among the declining pottery towns of the Midlands, where it would reuse superfluous rail systems and regenerate life within the region. There were to be 40,000 students studying in various locations and faculties but living among the existing communities in order that education should not become an isolated condition of life. The physical requirements of the faculties were to be indeterminate in the sense that there would be no fixed building as such of stone and slate, to a tasteful and noble design, but an open set of disposable components, that is designed for short life use. These could be assembled as necessary by the scheme's most permanent feature, a series of large tower-cranes located beside a railway siding, the site of a faculty. So the idea and the process were all-important. And as with a living thing, it would be possible to tell when the life had gone out of it, because then it would stop moving. It would probably be fair to say that for Price, our architecture should promote change; when it inhibits change, it should be discarded. A mind that learns but a body that never ages — a curious religion.

Out of these events our current position evolved. Architectural debate has turned into a grand banquet of styles and theories, but the staple diet of architecture is still the 'no nonsense' work of commercial developers and local authorities. 'No nonsense' is the euphemism for expedient.

Suffering under a bombardment of criticism from the public, the press and finally from themselves, some architects decided it was time to ingratiate themselves with the People. Accused of being inhumane, they decided to be sensitive. No more tower blocks! Back to the simple values of village life. No more plain surfaces! Coloured bricks, arches over the windows, maybe; if the public wants decoration, we can put columns back on to buildings; give people what they want, what they need. And so this passionate reaction justifies abandoning those ideas which had recently seemed all-important. Awkward plans and bad detailing were considered to be almost positive values, since they didn't intimidate the public (poor things) with claims to superior knowledge and ability. This patronizing 'style' put architecture right back where it was in the early 1950s.

It is the common practice to end discussions of modern architecture with hopeful remarks about the future: a new generation of young and enlightened architects will use their acute sensitivity to build us the world we have been waiting for. I would rather end with this quotation:

> . . . in his right hand he held the past: in his left hand the future. These two occupied his whole grasp, but hand in hand with them he felt at last his existence. Together they formed a triad of which he was the present, and this brought to his mind that figure of the Three Graces, woven together inextricably in an active ring, a cycle of giving, receiving and returning. He thought of this position as necessary, but not a pose. How many people played the role of Past or Future! The foolishness of that, to duplicate one position within the triad and leave another vacant — a useless ring, not a ring at all. To give, to receive, to return. The thoughts circled in his mind, and as they did he became aware of one certainty: that his chief duty was to perception.
>
> Robert Carpenter, *The Modern Bride*, 1972.

6
Reflections on Technology

... God became angry with Adam, and had him driven, him and his companion, forth out of Paradise, saying to them: 'Inasmuch as you have disobeyed the command which God gave you, by your struggle and exertion you shall carry on your lives.' And so Adam, recognising the error which he had committed, after being so royally endowed by God as the source, beginning and father of us all, realised theoretically that some means of living by labour had to be found. And so he started with the spade, and Eve with spinning. Man afterward pursued many useful occupations, differing from each other; and some were, and are, more theoretical than others; they could not all be alike, since theory is the most worthy.

Cennino d'Andrea Cennini, *Il Libro dell'Arte,* 1437

And so Plato casts his shadow across our modern world. But let the quotation stand, for this is a chapter of anecdote and exploration, not one of consistent or all-embracing philosophy. Cennini was a Florentine painter, who wrote the *Libro dell'Arte* as a handbook of technical skills for artists. The point of his introduction, quoted in part above, must be that theory and practice are welded together by the very nature of our human condition. Our physical necessity causes us to labour, but by means of that labour we are able to manifest the theoretical ends that are a spiritual necessity. The brick and tile barn on the edge of Shropshire (p245), or Paycocke's, a merchant's house at Coggeshall, Essex, might stand as illustrations of the principle. For those who built them, it was a way to make a living, a job, and they did it in such a way that the buildings became more than just a collection of materials. It was materiality embodying ideas, the product of technique. This is the technology of architecture.

Paycocke's House, Coggeshall, Essex. Built for a local merchant, this house shows how the everyday methods of building can be raised to a higher level simply by a more careful handling, a closer attention to detail. All is accomplished with just the three materials of oak, brick and glass

The stables of the Royal Hospital, Chelsea, designed by John Soane in 1814

In etymological terms, 'technology' is a fusion of the Greek for 'art' and 'words', and one of its main English meanings, until quite recently, was a terminology of, or discourse on art. It is not far-fetched to say that technique is of a linguistic nature, whether as the terms employed in any craft, or as its component parts. People speak of the 'language' of brickwork, and that is right. There is nothing quaint or unsophisticated about brickwork or carpentry. Just as a garden designer would be lost without a good knowledge of plant names, so these crafts have large vocabularies, which are a means of understanding what one sees in existing buildings — which could be called analysis — and for expressing ideas in building new ones, which is synthesis.

One may see this in John Soane's stables at Chelsea Hospital, where the success of the exercise depends upon a high knowledge of brickwork construction.

Only to take a list of manufacturing faults that may be found in bricks is revealing: hearting, bloating, chuffs, crazing, crozzling, efflorescence, grizzling, iron spots, laminations, lime nodule, scumming, shippers. Strange names, but a list like this denotes a wide range of observation and dis-

(*previous page*) Two medieval barns at Cressing Temple, Essex, built for housing wheat and barley. The constructional systems by which they are built were common to both church and secular architecture, in a sense value-free, abstract principles. Only when put into use do they take on a cultural meaning

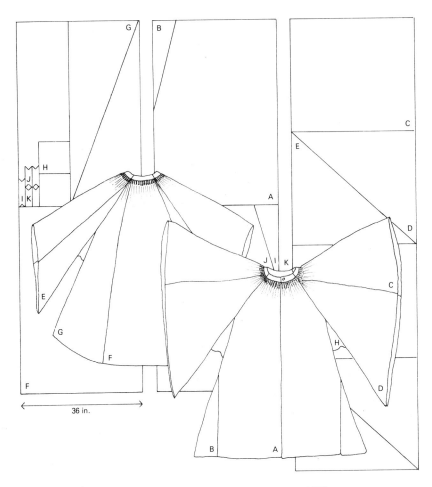

An English surplice and its cutting pattern, *c*1865

tinction, as indicative of our cultural preoccupations as the famous twenty-five Eskimo words for snow are of theirs. The fewer means of description or expression at one's command, the less detailed is one's experience, the less readily absorbed. Observation depends upon descriptive power and the ability to manipulate a language. Paul Valéry wrote that 'A man is a poet if the difficulties inherent in his art provide him with ideas; he is not a poet if they deprive him of ideas.'

Returning to Cennini and the art of earning a living, many fine examples can be found in simple designs for clothing. A nineteenth-century English surplice, or a man's shirt, show instances of what might be called the inventiveness of necessary selection. The cloth width is given by loom dimen-

159

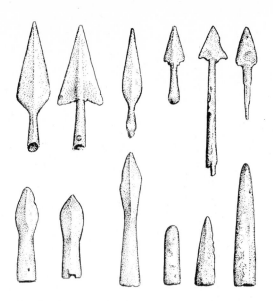

A selection of medieval arrowheads, showing various techniques for killing things

sions, the material is flat, and there is very little wastage, yet the clothes that are produced are of the most exquisite refinement, the intractable rendered docile. One sees buildings like that, chiefly, but not only, vernacular buildings. Again, the Chelsea stables come to mind. What is so striking is this discrepancy between simplicity of means and complexity of the finished article, promoting mere labour into the realms of theory: art. That technique has its complement. Consider the longbow, an English weapon, but originally a Welsh invention. Edward I in his Welsh campaigns, saw the longbow's potential for refinement, and hence its increased shooting power. By considering and sophisticating each technical component, he transformed the longbow into medieval England's supreme military weapon. Yew is a particularly good wood for bows because of its capacity to release stored energy very quickly, and the best of it comes from southern countries where it grows with a fine grain and hard texture. (In some periods each cask of Spanish wine had to come to England accompanied by a certain number of yew staves.) For bow strings, however, one went to Flanders, where the best spinning was accomplished with the finest flax. Beeswax was of course English, if one can distinguish amongst bees. The longbow was a simple idea, then, with complex means for its fulfilment: the necessity of inventive selection. Things put together in this way tend towards the mechanical; one thinks of bridges, instruments and so on, where a device's mechanical function sets standards of efficiency.

A detail from the base of Yardley Parish Church, Birmingham, disfigured over several generations by the sharpening of arrowheads before Sunday practice in the churchyard

'That a man can interrogate as well as observe nature', wrote Sir William Osler, 'was a lesson slowly learned in his evolution.' The progress from the static machine of observation like Stonehenge to the dynamic exploratory devices of modern science has confronted us with a fearsome vision of technology as an independent vital force. During the 1960s and 1970s, a great deal of intellectual energy was spent attempting to prove technology to be an evil thing, and perhaps not quite as much in advocating its ideological rightness. Writers of the first school include Theodore Roszak and Charles A. Reich, author of *The Greening of America;* of the second Herman Kahn, whose *The Year 2000* was a best seller, and Buckminster Fuller, are among the better known. But the truth is, as we have seen, that technology is not an independent force or thing, and cannot legitimately be ascribed a moral character. Like Euclid's demonstrations in geometry, the great barns of Essex are strikingly beautiful, but their structural principles as such are devoid of meaning. To identify technology with the ideology of machine culture is a mistake, for we do not suffer from technology but from its disagreeable ends; from the fact that it is poorly understood, narrowly defined and kept inaccessible by those who might have reason to fear its wider application. As a parallel to this one might recall that the medieval Church thought its best interest in power was vested in maintaining illiteracy among the laity, and forbade the clergy to teach reading or writing. Like language, technology cannot be an ideology; it can merely express

161

ideologies. This must be understood if we are successfully to fight the deterministic scientific element in our culture, to deepen our attack by study and broaden the field of battle with knowledge. The attitude of many men of Roszak and Reich's generation is that of the Bellman and his crew in *The Hunting of the Snark:*

> He had bought a large map representing the sea,
> Without the least vestige of land:
> And the crew were much pleased when they found it to be
> A map they could all understand.
>
> 'What's the good of Mercator's North Poles and Equators,
> Tropics, Zones, and Meridian Lines?'
> So the Bellman would cry: and the crew would reply
> 'They are merely conventional signs!'
>
> 'Other maps are such shapes, with their islands and capes!
> But we've got our brave Captain to thank'
> (So the crew would protest) 'that he's brought us the best —
> A perfect and absolute blank!'
>
> This was charming, no doubt: but they shortly found out
> That the Captain they trusted so well
> Had only one notion for crossing the ocean,
> And that was to tingle his bell.

Our real complaint against 'technocracy' is the same as that we have against bureaucracy: unaccountability, capriciousness and a solitary interest in self-preservation. For although the 'expert' is suspect, we hold a place of high regard in our imagination for the craftsman. And who, if not he, could be called a technologist?

The value of technology is in its utility to art in creating deception. There is no value in displaying technique *per se,* and a skeleton without its covering body is more preposterous than beautiful. Art deceives, and if it is to do this with any success, it must to some extent hide its means. Only plumbers are interested in pipes. 'I have observed', wrote Burke, 'that colonnades and avenues of trees of a moderate length, were without comparison far grander than when they were suffered to run to immense distances. A true artist should put a generous deceit on the spectators, and effect the noblest designs by easy methods. Designs that are vast only by their dimensions are always the sign of a common and low imagination. No work of art can be great but as it deceives; to be otherwise is the prerogative of nature only.'

The comparatively small villa at Chester by James Gowan could have been designed with this passage in mind. Almost all of its architectural effect

Villa at Chester by James Gowan. As in the preceding example, the technology that holds this house up is quite independent of architectural meaning. At Paycocke's in Essex, the elaboration of structure *was* the architecture. Here, the structure is almost invisible, and acts only to hold up certain forms and materials. In a way this is the most generous kind of architecture, that does not expect to make every penny spent show on the surface

derives from the use of a steel frame which is completely effaced in itself as an element in the building. Its large spans and overhanging gable are striking just because their means of achievement are not apparent, and this formal effect sits restlessly in the subconscious beside the beguiling and innocent use of quite traditional materials — oak, stone, slate and handmade brick.

A great deal of polemic from the eighteenth century onwards has been directed against what has been thought of as the essentially frivolous nature of this kind of architecture: the mask is deceit, deceit an ethical wrong. As long as the remnants of this attitude last, there will be architects who consider the 'mask' in their art as unserious, no matter how important they claim it to be. The American post-Modernists — Graves, Eisenman, Moore *et al*

— are their own victims in this case. Though apparently the deepest care and thought go into external appearances, the buildings they design are generally poorly built, and the usual excuse for this is that the exercise was tongue in cheek from the start, ephemeral and certainly not to be taken seriously in its demise. But where is the fun in rain-sodden *papier maché*? The British partnership of Conell Ward and Lucas found themselves with much the same problem in 1930s as they built their clean white houses in the International Style. Concentrating all their energies on producing a photogenic building, they took some unwarranted technical liberties, for instance using render on the wrong sort of brick, or steel in contact with antipathetic metals. The result was a fine set of pictures for the architects and daily desolation for the rest of us. The fault, although it may seem paradoxical, is that of not taking the mask sufficiently seriously.

This problem of technical bravado has as a corollary the issue of unprecedented design solutions, which, since the last war and the pervasion of plastics, has become crucial, though for the most part unremarked. By now it seems obvious that far too many innovations have been introduced without much thought for their specific consequences. Old techniques are seldom perfect, but our limitless optimism should not deceive us into thinking that purely abstract solutions (those untested over the years) will lead to a higher degree of perfection. One feels that the petrochemical industry must bear some responsibility for using their enormous influence in advertising to sell unproven goods, lowering the demand for traditional materials and thus making it an easy matter to buy up and shut down traditional manufacturers. Polythene sheet, for example, is now widely used underneath concrete floors as a method of damp proofing, whereas twenty years ago the usual method was to apply an asphaltic paint beneath the floor. It was fairly easy for advertisers to make this traditional method look silly: the paint was black, it was applied with brooms and brushes, it was sticky, and so on. Now polythene was clean, flat, new and shiny: the perfect modern answer. Only today, having for years accepted with credulity the plastics sales pitch, are architects beginning to realise that there may be more problems associated with this material than it is worth. The middle of a polythene sheet presents no difficulty — provided it hasn't been stepped on and punctured — but what about the joints, the edges, the holes where pipes pass through, all the details that are so critical? There is an enormous amount of information about dealing with these matters with sticky tape used in clever ways, but the whole thing is a bit makeshift, and to expect the ordinary builder to succeed in this technique where painting was considered too difficult for him, is absurd.

The truth is that all building is a compromise. It may be possible to make buildings that don't leak, but it isn't considered to be worth the expense, certainly not by local councils, seldom by private builders. It is more usual to design a building in which small errors, failures and tolerances don't produce disastrous results. If the traditional pitched roof has any advantages over flat roofs, it is not that it is more watertight; it is that any water entering it does not pass straight into habitable space, but staying in the roof void is able to dissipate in drier weather. The choice between flat and pitched roof types is possibly more political than technical.

Familiarity can often blind us to the arbitrary nature of the artifacts we make and use and the meanings that we give them. Forcing materials into configurations with new meanings is a difficult task — and it is the task of technology. Wittgenstein wrote that 'Every sign by itself seems dead. What gives it life? In *use* it is alive. Is life breathed into it there? Or is the *use* its life?' The use of signs, the manipulation of materials: these are matters concerned with forcing familiar objects into new relations, making them at the same time both familiar and newly significant. Man had to wait for Darwin before he was related to the ape: a relationship unwillingly accepted at first, but eventually creating a quite different reality for us, if not for the apes. To generate relationships, architecture often uses metaphor , whose logic can force unlikely elements into conjunction. The cross plan of cathedrals, guarded on the west by city gates and at each corner by a tower: these are clear metaphors which become so conventional to us that they cease being fragments of other ideologies such as city and kingship, and become for us

At Bury St Edmunds, the west front of the ruined abbey has been given new meaning and use as a terrace of houses. The date of each addition can be fairly accurately judged merely from the different window types

165

An idea in stone. Thomas Tresham, whose initials can be seen acting as anchors to the two iron bars that pass through the building, used architecture to transform his religious notions of the Trinity into stone. Ideology here seeks out the aid and stimulus of technique, and turns the necessity of construction to good use. Gables, for example, become more than just a way to end the roof

The west front of Wells Cathedral, or rather part of the west front that curls around the corner and faces east. Images are placed in space, each with its separate character, each available as a reminder or reference to the people who used the building. Compare these stones, carved in the images of religious figures, that is, people of spiritual importance, with the giant stones of Avebury in Chapter 1

simply 'cathedrals', in its turn food for new imaginings. The continuous breaking down and regeneration of meaning is not a progress towards a final goal, but a necessity to establish personal meaning and order in the observed world.

In Northamptonshire stands a small triangular lodge, built by Sir Thomas Tresham in the last decade of the sixteenth century, a blizzard of metaphors on the Holy Trinity. Each of Rushton Lodge's three sides is 33⅓ft long; of course there are three floors in it and thirty-three steps connecting them. Even Tresham's name — he was sometimes called 'Tres' by his wife, apparently — is punned upon in the inscriptions. For those who may doubt the serious intention and depth of knowledge of early Renaissance English architects, Tresham's work provides proof to the contrary. Although this is not the place to explain at length the iconography involved, every feature of this building is generated by the idea of the Trinity and the subsequent elaboration and expression of that idea in terms of hermetic and classical reference. Significantly, Tresham was a Roman Catholic, and did not have the Protestant fear and detestation of icons and symbolic meaning. This is a point brought out by the late Dame Frances Yates in her work on artificial memory systems. Using such systems, a person wishing to remember a speech, say, would associate main points in his speech with specific objects (a sword for war, a cornucopia for agriculture etc), in a place that was known to him. Then, when it was desired to recall the speech, he would mentally move through the space, find these images and thus remember what he wanted to say. There appears to have been a tradition of such systems from earliest times until about the seventeenth century. Clearly architecture takes on a quite different role in this system, as the context for memory, a palimpsest on which various images could be mentally inscribed. Buildings themselves would become redolent with systematic memory images, micro-cosms of the substantial universe. Yates maintains that the destruction of such systems paralleled the destruction of symbolic architecture in churches and cathedrals by puritanical iconoclasts. Images, within or without, were intolerable, and Wells Cathedral in stone marks the dilapidated condition of our powers of imagination.

Yates indeed claims that Shakespeare's Globe Theatre was built according to the classical Vitruvian description of the ancient theatre, itself designed as a world in miniature, adapted to the multi-level stage of the English medieval theatre. Though it is commonly thought that Inigo Jones was the first British architect with a knowledge of classicism, he seems merely to have imported the style or appearance in the early 1600s, but the sense and principles had arrived years earlier when parts of Vitruvius were translated, in a book for craftsmen, in 1570. There was a famous and long-standing quarrel between Ben Jonson and Jones about who was in charge of the theatre — architect or playwright. Jones in the end won, and his victory was that of the eye over the ear, the spectacle over its meaning. For Vitruvius was clear that a theatre should do all it could technically to help a play be heard and understood in universal moral terms, and the Globe seems to have combined this advice in its symbolic representation of microcosm, theatre of the world. These plays were of course themselves symbolic, and they were acted on three levels of staging: heavens, world and underworld:

> . . . can this cockpit hold
> The vasty fields of France? or may we cram
> Within this wooden O the very casques
> That did affright the air at Agincourt?
> O, pardon! since a crooked figure may
> Attest in little place a million;
> And let us, ciphers to this great accompt
> On your imaginary forces work.
> (Shakespeare, *Henry V*)

It seems fitting, perhaps inevitable, that Elizabethan drama should have called into being a new architecture, albeit soon abandoned, that could match its language in richness and significance.

After a description of symbolism, to which some people may be apt to react with scepticism, I would like to present an extreme of practicality, Alberti's description of how a house may be rid of 'troublesome vermin'. 'For it is certain to be wished', says he, writing in the mid-fifteenth century, 'that a building could be free of all manner of inconveniences.' Though we have indoor WCs, refrigerators and fresh water on tap, quite profound elements, consider the architectural implications of these: 'the Assyrians, by means of a burnt liver, together with an Onion and a Squirrel hanging over the Transom of the Door, drove away all poisonous Animals . . . the Weasle flies from the Smell of a roasted cat . . .' Those living on the Isle of Thanet will be interested to learn that their lack of serpents is no accident, for: 'Solinus says, that strewing a Place with some of the Dust of the Isle of Thanet in Britain, will perfectly drive away serpents . . . Against Canker-worms we are directed only to stick the Skeleton of a Mare's Head upon a Post in the Garden . . . If you sprinkle a Place with Goat's Blood, they will march to it in whole Swarms', and finally: 'Broad flat Vessels full of Water set about the Floor are dangerous Traps for Fleas that take their leaps too daringly.' Not only, I imagine, for fleas.

Technical matters. But a building designed to utilise and take account of these methods would be a strange device indeed; analogous to a cathedral, perhaps. Our own houses accomplish these ends by different means, and those means are so familiar to us as to seem natural. Yet they are not natural, they are creations as artificial and as useful as those symbols of which the Triangular Lodge is composed.

So the generation of architectural form and meaning involves many varied techniques. One of the more popular in the days of the Modern Movement, which perhaps culminates the general love of 'movement' begun in the eighteenth century, has been the tracing of circulation patterns of vehicles and people, making buildings respond to, signify and control these routes and turn their meaning into architecture. Recently, less material, more conceptual methods have been used: for example, purely abstract lines — that of a vanished street or field, orientation towards some monument near or far, perhaps out of sight. Such methods aren't new, but inasmuch as they attempt to connect buildings with the ideas and images which surround them, and to recognise in built form influences other than the merely physical, they are only recently being re-employed. A church, for example, is traditionally orientated.

Scientifically speaking, there is in England a building that must be considered a type of Jerusalem, for although spaces are not (as far as I know)

Even if parts of it are Victorian, the style is that brick-and-sash window combination that can be called Georgian. A quiet domestic terrace; but that roof on the left? A simple row of houses; but that slot running down the middle? Well, then it must be the Royal Observatory at Greenwich

This detail is to be found at Winchester, but similar examples can be found throughout the country, where a simple function has been performed with grace and generosity

orientated towards it, time is. This the Royal Observatory at Greenwich, through which runs the Prime Meridian, an invented line with considerable power. People stand with one foot on either side of it and have a slightly giddy sensation, unsure if their gesture is profound or trite, while friends snap their photos. Ships, aeroplanes and spacecraft are constantly related to it by GMT. And the building from which this potent line is produced, this universal technical hinge, is it a masterpiece of engineering, a celebration of high technology? Not at all. Rather it is a contraption. Not even an expressively round dome exists to house the fine telescope which traced this line around the globe. Instead we have a building a little like one of the grandfather clocks that hang in the museum collection, a precise mechanism sheltered by an ordinary Georgian building. Well, perhaps not quite as ordinary as it looks. For here one can open a few doors, crank back the roof ridge and peer at the stars. A small technical change that completely alters our understanding of what 'simple' Georgian architecture is and can be. English understatement, no need to make a big thing of it. Even the Great Equatorial Building is a sort of conversion, its onion dome sprouting to replace a more conventional roof when a larger telescope was installed. Very accommodating, this bricks-and-mortar architecture; even science can't frighten it.

So what are we to make of the High Technology style, with its various manifestations of abstract engineering in recent centuries? What of the Sainsbury Centre for the Visual Arts at the University of East Anglia,

171

One side of a little column capital in the Shambles, York; on the other side is written the year of its construction

where looking at objects would seem to have demanded a technical miracle of a sort considered unnecessary at Greenwich? All one can say is that it too is a style, though whether any more accommodating I wouldn't like to say. The heavy mechanical bits, the heart of the Centre, are buried underground. Only certain pieces of hardware are considered fit for display, so there is no great sincerity about the building, ethical superiority or necessity for it to be as it is. Architectural values must be had from somewhere, and technique as a source has been partly the subject of this chapter. But it could be that here one is being beguiled into a mistaken identification of technique with architecture, being offered a one to one correspondence between what a thing does and what a thing is. An observatory that looks like a house is no less of either, but the confrontation of the two propositions gives a layering of meanings and a source of intellectual speculation that is surrealist.

If one looks for a moment at Decimus Burton's Palm Stove at Kew, built in the 1840s, one sees a building often thought of as a forerunner to modern High Tech architecture. And yet, this is a deception. The Palm Stove was produced without the benefit of advanced technical means. What is more, its technical performance, though suited to its purpose, is remarkably low. It leaks, loses and gains enormous amounts of energy, is costly to maintain, and so on. The very reason it can appear so insubstantial is that it does almost nothing technically as a building. But that, of course, needn't limit what it does architecturally.

The most sophisticated objects with which most of us are familiar are aeroplanes. Yet walking through an aircraft factory one is struck by the fact that these objects are virtually hand-made; unlike automobiles, they are craft products, and that is their beauty.

The Palm Stove at Kew Gardens

172

A small pub in Shropshire, showing industrial forms
returning to the common language of architecture

173

An ambiguous technical assembly at Fountains Abbey, Yorkshire. This might stand as an English evocation of the house Adam built for himself after his expulsion from paradise

It may be significant too that the cost ratio of labour to the total cost of an aeroplane is roughly the same as for medieval buildings. When one thinks of the technical demands made on aircraft, it would seem foolish to make buildings compete on the same level of engineering; neither the performance demands nor the potential for their fulfilment exist. The lessons of what architecture is and can do, its raw materials and potentials, are more accurately expressed at the Royal Observatory than in High Tech architecture.

Let us return to our primogenitor Adam, evicted from Paradise where all had been provided and obliged to work for a living. He did not forget Paradise, but kept it in his mind, as an image; and he invested his work with that image. He could not hope to regain Paradise in this life — that was to be promised after death — yet he wanted to retain the memory. There was a time, particularly the first half of our century, and in some areas continuing, when we tried really to build Paradise, a mechanical world where we had, again, nothing to do: *leisure*. But the human truth is that we must work. The preposterous concept of unemployment, which says that simply because people are not required to build cars we must consider that there is nothing for them to do, needs to be discarded. Paradise is an image to remember; we can construct metaphors of it, but never the thing itself.

7
Chess Games of Power

In chess-boards and tables we yet find Pyramids and Squares. I wish we had their true and ancient description, farre different from ours, or the Chet mat of the Persians, which might continue some elegant remarkables, as being an invention as High as Hermes the Secretary of Osyris, figuring the whole world . . .

Thos. Browne, *The Garden of Cyrus* — 1658

. . . a testy cholerick game, and very offensive to him that loseth the Mate.

Robt. Burton, *The Anatomy of Melancholy* — 1621

Descriptions of architecture in terms of power normally concentrate on psychological force, and an 'aesthetic' power to express relations or instil moods. We looked at this type of power briefly in Chapter 4. In this respect architecture can tend to become a neutral thing, its message either accepted, rejected or ignored, but not necessarily taken to heart. Discussion may be reduced to likes and dislikes — taste — but may not affect one's passions, or one's health. What I want to discuss in this chapter is architecture as a type of game, with winners and losers, not merely spectators. It is a subject less to do with taste than with passion, intellect and desire. For there is a tendency to think that buildings, especially those of past ages, were erected primarily for aesthetic ends. This is far from true. Buildings usually have functions not associated with aesthetics, and far beyond the architect's domain of control.

In chess, a game of ancient and symbolic origins, the different pieces represent differing kinds of power. The king, for example, is a piece powerful not through its action so much as through a radiant influence which carries to each square of the board. I don't want to hammer the analogy too hard, or too directly, but it is a happy coincidence that a good illustration of this radiant influence is found in an English monarch, Elizabeth I.

A visit from Elizabeth to one of her subjects was like a command to build. As she announced the itinerary for her summerly tours of the kingdom, to visit the more important of her subjects, hundreds of carpenters and masons would start to work, enlarging and enriching houses to accommodate her and her numerous retinue. There was no question of declining to entertain this sovereign, who could 'command where she adored', and, indeed, where she didn't, although there were those who attempted to forestall these ruinously expensive honours.

Sir Christopher Hatton wrote to William More, of Loseley, advising him to, 'come and declare unto my Lord of Leicester your estate that majesty might not come unto your house'. Whether More had any luck in avoiding this threatened honour or not, is unknown, but certainly Hatton knew what he was talking about. His house, Holdenby, was among the greatest of any age, specifically built to honour 'that holy Saint', the Queen. There may have been mild irony in that description, for Lord Burghley found himself pushed to build and build: 'My house at Theobalds was begun by me with mean measure,' he wrote in 1585, 'but increased by occasion of her Majesty's often coming.'

From all this it would seem that Elizabeth was not a patron as the eighteenth century would have understood it. She didn't commission buildings, and was, in fact, known to be rather mean. More cleverly, she forced men to spend their own money on buildings which they may not have had any great desire to possess. Nor was artistic patronage evident on the part of the wealthy builders, as it became in James's reign when Inigo Jones was the court architect, responsible for establishing canons of taste in architecture.

As Summerson says, these Elizabethan houses were 'assembled' rather than 'designed', usually by their owners. This was certainly true of William Cecil, who apparently had an extensive architectural library and drew many plans and sketches for Burghley House. Elizabeth, like the chess king, influenced events merely by manifesting herself. These manifestations precipitated buildings, masques and splendid costume, and even if she might have found much of the masquing tedious, it at least kept people busy on her behalf.

Busy-ness may be the key to the architecture of this age, whose profuse detail and obsessive elaboration seem never to have been fully explained by aesthetic theory. Though someone has called it conspicuous consumption, that expression seems too crude, or lopsided, even if partly true. Clearly, if important men were stretched financially by their houses, and had to spend their spare hours 'assembling' them, little time or money would have existed for political intrigue, or competition. As the guide book to William More's Loseley Park points out, somewhat naïvely, 'It appears that Sir William (he was knighted in 1576) planned the house himself and was also "Clerk of the Works", supervising the work of his own direct labour. For a man with many

The courtyard tower of Burghley House, Northamptonshire, built in 1577–85
and designed by William Cecil, the house's owner

public duties to perform, this was no mean task.' Quite.

Elizabeth disliked it when people competed with her; that it rankled is evident in an anecdote of Lady Howard, a woman who possessed a 'fine border, powdered wyth golde and pearle, and a velvet suite belonging thereto, which moved manie to envye'. This included the queen, who one day contrived secretly to get hold of the garment and wear it herself. At court, she asked Lady Howard how she liked her 'new fancied suit', whether it was not perhaps too short and ill-becoming. Lady Howard naturally was obliged to agree. 'Why then,' said the Queen, 'if it become not me, as being

Popping out of the stonework, this lion is surprised to find himself in the middle of Wollaton Hall, now the City of Nottingham Natural History Museum and full of his cousins and ancestors. Though Wollaton presents nothing as elaborate as the hall screen at, say, Audley End, this strapwork in stone shows the kind of richness the Elizabethans pursued, and is a good deal easier on the eyes

too short, I am minded it shall never become thee, as being too fine, so it fitteth neither well.' That dress was not seen again in Elizabeth's lifetime, and the incident seems to be indicative of, rather than exceptional to, her character.

It may be said that this was competition of a different kind to that of politics; I would argue that it is merely on a different level. Where she saw rivalry in any field, she moved to stem it, and if among women she fought this kind of competition, against statesmen it was a different battle in the same war. Yet the way she could induce men into building these houses was to a remarkable degree feminine. One can almost picture Hatton, or perhaps more especially Burghley, in Malvolio's place: 'Sad lady? I could be sad: this does make some obstruction in the blood, this cross-gartering: but what of that? if it please the eye of one, it is with me as the very true sonnet is, "Please one and please all".' So the unhappy attendant tortured himself as he conformed to the supposed fancies of his mistress, 'not black in mind, though yellow in my legs'. Smiling 'his face into more lines than are in the new map with the augmentation of the Indies'.

One couldn't imagine a man scampering about and behaving like this for another of his sex. The opinion is hard to resist that these great Elizabethan houses were produced by the spirit that inspired Malvolio, though consciously cultivated by Elizabeth. They, too, seem to crinkle with enthusiasm to please, greatness, as it were, having been thrust upon them.

The fact that building may be a by-product of some other activity, not a goal but a means to an extraneous end, is an obvious fact (except possibly to architects) and perhaps most evident in modern speculative developments. One of our most insistent architectural difficulties is the attempt to find some reasonable way of redeveloping large parts of the city for developers' profit, while at the same time producing architecture of social importance; something which represents more than a lettable space.

'A game of chess', said Marcel Duchamp, 'is a visual and plastic thing, and if it isn't geometric in the static sense of the word, it is mechanical, since it moves; it's a drawing, it's a mechanical reality. The pieces aren't pretty in themselves, any more than is the form of the game, but what is pretty — if the word "pretty" can be used — is the movement. Well, it is mechanical, the way, for example, a Calder is mechanical [Alexander Calder, sculptor]. In chess there are some extremely beautiful things in the domain of movement, but not in the visual domain. It's the imagining of the movement or of a gesture that makes the beauty in this case. It's completely in one's grey matter . . . there is no social purpose. That above all is important.'

In the world of speculative development, the building of Centre Point enjoys a fame that parallels that of the more celebrated chess strategies. Its story begins in 1956 with an LCC plan to reorganise the road system at a critical point in London, the intersection of Tottenham Court Road, New Oxford Street, Charing Cross Road and Oxford Street. A roundabout was demanded by the plan, which in turn required the purchase of a good deal of property around the intersection. One man, unfortunately, refused to sell, holding out for a sum far higher than the LCC could afford under its statutory purchase powers. At this point the speculator, splendid in (metaphorical) handlebar moustache, enters from the wings; it is Harry Hyams, offering to buy out the opposition on behalf of the LCC. He would give the LCC what land it needed for its road in return for certain favours; specifically, permission to transfer building permission for the whole site on to what remained after road requirements had been satisfied. This was an unwritten, but fairly common, way for the LCC to acquire land for roads. It rather made nonsense of planning principles, because although overall density was maintained, it resulted in buildings in this case double the size originally considered desirable, beside a traffic route tending toward the motorway class. However that may be, Hyams got his planning permission a few days before a new act was passed that was to require holders of planning permission (who need not have owned the land), to notify those who did own property affected by any permissions.

Thus was Hyams able to buy up most of the land quite cheaply from landowners ignorant of a permission which would have greatly increased the value of their property. Having bought the land, Hyams gave it to the (now) GLC, from whom he leases it, at a fixed rent of less than £20,000 a year, for 150 years. Quite how he managed that manœuvre isn't known, but the thoroughness of the GLC's defeat in this game is indicated by the fact that by the time of the building's completion, the traffic master plan had been changed and the roundabout was no longer required.

It is well known that Centre Point remained unlet for many years, and in a period of rapid inflation this makes sense. Rather than lagging three years behind inflation, waiting for lease renewals, the capital value of the building could keep up with the general progress of letting prices. This was an asset to someone who might want to borrow large sums of money for his developments. The initial profit on the building was some £11 million. So in effect, (and this to me is a very beautiful idea) it could have been made of cardboard, or projected as an insubstantial image. When the attention of the country focused on Centre Point in its anger against developers in general during the 1960s and 1970s, the architecture was useful as representing a certain power

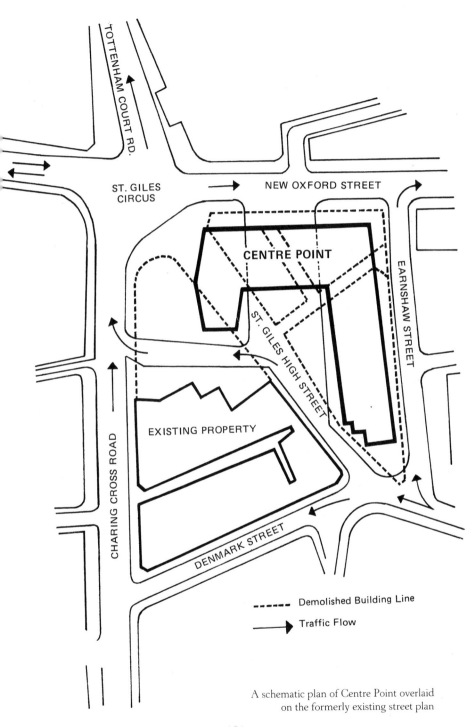

TOTTENHAM COURT RD.

ST. GILES
CIRCUS

NEW OXFORD STREET

CENTRE POINT

EARNSHAW STREET

ST. GILES HIGH STREET

EXISTING PROPERTY

CHARING CROSS ROAD

DENMARK STREET

- - - - - Demolished Building Line

→ Traffic Flow

A schematic plan of Centre Point overlaid
on the formerly existing street plan

game. One remembers conversations lasting many hours concerning Centre Point and in the end someone usually asking, but what do you think of it *as architecture?*

But it is not only through games with speculators that buildings come to represent such strange purposes. For their own ends, governments often make the most curious and contradictory demands on architecture. The Old Testament book of *Leviticus,* which sets down many laws and regulations for daily life, describes a leprosy of houses, which was in fact an efflorescence of saltpetre, that appears on stone and brickwork in damp, urine-soaked soil. Houses divided between animals and humans, farm houses, are obviously liable to such efflorescence. Leviticus describes the treatment of this 'disease' and if it persisted, a house had to demolished. But saltpetre, of course, is a chief component of gunpowder; though worse than useless in ancient days, its value changed with the growing use of artillery in the modern period.

Several proclamations were issued in sixteenth-century France regarding saltpetre, which gave government agents the right to enter buildings, and to collect any saltpetre found in them, and further, prohibiting the population from removing it themselves. So we have a curious development where domestic buildings come to be used as primitive munitions factories, and useful as such only as long as they remain uncomfortable as houses. The state could be said to have been promoting unhealthy houses for its own military purposes; this can only happen where the idea of 'state' is of a thing independent of the people who comprise it.

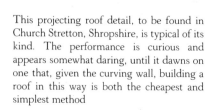

This projecting roof detail, to be found in Church Stretton, Shropshire, is typical of its kind. The performance is curious and appears somewhat daring, until it dawns on one that, given the curving wall, building a roof in this way is both the cheapest and simplest method

182

Centre Point, seen shooting up in the distance, replaced an area of buildings much like the ones in the foreground of this picture. For years it stood empty, merely an irritant splinter in the city's flesh, for even at its base the pedestrian can no longer use this corner, which has no pavements. The building is now occupied but the roundabout of which it is a by-product remains unused

183

An English equivalent might be the window tax, originally levied in 1696 by William III to raise money for the French wars. It was introduced for a period of seven years, but a tax once raised soon becomes inalienable tradition. Increased several times during the eighteenth century, it was not finally abolished until 1857. Houses with six or more windows were liable, and the tax reached a maximum at fifty windows. So we find Mr Thoresby writing in his diary for 1710 that he was, 'all day attending workmen, making up windows, to prevent the extremity of an unequal tax, that would else equal me in payment with the greatest nobleman'. This was the negative approach, and a new building need not necessarily have taken the imposition at face value. At Low Pavement, Chesterfield, that town of distortions, is a single window three storeys tall that once lit a spiral stair, and which, by this clever counter-move, must have avoided or at least reduced considerably liability for the dreaded tax. Incidentally, it produced a rather fine piece of design, though recently 'restored' rather crudely.

'And so I came away, having seen everything in the Zoo except the most advertised animal of all — the pick-pocket.' This was E. V. Lucas, writing in 1907. 'To see so many visitors to the cages wearing a patronising air, and to hear their remarks of condescension or dislike, as animal after animal is passed under review, has a certain piquancy in the contiguity of this ever-present notice: 'Beware of Pick-pockets', warning man against — what? — man. Lions, at any rate . . . pick no pockets.'

In spite of the deviousness of the examples so far presented, one can't help admiring the inventiveness of the strategies involved. It may be that they seem somehow sporting, or it may be that vicious determination is, at a distance, attractive. They are wars one observes with the analytical detachment of Thucydides. But there are games in which one's own feelings have been caught up, in which one is found to be on one particular side and fighting hard. Even Thucydides had his own life to lead, where things were far from neutral. So we come to the subject of architectural competitions.

When proposals were first put forward for a building on a site in Lambeth, by Vauxhall Bridge, the nickname 'Green Giant' quickly attached itself to the whole project, which intended to build on it a 500ft high green office building of some 600,000 sq ft. Meanwhile, on a site under separate ownership, just across the bridge's approach road, permission was being sought to construct 400,000sq ft of offices and some 250,000sq ft of housing. Public enquiries were held and a rather heated atmosphere created, but this was dissipated by the then Secretary of State for the Environment, Michael Heseltine. Since coming to office, he had both promoted the acceptability of

Chesterfield, city of distortions . . . The tall window in the centre of the picture used to be glazed top to bottom, but its recent restoration by the shop to its right changed that. By designing the opening as one window to light a staircase, rather than using three or four smaller ones, the builders avoided window tax, and as an added bonus created a rather splendid piece of design

architectural competitions and cut to almost nothing government building programmes. Only a cynic would care to connect the two enthusiasms, and suggest that competitions keep dozens or even hundreds of architects working, for nothing, on one project, each ever hopeful of his own favoured destiny. In Hazlitt's words, 'there is a strong tendency in the human mind to flatter itself with secret hopes, with some lucky reservation in our favour, though reason may point out the grossness of the trick in general'.

One might express this attitude in another way, and compare competitions to that bicycle race observed by the astute Irishman. Asking why a hundred people were spending so much energy going around and around in circles, he was told that the winner of the race was given a thousand pounds. 'Well I know that,' he said impatiently, 'but why are all the others doing it?'

The intention was that this competition would produce a building of such high quality (a building to cover both sites, for one owner had digested the other) that a Special Development Order should be passed through parliament, avoiding the need for public enquiries and appeals, lengthy and expensive as these operations are. But even this might have been too blunt an instrument with which to wound the public's self-esteem, too crude a move in a subtle game. Out of the hundred or so entries received, six were short listed and models of the schemes displayed in a tent on the site.

The amount of accommodation required in the brief was as before, and that was large. None of the schemes did much more than simply get it all on. Yet each member of the public who visited the exhibition was presented with a sheet of questions, which, in the end, came out with the vital phrase: 'Which scheme do you like best? (Write letter in box)'.

There is a strong tendency for people to feel that any question deserves an answer; questions like this one are especially tempting because they flatter our vanity by ostensibly seeking our advice and approbation. But some questions have no answers in the terms in which they are framed; we are all familiar with examples of a more awkward kind, the traditional one being, 'Have you stopped beating your wife?'. Such demands can be answered neither yes nor no without serious compromise. Even hesitation is seen as just a play for time. So it is with this competition. One sees how clearly the process works: the developer chooses the size of his development in square feet. A hundred architects submit designs showing how it can be done, a jury chooses the short list, and the public chooses the one they like best from this highly pre-selected group. In the end we will have an enormous and enormously profitable development apparently chosen by us, the public, and we should not, therefore, protest. In reality we have had no choice and have merely been compromised by our own vanity.

186

Perhaps the most amusing story of combat with the weaponry of architecture is that of the quarrel between Sarah, Duchess of Marlborough, and Sir Robert Walpole. It is a tale that was unearthed and first told by Hugh Phillips in his inexhaustibly rich book on mid-Georgian London. The duchess, as is well known, put the backs up of both Wren and Vanbrugh. The latter had been dismissed without payment from his work at Blenheim, and had to appeal to Walpole for help with money. Walpole went further than sorting out Vanbrugh's financial difficulties with the Duchess, taking out his personal dislike of her by cutting off her carriage entrance to Marlborough House in St James's, built for her by Wren, and foiling her every attempt to form a new one.

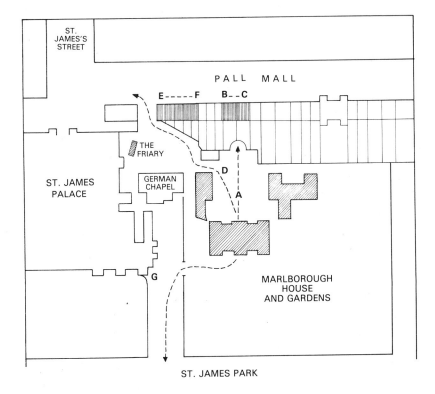

A schematic plan of Marlborough House, based on Hugh Phillips' book *Mid-Georgian London*. A: Where the Duchess wanted to go. B–C: Houses in Pall Mall which she hoped to acquire and demolish to make her entrance. D: The narrow passage she was forced to use when B–C were blocked by Walpole's machinations. E–F: The houses she tried to acquire after B–C were full of Walpole's relations. G: The Duchess's original carriage entrance before the withdrawal of privileges

187

In 1726 George I, at Walpole's request, revoked her privilege of driving in St James's Park, which had provided the chief access to her house. This forced her to use the service entrance, and though there is something amusing about her description of it as a place so narrow that 'a coach and six horses can barely get out', it was in comparison rather pokey, and apparently always crowded with people. She appealed to the Princess, who appealed to the King, who refused to renew her privileges. Her plan then was to build a new entrance, into Pall Mall, by buying up and demolishing two houses opposite her own. Wren's design had in fact foreseen just such an entrance, and had provided stabling and entrance lodges ready for its execution. These houses belonged to the Crown and were leased out.

But Walpole was there first. Initially he convinced the leaseholder to apply for an extended lease, which was granted for thirty-six years, additional to the fourteen years that remained of his original agreement. Walpole then had the lease transferred to his brother, Lord Walpole of Wolterton, and took the adjacent house for his own son. Not only was Sarah denied her entrance, but was now further galled at being blocked by a very nest of Walpoles.

Her final attempt was to build an entrance to the west at the end of Pall Mall and quite off axis with her house; better than nothing, but nothing grand. It was now 1733 and the leases to the houses which stood in the way of this project were to have expired in 1740. The Duchess visited the houses with the intention of buying them for demolition, only to find that Walpole, seven years earlier, had extended these leases as well, until 1778. Testy and choleric are polite words to describe what must have been her humour.

Walpole was, however, caught up in a rather larger game, and when he fell from power in 1741, 'old Sarah' finally got her way. The Crown tenants were evicted and her side entrance was built. But for fifteen years Walpole had kept her at bay, and she only ever gained a rather undignified approach. And, too, she lived to enjoy it only until 1744; so Walpole had a good run for his, or someone else's, money.

Finally, the *Gentleman's Magazine* in 1772 reported that, 'the remains of the late Lord Baltimore, who died abroad, were carried from Exeter Exchange, in the Strand, where they had lain in state, in order to be interred in the family vault at Epsom. His Lordship had injured his character in his life by seduction, so that the populace paid no regard to his memory when dead, but plundered the room where his body lay the moment it was removed.'

A mob is a mysterious being, coming into existence at the calling of some strong passion, dissolving into air when that passion is spent. It is, perhaps, the most striking example of an idea objectified. The mob's epoch appears to have been the eighteenth century, and its creation was not always a result, as today, of simple desire to destroy; rather, destruction appears to have been an expressive force. One person breaking up the furniture of a room, or 'plundering' it as the magazines had it, would have had a quite different meaning to the mob's action. They were not people angry at personal loss, or merely frustrated at the loss of a football match: they were a kind of moral violence. The mob was an instrument of general utility, sent out on a wave of public feeling to demolish the houses of errant citizens or the seats of malignant institutions.

The Round House, opposite St Martin-in-the-Fields, was a headquarters of watchmen, where people were kept overnight before being brought before a magistrate. Here, in 1742, a party of drunken constables held about twenty-five of what they had rounded up as 'disorderly persons'. Most were

People's architecture it may be, but the National Theatre cannot escape its monumental purpose as state architecture. One of the contradictions that modern architecture has pointed out, more by accident than by intention, is that institutions created as distinctly separate from popular culture, whether theatres or government agencies, cannot be made 'popular' simply by wearing different clothes. The little building in the background on the left shows an acceptance and use of this fact

quite innocent, but by morning half a dozen were dead from want of air, and another dozen were badly ill. The cruelty of this event enraged the public, and it responded by gathering and pulling off the front of this house, leaving floors hanging in space and rooms with three walls open to general gaze.

How indicative of both the strength and frailty of architecture is this 'public'. It could be argued that the preciousness of an object relates to its delicacy, the ease with which it may be broken, and that these eighteenth-century houses, with their thin walls and delicate (some might say shoddy) construction, were extremely susceptible to the fluctuations in fortune or favour of their inhabitants. Today we have abstracted this into a legal process, which I suppose is more civilised, but takes some of the edge off architecture.

Paris streets, to give another example, made as they are of paving stones, have for generations provided material for building barricades and the missiles projected from them, but simply by constructing roads of asphalt this function is removed. The road means less, has less expressive value, and becomes both less dangerous and less interesting.

It is worth noticing in this context that public buildings have always promoted a monumental image, as an attempt to preclude equally the inter-vention of the mob and the passage of time. They are built to last, and even the South Bank complex and National Theatre, put up during the 1960s and 1970s, those years of homage to the *hoi polloi,* are of an indestructible rein-forced concrete. The mob who succeeded in razing Newgate prison in 1780 would have a hard time here. Yet when the National Theatre opened, I remember, there were posters which imitated graffiti-written brickwork, pasted on these concrete walls, which told us that 'the National Theatre is your theatre'. Yet anything that a mob can't destroy belongs not to men, but to time. There was an obvious nervous uncertainty here on the part of the state, unwilling to be seen as the source of authority, but unable to avoid that reality.

Newgate prison itself presents a curious tale. George Dance's design for the building which replaced that destroyed by the rioters, is often regarded as a building expressive of its purpose, full of inspiring gloom and a 'memento delicti'. If this is so, it replaced with symbolic force a building that had impressed this force in actual fact. Of the condemned cells in the old prison, we are told by Howard that 'criminals who had affected an air of boldness during their trial, and appeared quite unconcerned at the pro-nouncing sentence upon them, were struck with horror, and shed tears when brought to these darksome solitary abodes'.

The rabble that destroyed Newgate, and many other buildings in the

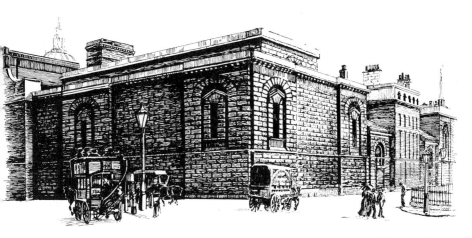

Newgate Prison, built by George Dance in the 1770s after the Gordon Rioters had destroyed its predecessor. It was itself demolished in 1902

Gordon Riots, soon turned to pillage, where Doctor Johnson found them, 'plundering the Sessions-house at the Old Bailey. There were not, I believe, a hundred; but they did their work at leisure, in full security, without sentinels, without trepidation, as men lawfully employed in full day.'

So the pawns were taken, distracted by mere goods from their journey towards the seventh square of power and enlightenment. The mob which might have used its force to some purpose, to achieve power at a higher level, here broke up into individual desires. One might paraphrase Queen Mary's response to a soldier, who, being presented by her with a medal had muttered to his companion, 'No more bloody wars for me, mate . . .'. 'No more bloody wars,' said the Queen, who had overheard, 'no more bloody medals.' No more revolutions, no more power . . .

8

Handmade Nature

> . . . a special ready-to-use modelling material. Hardens in a well-ventilated place . . . To keep unused material, place in a plastic bag. Non-toxic.
>
> (Description on a package of modelling clay)

We find ourselves, in the world of architecture, using the materials of nature to create what objects we desire and need: stone to build walls, wood for floors and slate on roofs. Clearly what we do with these natural materials, either consciously, or done without thought, can give us insights into our relations with nature in a more abstract sense. Though we now have steel, glass and concrete, there are simpler materials which characterize a long period of our culture, and have not changed throughout history. The various purposes to which they have been put, both practical and idealistic, are creations of the mind.

The 'raw nature' of land was itself a vital resource at one time, now replaced, at least in towns and cities, by artificial networks of services. Even remote rural areas depend much less on the land than they would have done two or three generations ago. It is well known that in times past you didn't choose to build a house with a fine view if there was no water available; you built near a well. Without good roads you built where you had to work; and you also used local materials for the same reason — lack of cheap and easy transportation. It seems fair to suggest that although these matters all require thought, they are practical confrontations with the natural world. Their frequency and immediacy would have made it difficult to use practical buildings for idealized purposes. Any idealization of nature would not be domestic, but, more likely, religious.

Now in our age, land is most highly valued not as a practical affair of water supply and brick-earth; nor as a medium through which we can work out spiritual relationships with the world. We want it, above all, Natural. This means untouched, primitive; it means the one way we can't have it. So in turn this becomes a search for the ideal.

Stone accepts its fate at the hands of time, and does so with some style. St Giles's Church, by Henry Flitcroft

Land is a convenient example to start with, as the 'natural' world we live on, and it provides immediate illumination of intellectual and practical attitudes. From this point the conversation will be illustrated with gardens and buildings, which parallel these more general feelings and exist, by and large, to make such feelings manifest. Since by exploiting the natural world we necessarily alter it, we have sought ways to perform practical functions in a way that adds a dimension of meaning to our tasks. Digging gravel out of the ground alters the world. We can leave it at that, and in this example usually do: the task is a physical process with known ends. On the other hand laying the corner-stone of a building is a simple task, but has ceremony added to it, in order that we give significance to the actions which alter the world.

And so this chapter concerns the ways in which men have put the natural world to use in achieving certain practical ends. There are four examples here, some of which illustrate the simpler domestication of nature, others its use as a political tool; others are concerned more with the material quality of architecture in its own right, nature as it were illustrating nature.

Earliest of these examples is Hampton Court, not a typical house by any means, but a summation of medieval ambitions and an indication of the quality of that age. The existing manor was bought by Cardinal Wolsey in 1514, and within a decade he had turned it into the most magnificent of all English palaces. In a last attempt to regain lost favour with Henry VIII, Wolsey presented the palace to the king in 1529. But of course the ploy didn't work; art could work no change in Henry's nature. That did not prevent him from enjoying Hampton Court, and he added extensively both to buildings and gardens throughout his reign. None of the gardens from this time still exists, but reconstructions have been made in this century, making it possible to get a good idea of what was here four centuries ago.

The second great building phase came during the late seventeenth century, when William and Mary employed Christopher Wren to design the building which, it was hoped, would rival the palace at Versailles in grandeur and magnificence. A great deal of the earlier building was demolished for the cause, and it had been the intention to knock it all down, until William had the bad luck to die. But perhaps that was good luck for us. The palace and its grounds are now cared for by the DOE, whose tidy-mindedness is perfectly suited to the maintenance of such a place.

An important fact to remember about Hampton Court is that, when built, it was the home and workplace of some five hundred people. Not only did this make it the largest household in England, but also made it a kind of

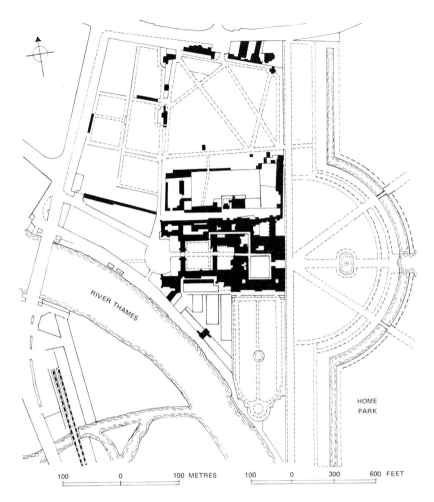

A general plan of Hampton Court. Wren's work was concentrated about the eastern courtyard

village or town, and a decent-sized one at that. To call it 'Wolsey's Palace' makes us think of it as one man's house, yet the part he or any of its successive owners occupied was a small part in relation to the whole. Looked at in this way, the house becomes a substantial social organization, not a mere private domain. Architecture is employed only in one or two rooms as the exclusive territory of the owner. The Great Hall and all the various courtyards were places open to five hundred people. Beyond that, the building's power is expressed as an enrichment of practical objects rather than a proliferation of useless ones. The dozens of brick chimneys are beautifully

At Hampton Court, the number of chimneys alone is some indication that we are dealing more with a town than a single house

carved to form impressive picturesque displays, but this is a quality deriving from the practical turned pretty.

Inside, one of the noticeable features of Hampton Court's plan is that there are no corridors, which means that only by passing through a number of rooms can any other room be reached. The words, room and corridor, have to be reconsidered in such a context, because they are being applied to spaces quite different to those of modern houses. Corridors as they later developed were somewhat negative spaces, roads between rooms with no use of their own as spaces beyond that. As it happens, Wren followed the older system in his rebuilding works, though the modern 'corridor' system was being developed in his day. It was taken for granted, then, that servants and their masters used the same space for moving about, a principle made concrete by the architecture itself, which allows no choice in the matter. So the house is a town under one roof, where industry and its workforce, religious and government activities, are all accommodated.

This point is clearly made by the Cartoon Gallery, so named because it was originally designed to house the Raphael Cartoons, now at the Victoria and Albert Museum. Its walls are panelled with columns and entablatures, suggesting a town square with building façades surrounding it. Even today the room has a public feeling about it, as groups of visitors talk among themselves, oblivious of the other people walking purposefully through on their way somewhere else, while others still wander vaguely about looking at the walls and taking in the scene. What a lovely gallery it would have made, not an Arts Centre away in a lonely corner of the grounds, nor a picture gallery standing silent at the end of a dark corridor, closed off by a heavy door. Here it lay instead, part of a route between other places but itself possessing a distinct character as space.

One last point about the Gallery's imitation of outdoor space is made in the construction of its ceiling. Each room has dark panelling topped by timber cornices, and above this the wall steps back and becomes white painted plaster. Instead of meeting the ceiling at right angles, the two surfaces are joined by a gentle curve, making the junction so soft as hardly to be noticed. Effectively the room stops at cornice level, above which ceiling and walls become a vague area more like the sky than any hard surface.

So much for the outdoor quality of internal spaces. It would be surprising if at this period we could not also draw some parallels between external and internal in relation to garden spaces. The earliest gardens at Hampton Court were of about 1525, and are represented by modern reconstructions of the Pond Garden, Herb Garden and Knot Gardens. To the busy spaces of the palace and its many inhabitants, these gardens offer an ideal complement. In comparison to the indoor public space, the gardens offer solitude. Each is entered from a corridor-like path that links them all, each by a single gate, and none is connected to any other space. The fact that there are gates at all is a significant difference from the palace. Here there is nothing haphazard or chancy; they must be entered for themselves alone. But once entered they seem more peaceful, contemplative, even domestic, than the palace apartments ever could, rooms of nature, where hundreds of plants are intricately presented for reflection.

But when new gardens were laid out for Charles II, William and Mary and Queen Anne, nature had taken on a different significance. More important to them than the seclusion a garden gave was the visible mark of their dominion over land. Standing inside the palace and looking out over the Long Water, one feels that this single idea was being pursued to the exclu-

How well the Elizabethans understood the possibilities of
architecture can be seen in their gardens. They appear to be
like rooms, but rooms made for contemplation rather than to
serve any specific activity

Another of the Hampton Court gardens. Their architectural
nature is evident from the fact that one is not permitted to
enter them; like the State Rooms, one can only pass by them
and look

sion of all else, and indeed it was. Here was the beginning, in England at least, of that effort to extend one's grasp and claim nature as a possession. Not to sit among it reflectively, but either to regard it from indoors or to move about in it as a recreation.

But if the models for this kind of design were French, mostly those of Louis XIV's gardener Le Nôtre, the English version falls far short of the originals. Wren's façade to the garden keeps promising grandeur but never quite gets around to delivering it, which as the centre of the piece it ought to do. And then in front of the façade we have, instead of the semi-circular and fountain-covered parterre originally intended, a rather dull patch of ground that might justifiably be regarded as the father of municipal parks. Add to this the fact that two hundred and fifty years have left most of the trees mature to the point of senescence, and the sight is a little pathetic.

Yet here was a garden with this dual character: it was either viewed from indoors as it progressed mechanically towards infinity, a picture in perspective of the natural world under control; or it was used as a mapped territory of the natural world, with roads and spaces carved into it, to be ridden through on horseback: figures in a landscape. From indoors it was a map of one's outdoor activities, and in this way introduced the possibility of using gardens as narrative devices. The eighteenth-century landscape gardeners were to exploit to the full this ability to tell stories by an ordering of nature. Just as a city remembers its past with statues, squares, street names and occasional processions, so too Hampton Court Park uses avenues, statuary and natural forms to evoke images of power, not as the arbitrary possession of a small group but as Power historically developed by kings. The French found this perfectly clear and designed their gardens with an appropriate forthright clarity. It was less clear to the English who used this layout more in imitation than understanding.

Our perception of Hampton Court today is a strange one. We outsiders from a crowded city flood into the empty palace, which was once a densely populated house in a rural emptiness.

Some distance from Hampton Court, and now standing in a true rural emptiness, are the ruins of Kirby Hall in Northamptonshire. Built at the end of the sixteenth century, it carries the marks of that radical transformation from medieval to Renaissance architecture, which left it one of the most remarkable buildings in the country.

Kirby Hall sits in a hollow, so the first sight one has of it is its enormously tall chimney stacks ranged in two long rows. The house was begun in 1570 by Sir Humphrey Stafford and was probably finished within the decade.

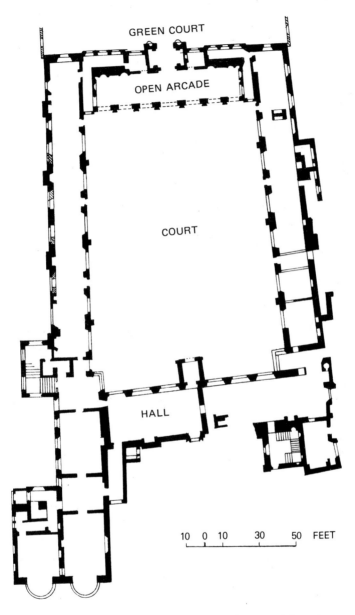

GREEN COURT

OPEN ARCADE

COURT

HALL

10 0 10   30   50 FEET

A plan of Kirby Hall, Northamptonshire (North is toward the top).
The formal gardens are to the left of the large courtyard

(*above*) Facing north, the great entrance porch of Kirby Hall is a cake-like invention of classical detail. At first-floor level, trying to turn things more serious, is the window added by Inigo Jones. To the right was the Great Hall

(*opposite above*) The south façade of the courtyard at Kirby. Here Jones has added windows right across the width of the building, giving rhythm and movement to the façade, compared to the still flatness of the wall in the previous photograph, which it faces

(*opposite centre*) Kirby's west front is made of clearly cut stone forms. Apart from the gables, everything is rectilinear, and even these gables are very flat surfaces. In the foreground, thick hedges are cut to chest height; when seated, one cannot see out of the individual 'rooms' that they form

(*opposite below*) Kirby's great bow windows stand not overlooking the formal garden, whose quality is too private to be able to tolerate such an intrusion, but instead turn their attention towards what was once the 'wilderness garden'

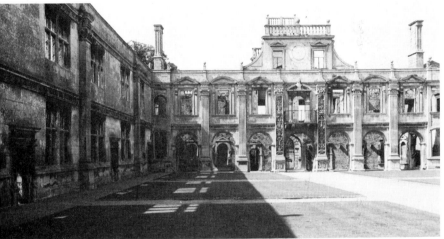

Then it was sold, in the 1590s, to Sir Christopher Hatton, and when he died the house went to his nephew. It was he who made Kirby famous, entertaining both Anne of Denmark and King James here at various times, but subsequently the house slipped in importance and physical condition, until it reached the state we see it in today. The building is mostly a ruin, but because of that a good example of architecture detached from function. Only the essence of architecture remains, useless, and a financial liability to the public who pay for its maintenance.

The transition from medieval to Renaissance architecture is neatly summed up in the design of the inner courtyard. Straight ahead as one enters it, on the south side, is a fantastical composition of Renaissance odds and ends. Although the central window and balcony were added in 1639, the rest of the porch is of about 1570. It is entirely decorative. None of the classical elements is in any way structural or in any but the loosest way related or linked to its neighbours. The enjoyment is obviously in the stone, in the carving and shaping of it, and the forms chosen as decoration are merely vehicles for the mason's art. Academic correctness didn't concern the builders, as they piled columns, entablatures and consoles on top of one another, and how could it have, since the designers worked only from the plates of architectural books from Holland, themselves more imaginative than correct? It says a good deal for the value of direct experience that when Inigo Jones went to Italy, the first English architect to do so, he returned with a more or less complete and personal knowledge of Italian Renaissance architecture. But in the 1570s classicism was used to delight, not to display rational thought. Texture is everything, the work being intended either for close examination or as a background. There is little rhythmic interest, and the windows on either side of the porch have an unarticulated, motionless quality that is more suited to the presentation of materials than ideas.

If one now turns to look at the north façade, it will be found to be again of the 1570s, but with one profound change: a row of windows on the second storey, added in 1638 by Inigo Jones himself. Compared to the south façade, the wall is full of movement, so much so that its nature is quite different to the rest of the courtyard. Each opening in it is clearly defined, contained by its edges, unlike those to the south with their seemingly indefinite spread. The mouldings are also different from one window to the next, and this indicates a different use of carving to the simple exposition of surface. It creates effects of form and rhythm independent of the building's material nature. But somehow they harmonize, these two phases of building, these two ideologies. The same stone helps to unite them, but Jones must have still understood the old architecture, and he didn't destroy it with what he built.

This simple flight of steps leads from the civilized 'garden of rooms' at Kirby down into the 'wilderness garden', once filled by exotic trees from all over the world, but later cut down to pay off debts. The fact that this transition is understated makes the line between gardens all the sharper

If one now enters the house under that ornate porch, there is a second harmony between ages to be met with. For in spite of a straight axis through two courtyards and a centrally placed entrance, a route completely foreign to traditional medieval plans, the entrance of the hall itself, and its plan, are of a virtually standard medieval type. Future developments were to diminish the role of the hall to a mere extension of the porch, a central vestibule, the idealized relic of a way of life. Sir Humphrey Stafford obviously still saw the hall as a practical room. The point is that Renaissance designs have often been seen as too rigid to accommodate medieval house plans, so that the plans were changed to suit symmetrical elevations. Kirby illustrates that this was not necessary, that a symmetrical composition was possible which included medieval practicality. It is only 'transitional' in the sense that soon the hall, as useless as a room as Kirby is today as a house, was to be idealized, and therefore repositioned centrally as the symbolic heart of a house.

To return to the exterior again, and take another look at the application of classical elements to the house, we see how very flat they are, almost painted rather than carved. The west elevation, facing the garden,

Heavy modelling at St George in the East, London, by
Nicholas Hawksmoor, 1715–23; the product of rain and grime

demonstrates this effect, stepping in and out along its length, but very
slightly, and always the whole surface rather than just a part of it. Again this
is the result of classical architecture reaching England in the form of books,
that is on flat papers rather than boldly shadowed in an Italian landscape.
Yet the mention of shadow here is important, because it never can be the
greatest asset in British architecture. We lack the basic element, sunshine.
While Italian buildings are usually designed to throw strong shadows, and
in this way to change their modelling with the moving sun, British buildings
must be built to respond to changes in the quality of light itself, so frequent,
subtle and dramatic. Where an Italian building sits under the sky as under
a vast roof, the British sky is low and ever changing, always in contact with

the ground. Intensity of light, depth of space and colour have constantly changing values, and for these perceptions heavy modelling is unnecessary. A good stone surface is the best reflector of these qualities, and Kirby had the good luck to be built adjacent to one of the finest stone quarries in the land, Weldon. The other common trick in England has been to use the rain to cast shadows. Portland stone is a brightly white limestone, which goes brown to black in time according to the purity of the air. On surfaces exposed to rain or wind, though, it is kept white by the rainfall, and the effects of this black and white are not a bad substitute to give a building form.

A detail of Kirby's stonework

An important part of any English house is its garden, and the gardens of Kirby, first laid out in 1685, are no exception. Like those at Hampton Court, they are modern reconstructions, but accurate, laid out on the original curb-stones that were recently discovered. The arrangement is strictly formal, basically four outdoor rooms, with walls formed by continuous hedges. But these walls only rise high enough to give privacy to someone sitting down; when standing, you are again in public territory, and can see anyone else who happens to be standing. Two hundred years ago the sensation must have been yet odder, when standing up would have put one in the company of the dozens of statues that once peopled the garden. Only a fragment of a single statue now remains, which is not much company.

At the southern edge of this garden, this group of rooms, is a set of semi-circular steps, leading to what was once called the 'wilderness garden', full of exotic trees collected by Christopher Hatton III in the 1680s. These were felled in the eighteenth century to pay off gambling debts, apparently. The narrow passage from one space to the next, and the steps descending as into the sea, are quite simple devices that put the spectator on the edge of civilization, confronting the wilderness of nature beyond. It is a precise edge to create a dramatic moment, and makes an interesting device to compare with the easy transitions from place to place, the more 'natural' landscaping of fifty years later. Before going on to that, though, there is another architectural story to tell.

That story is of the Queen's House at Greenwich, begun in 1616 for Anne of Denmark by Inigo Jones. It was Jones's first building after his return from

207

Italy, and although a little sombre for some tastes, it is the earliest purely classical building in England. Unfortunately the building has been considerably altered since its completion and the surrounding land has been rather crammed with more architecture in the intervening years. The information is there, though, and the effort of mentally peeling away the accretions is repaid by the discovery of a building that employs its architectural means in a striking way.

The house originally stood in the grounds of an existing royal palace, later demolished and rebuilt by Charles II and finally given over as the Royal Naval Hospital. The palace was built by a pupil of Jones, John Webb, and then additions were made to the hospital by Wren and Hawksmoor among others, to form the group of buildings that stands north of the Queen's House facing the Thames. Each architect in turn looked for some way to terminate the series of enclosures visually without spoiling that little house, but none found the answer. It stands today, a little absurdly as the climax to a grand baroque conception of architecture. The long colonnades extending east and west from the house were added last century and are perhaps the weakest part of the whole scheme; and yet, as early as 1661, the house was being substantially altered by John Webb. That is a brief catalogue of the changes at Greenwich, but to see their importance, one must try to understand the original purpose of the house.

Between the palace gardens and the royal park to its south, ran the main road between Deptford and Woolwich. Jones chose to build in a rather odd

The Queen's House, Greenwich: south front. It is difficult to imagine this house as built, without the colonnades and with its clear division where the Dover Road passed through it. But this façade gives no hint at the house's strange plan or function, putting on a face of pure formality for its owners

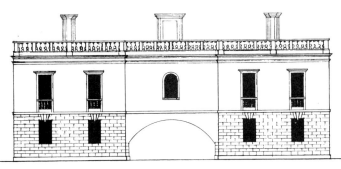

Queen's House, Greenwich; east and west elevations (reconstruction)

manner — on the road itself, which passed straight through the middle of the house. Although this is strange, it is not as lunatic a proposal as it first appears. Its effect was to join palace garden to royal park, and to do so in a way that made the road almost unnoticeable. Whether his inspiration for the idea came from Sir Walter Raleigh's legendary act of chivalry in throwing his coat in the mud for Elizabeth, which is said to have occurred at this very spot, is speculation. At least Jones finished life with his head still on his shoulders, better rewarded for his gesture than Raleigh was for his. At any rate, the original plan shows a ground floor of two rectangular blocks with the road between them and an identical first floor with the addition of a single narrow bridge linking the two blocks.

Jones could have made this bridge the main element of his design. Similarly he could have concealed its existence or suppressed it, as Webb did later when he filled in the gap between the two blocks at first-floor level. Instead, he chose to split the building in a severe way, dividing the two blocks as if cut by a knife and then pulled apart. The house is therefore a complete house, or gives the impression of being so, only for those to whom it belongs. Those façades facing north and south are not terribly interesting, but they are proper little building fronts, and inside the house even today one is unaware of the split. The flow of space takes one up and over it quite easily. But think of being on the road, coming upon this fractured object, more like a ruin than a royal residence. There is no triumphal arch or pleasing classicism for the traveller, only two precipitous walls squeezing him in as he passes. This is a cold and calculated building, quite unemotional. It represents the solution to a number of problems, and that Jones should have started his career with a building like this is indicative, for this is the role architecture was to play more and more.

Jones's achievement was as much in the field of theory as practice. The ideas he displayed in built form, of this cold and unsentimental approach to

209

design, spread quickly, and the naïvity of English architecture, as seen at Kirby, was soon lost. Turning the naïve into the intellectual was a general tendency of the age. A desire grew to discover the underlying principles of common activities, such as economics, or to impose theoretical systems, such as numerical proportion in architecture. Classical architecture at this time was thought to be as old as mankind, a gift from the gods, that had been lost for a long period of society's ignorance and corruption, now to be re-established in a new, enlightened age. Its origins claimed a mythology more ancient than all others, replacing rapidly diminishing local customs, myths and traditions. When Roman and later Greek culture freed myth from local conditions and associations, classicism became as general a thing, and as portable, as Christianity had been in medieval Europe.

Finally in this chapter, there is the garden at Rousham in Oxfordshire, one of the earliest, most complete and loveliest of all English landscape gardens.

Naturalistic landscape had become fashionable in literature long before its realization on the face of the earth. Milton had pointed out its basic picturesque qualities in *Paradise Lost,* and went on to suggest that gardening was at least as old as any other profession:

> On to their morning's rural work they haste
> Among sweet dews and flowers: where any row
> Of Fruit-trees overwoody reached too far
> Their pampered boughs, and needed hands to check
> Fruitless embraces: or they led the vine
> To wed her Elm . . .

An Eden where nature had done, on the whole, not badly, needing only the odd hand, and clip from primitive sequeteurs, to reach perfection.

But it was left to Pope, Addison and that circle, with their didactic writings and wealthy patrons, to produce gardens with the romantic appeal of Milton's poetry or the painting of Claude and Gaspard Poussin. General James Dormer was one of this group, a friend of both Swift and Pope, so it was a matter of course that when he wanted his gardens remodelled, he should have employed the group's favourite artist, William Kent. His scheme, carried out between 1738–40, produced one of the most complete examples of landscape gardening in existence, now old, but still essentially as it was then intended to be. It is one of those works common in England, an amateur work of art; but uncommonly, it is completely successful.

The age was fond of the 'serpentine line', the double curve, Hogarth's 'line of beauty'. It was the essence of Rococo art, and all but one of Rousham's paths use it — some twenty in a small area. The one exception is a perfectly

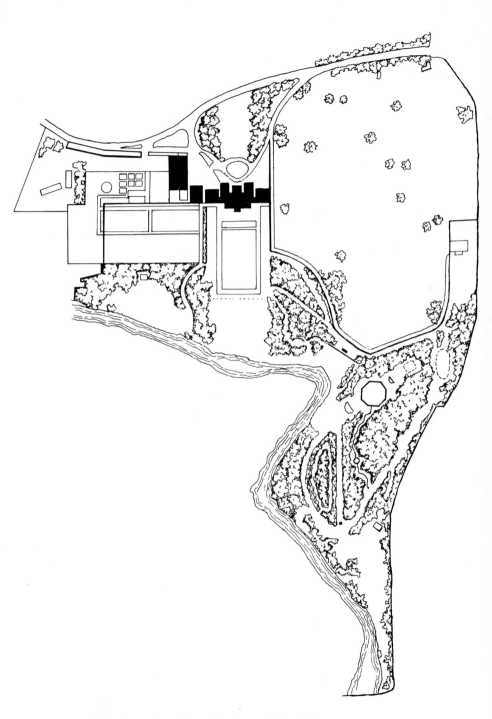

The plan of William Kent's gardens at Rousham in Oxfordshire

(left) This is the gate at Rousham where the servants of those who were being given a tour of the gardens would be admitted and given their beer and cheese. Their masters, it seems, were given wine at the house, and I daresay their portion of cheese was cut from nearer the centre
(centre) The Dying Gladiator lies at the outset of the tour at Rousham, setting a tone of melancholy speculation that pervades the whole journey
(right) The Praeneste arcade at Rousham. Here one can stop a moment and gaze across the River Cherwell, undisturbed by any specific images of classicism. For there are no statues here, or 'worthies' as there are at Stowe. The intention is for a more generalised romance

straight avenue of trees. The serpentine path has the advantage, when one is unfolding a story or revealing scenes one by one, of concealment. It avoids the necessity in a straight path of setting up a picture and then marching towards it. Here the notion of moving through a landscape, hinted at in Hampton Court's later gardens, is picked up and developed as a device of some sophistication. The purpose of the garden has become that of transporting the viewer or participant, by means of space, through time, to paradise. Progressing from place to place one sees now a ruin, now a medieval bridge, next a Roman temple, and so on, in a sequence that purges

the mind of daily thoughts, fills it with reflections and allows it contemplation. Nature here is the backdrop, no longer confronting harsh barbarity with manmade civilization, but creating the illusion of a benevolent natural world. And then along paths, standing by pools and cascades, the imagination peoples this landscape with figures of antiquity; with them come thoughts of perfectability, of the order of ancient Rome, of the British Empire . . . and these figures are seen not as strangers, but companions.

That at any rate is what the eighteenth century wanted to see. Our pleasure here is rather different, much the same as one has touring the giant engines that used to power Tower Bridge, or old abandoned mills. It is a giant machine, whose use is no longer required, and its parts are rusting; we can only stand in wonder at the skill that built it, and marvel at the necessity it satisfied. That sense of nature being benevolent, of the natural order being essentially good, is a main principle of the art of landscape. And how not? The Whigs who built these gardens had done well enough in life — done well enough at business, blowing their South Sea Bubbles — to buy land and make the world look as enchanting as they felt it should appear. Rousham was not designed for idle wanderings. A particular route was set out for the many people who would have toured the grounds even when it was built, and the journey was designed to prepare one little by little for a vision of Eden, paradise regained.

The English are fond of anecdote and stories. In particular the eighteenth century saw narrative become very important to painting, as Hogarth bears witness. It was a method of moral instruction, and interestingly, William Kent was himself trained as a painter. But perhaps even more significant was the novel in literature, developed and refined during the 1700s by writers like Fielding, Smollett and Sterne. So that when gardens also take on a moralizing narrative air, the fact should not seem quite so extraordinary.

Of the original formal gardens designed by Charles Bridgeman only two items remain, and from the first of these, the Bowling Green, a tour of Rousham starts. The green itself slopes away sharply towards the river Cherwell, revealing in the distance two sham ruins. From this point one plunges into the trees and emerges on to a balustraded terrace, with a different view of the river. Into the trees again, and out again, but now a long valley stretches out, containing a series of ponds linked by cascades, which eventually reach the river. Already one has passed through three open and two enclosed spaces, had three views of the river, and changed direction about ten times; and this is only the beginning. Compare this progression through space to that through a Tudor or Jacobean garden, and the mechanical quality of the garden is clear. The raw material is the visitor himself.

From the cascading valley one re-enters the woods and immediately is presented with one of the greatest delights of any English garden. Here one finds a tiny stone aqueduct set level with the earth, wandering along the path in sinuous curves until it reaches a large octagonal pond (where one's only disappointment is that there is no mad hermit to dash out and hurl himself into the icy water). From here it continues on to an open field. All the richness of significance which the double curve contains is apparent here. Its wave-like motion not only conveys the rhythmic motion of water, but it makes us follow its bends, taking up that motion. It recalls, too, man's watery origins and the biological rhythms of existence; even the stone of which the channel is made, a sandstone, echoes the line of waves that moved a million years ago.

The end of this path leads out to a small temple, inside of which is a Roman tombstone, a fragment of the real thing. Once again the river appears, this time with the medieval Heyford bridge, and peels another layer of time from the visitor's mind. This long sequence of 'informality' brings us

Looking down Rousham's serpentine aqueduct, across the Cold Bath

On the left, Apollo looks out towards the Heyford Bridge. The little temple on the right houses a small Roman funerary cask: the dying gladiator is laid to rest, Apollo stands immortal

The rushes growing in the River Cherwell also tremble and move with the motion of water, and the poetry of Rousham's art is constantly verified by nature

to the second remaining feature of Bridgeman's garden, the straight avenue, a double row of trees leading up to a view of a classical arcade. This marks the start of the return journey. This is clear not only because there is a formal element at either end of the trip (which began with the Bowling Green), but because it shows us the time machine rapidly pointing out its own future decline: Bridgeman's garden lasted only a few years. These techniques are of course subtle, and are not as bad as I have made them sound.* They are not always consciously perceived, but they are felt, and the feeling of this unfolding story or order in nature rather than its forthright exhibition is what marks the landscape garden as different from its predecessors.

Though from this avenue one can see the classical arcade, the journey to it takes the visitor past many of the scenes of the outward trip. Beyond the arcade, the sight of the Bowling Green tells one the cycle is complete.

* The little serpentine stream, for example, flows against our direction of movement, so we are going back to its source, exploring it.

I hope that by describing four buildings in some detail, and attempting to analyse their material construction and disposition as methods of conveying ideas, I have made the point set out at the beginning. The nature we use as a contrast or comparison of our civilization is quite as artificial and man-made as the buildings we place within it.

> Our walls aren't made of brick:
>   Thick though they are, they are made of dreams.
> Our floors aren't made of stones:
>   Bones sustain our daily schemes.
> Our roofs aren't made of lead:
>   Instead we are ceiled by remote extremes.
>   (George McLeod — 1950)

The Temple of Gas

9
The Practical City

There was one that found a great mass of money, digging underground in his grandfather's house, and being somewhat doubtful
of the case signified it to the emperor that he had found such
treasure. The emperor made a rescript thus: Use it. He writ back
again, that the sum was greater than his state or condition could
use. The emperor writ a new rescript thus: Abuse it.

Francis Bacon, *Apothegms*, 1624.

In this chapter, I want to introduce a discussion of cities, those collections of
buildings which we perceive as serving a larger idea, something intangible
but real. Discussions of cities can quickly become so abstract as to be inaccessible, so what I propose to do here is to illustrate my comments with progressively larger built examples. Each contains some urban idea, though some
are not what would be called cities, and beyond that each is based on a
remnant from the Roman occupation of Britain. It is often said that in
comparison to, say, France, the Roman influence on these islands was slight,
and in a direct way that is true. We have not the Roman system of law, and
the additions from Latin made to our language were partly a sixteenth-
century phenomenon. Yet the Romans left behind them an enormous
amount of building; that might be called buried treasure. It is the use, or
abuse, of that treasure, the ideas we have had for spending it, that is the
subject of this final chapter, and its main argument will be, that our greatest
successes come from an inventive manipulation of what we find about us.

At East End, a small Oxfordshire village, lie the fragmentary remains of
a Roman villa, built in the second century AD, in the valley of the River Even-
lode. This villa was developed over time into a courtyard house, quite large,
with all the comforts of baths and central heating that a Roman might have
expected in Italy. It was, in fact, a piece of Italy in England, for as a courtyard
house it made no concessions to the English climate, nor did it adopt native
techniques of house building. Obviously the model of civilization, the idea
of what it was to be civilized, was physically embodied in these houses,
which were repeated fairly regularly throughout the Roman Empire. It is
here that the question arises of the Roman influence on civilization, for
although there is some evidence that this villa was built not for a Roman, but

Fragmentary remains of the Roman villa at East End. These simple patterns on the ground may contain more material for invention than we imagine. Who knows where the contemplation of ancient empires might lead?

for a romanized Briton, the spark did not take light. When, in the early fifth century the Romans officially withdrew from Britain, their ideas of civilization did not endure. It was not a question of primitive barbarians knocking down the villa in frenzies of unbottled rage; but slowly, as their desires and needs changed they changed and modified those buildings accordingly. Eventually perhaps, sheep were housed in the villa and the farmers built wooden huts for dwellings in the near vicinity. No one knows what happened in detail, though it seems clear that a different and less complete notion of civilization took over. But to say this modification according to local usage was barbaric would be to repeat the Roman error, that everything not of the Empire was savage and anarchic.

Here at East End there is very little left to see, a few strips of stonework in the grass and that is all. The great effort of building was rewarded with what, two hundred years? of survival; and then ruins. This perspective of time is useful, for it indicates that if something is necessary to a civilization, there is no question, it must be built, however impermanent it may turn out to be. To build *as if* forever, even though common sense indicates another future, shows the commitment to an ideal necessary for civilization.

The irony is that now, useless as a house and not even useful as a sheep-fold, the ruins are likely to be better and longer preserved than the original house; prevented, in fact, from re-entering useful service. So let us turn to something less ephemeral, where the modifications made to the original are still to be seen.

Portchester Castle stands facing out into Portsmouth harbour, the major part of its original walls surviving from the second century AD. The Romans had obvious reasons for building a fort at this point, where the natural conditions for harbouring ships are so good, but our interest is in this, that the fort's purpose ending when the Romans left, the fort itself remained behind. It was then available as a structure free of purpose, an 'as found' object to be re-employed and adapted to whatever uses, if any, it could be made to contain. These must have been many, for the fort appears to have been continuously in use until the last century, when it was employed to house French prisoners during the Napoleonic wars. Edward I, evidently warlike even in his signs of affection, gave the castle to his mother. A birthday present, no doubt.

The fort presented a typical Roman plan, an enclosing wall and a pair of roads crossing at right angles. This, in terms of forts and towns, is as fundamental to the Roman culture as the courtyard plan was to their villas. The interesting fact is that the walls alone remain as physical things but the roads have been retained notionally in that the space is still divided into four quarters. But I wonder what the Romans would have made of the uses we see today in those sections: a Norman castle, a priory church and graveyard, a cricket pitch, and fourth, a scruffy area that could be pasture, an archaeological site or simply available land.

The Roman walls and bastions of Portchester have contained cohorts, conquerors, kings, prisoners of war, churchmen and cricketers

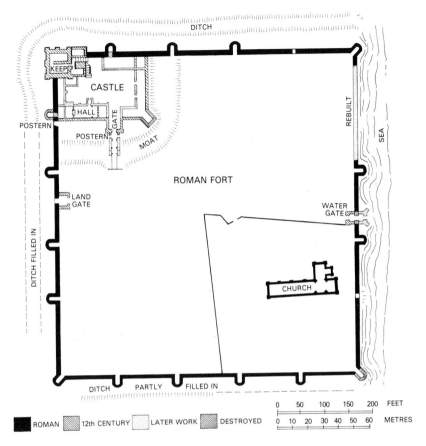

DITCH

KEEP

CASTLE

HALL

POSTERN

POSTERN GATE

MOAT

ROMAN FORT

REBUILT

SEA

LAND GATE

WATER GATE

DITCH FILLED IN

CHURCH

DITCH PARTLY FILLED IN

| 0 | 50 | 100 | 150 | 200 | FEET |
| 0 | 10 20 | 30 40 | 50 60 | | METRES |

ROMAN　12th CENTURY　LATER WORK　DESTROYED

Portchester Castle, Hampshire

Although the cricket pitch is the most relaxed re-use of space, just six stumps of wood, the Norman castle, occupying the other extreme of heavy permanence in stone, is in its way, too, a fine exploitation of the possibilities. On to the Roman idea of a fort Henry I imposed the Norman idea of a castle, that is, a kind of house rather than a garrison. The relationship between the two is especially well thought out, the keep sitting right on the fort's north-west corner and growing dramatically out of it. Within, an inner bailey extends as a smaller, but higher, repetition of the Roman walls. So the Norman designers exploited the object they found to its maximum, leaving it largely intact, adding to it, and turning it into a kind of forecourt, walled garden, or, perhaps, a town.

Adding this element of fortified house to the original object has changed the nature of the whole. It should be stressed that the Romans would never

221

Portchester's Norman keep replaces a corner of the Roman wall, a bastion of which is seen on the left, and in that one gesture gives the fort a new meaning

have conceived of building a thing like the Norman keep, any more than they would have conceived of playing cricket. We are speaking of the formation of different cultures, and it would be a mistake to think this could always be done with the transparency of a cricket ground. I don't think anyone today would regret the solid Norman keep, or attempt to have it demolished as being out of place. Its builders had a clear purpose; what they found they directed towards that purpose.

The other beauty of Portchester is just this ordered co-existence that we see among the four areas of activity. Each use occupies its corner independent of the others, but all are brought into relationship by the wall. That boundary wall, having been accepted as useful, though not purpose made, forms part of the circumstances of each activity. So while, for example, the rules and playing of cricket remain always the same, the playing of each individual game varies according to where it is played, the size of the field and so forth. One could say this is almost the opposite of the way the Romans planned their forts and towns.

Not far along the coast we come to the town of Chichester. There was a town here before the Romans arrived, but it was they who made, once again, the decisive cross plan, even in an existing settlement. As the region was

222

Pedestrianised Chichester. Where has the road gone? As the trees discreetly try to hide the identity of the corner shop, so the corner shop tries to hide the whereabouts of . . .

. . . its giant loading bay

welcoming and not warlike toward the invaders, the walls were not built until about a century after this.

Here, being a town rather than a fort, there was less necessity, or perhaps opportunity, for a grand change in the order of Portchester. In continual occupation, and suffering no natural calamity, the town was modified rather than rebuilt, and though its separate buildings were replaced over the years one by one, this only served to reinforce the Roman pattern. Again, as with the fort, different activities and different ages of building occupy separate quarters: cathedral, high quality housing, market, administration. This could not last forever. Around 1500 there was a fundamental addition made to Chichester, the Market Cross. I don't propose to discuss its qualities as an object, but the act of putting the very elaborate and presumably expensive 'cross' here, where in fact those Roman roads intersect, is a reinforcement of the usefulness of the plan, and a modification of it. By means of the Market Cross, the people of the sixteenth century could assert their mastery over the town, could make the plan do what they wanted it to do. This is what the act of architecture means; not content to tiptoe around the Roman ruins, the town asserts itself, and takes possession of this inherited pattern.

Unlike Portchester, the main axes here are defined by buildings on either side of them. In this way each quarter has become like a large house, with its inside masked by a façade that is more or less like all the others. This takes us about as far as Victorian Chichester. Beyond that we can say that the comparison of each quarter to a house is a good one, because they have been treated similarly in our own time. It is just those four main streets that the town has been most keen to preserve, the façade of a façade, and it is here that Chichester has lost its nerve and made its greatest mistake. For what goes on behind these tasteful façades with their tasteful signboards? If you wander into the hinterland of the north-east quarter, what you find is large plains of tarmac, and the deep projections of the national shops, their loading bays and monolithic stockrooms. The built parts are often ludicrously dressed — I was about to write 'disguised', but they certainly aren't that — in the local flint and brick, as these giant shops try to hide behind façades twenty feet wide that face these main important streets. But most of the space is given over to car parking, so that those streets may be 'pedestrianised' and held in a high state of preservation. One should look closely at these preserved streets and at the people in them. What are the activities this gesture has engendered? For the most part people may be seen shuffling about, eating ice creams, sitting vacantly on benches, and generally not knowing what to do. To me it all seems back to front: I have always assumed that we don't exist to serve buildings, but they to serve us. And yet

225

here we are meant to be watching them as we might watch television. It might be suggested that the modifications here are no different from the insertion of the Market Cross four and a half centuries earlier; but it is directly opposite. Where the cross was an architectural assertion, the modern changes have destroyed the 'innards' of the town, but there is no desire to turn these changes into an architecture. Rather, architecture of the past is brought into play only to conceal change, which hints more at cowardice than courage.

'Necessity', said Hume, 'is something that exists in the mind, not in objects.' He was referring to relations of cause and effect, and was attempting to show that such relations are illusory. In the end he succeeded, and is so said to have undermined empirical philosophy, with its dependence upon experience as a basis for future action. More simply, there is nothing 'necessary' about the relationship between these Roman remains and our towns; I have only selected certain cases to illustrate a point, and that point has to do not with empiricism but with practicality. That is, I am not trying to describe recipes for success, but only to look at the practical results of certain combinations of events, more as a lesson in method than in form.

When we come to Chester, we have a town that grew on the remains of another Roman fort, one that had been among the most important in Britain. Again, little of the actual Roman construction survives, and the present walls for the most part lie beyond the line of the first walls. But the name itself is evidence of the town's ancestry, as much as its patterning is; like the hammer that has had two new heads and three new handles, but is still in some way your grandfather's hammer.

Here, the use of those simple gestures, walls and cross-axes, is so different in effect from that at Chichester. The physical circumstances are of course different, the wall at Chester being of much greater importance for the working of the town. But this 'medieval' city, which is largely of Victorian construction, is an example of necessity as an idea, being carried through into reality, into architectural form. What does it matter the date, or even the appearance of the buildings? It is the idea that is of vital importance, and what we see are the means by which that idea is brought to life. The idea, of course, is a city.

The walls of Chester are places of peaceful elevation above the busy world of streets, providing a detached view of both city and countryside. Far from seeming old fashioned despite its antiquity, this system has been kept up to date by the imagination of those who use it

The Rows at Chester are a civilized creation, giving density and dignity to what is a fairly small area, packing it with people, and, in a sense, continuing the wall's vantage point right into the heart of the town

First, the walls provide a way of experiencing the city in a certain sense independently of the workings of the city itself. As you walk atop them, you are on the edge and become aware just what the extent of the town is; and then too, you have to left and right the absolute difference between town and country. Raised to a higher level, a little closer to the gods, you can look down on the world and judge it, or contemplate it; whatever it is you think the gods do. And occasionally on your perambulation you encounter steps, ramps and gates, fairly complex connections between the two levels, that offer to take you down into the busy world below. One thing more should be said about the walls, and that is that they take you behind the cross pattern of streets, and make this back area in a certain sense public — in that it can be seen — and as a result less accessible to surreptitious destruction. What at first sight appears to be a closed city has in fact many 'open' characteristics, and it may be worth bearing this in mind when examining the physical world with the intention of putting it to conceptual use. Things need not be as they seem: they are what we make them be. So it would be physically possible to fill the quarters with car parking; but would it be considered culturally possible? My feeling is that the inhibitions here, because of the town's form, would be strong against it.

The double height arch makes it possible to give a certain grandeur to a building composed even of rather small shops. No doubt a modern planner would throw his hands up in horror at a similar proposal for a new development: those stairs! and not even straight stairs! And undoubtedly the stepped bridges over the canals of Venice are inconvenient . . . but some things seem worth the extra effort

Behind the scenes at Chester there is still a density of service buildings rather than a desolation of car parking. It seemed too depressing to include a photograph of the same quarter of Chichester: all tarmac and sky

230

The famous Rows themselves are a fine trick, doubling shopping density with a simple gesture. Darkness under the galleries cannot any longer be considered an objection in these days of deep shops and artificial lighting. The more subtle fact of the galleries is their relationship with the ground level, which slopes quite sharply towards the river. If you were to walk into the backlands of, say, the north-west quadrant, you would emerge from ground level behind on to first-floor level of the galleried Rows, through Watergate Street. The point of this is again the sense of unity that endures between back and front, the formal or public face and the muscles that move it. Apart from odd exceptions, the backlands continue to be filled by workshops, houses and a network of access roads. But the relationship between cars and buildings seems to be in balance.

Nothing is perfect, of course, and Chester has been pedestrianised — such a charming word — but that could be changed tomorrow; the structure of the town is still there. To have gone as far as Chester has been taken, built up from Roman scraps, is remarkable. Inventiveness and practical skill were needed to accomplish it, and courage to accept that to be alive is to assimilate change, not exclude it. The walls have been used positively, not only negatively to exclude an alien world, but positively to promote a model of what a civilized town can be. Rather than sweep the pieces off the board, like a petulant child when losing a game, the people of Chester have seen that to play the game is what matters. They have played it with skill. It is precisely when things are working well that one cannot afford to relax, to attempt to preserve a state or condition, for the achievement of the present position has been a story of continual change and reconstruction. One can only, perhaps, preserve one's balance. And it isn't Utopia; it only works well, and only, as far as we can know, works well today. The game continues, and tomorrow will presumably bring new problems and difficulties into consideration. It is the struggle with those difficulties that will continue the life of Chester.

Now we have talked about a series of places, each more elaborate than the last. One of the elements common to all four has been the wall, at Chester and Portchester picked up and exploited to the full. The next example I want to use is pure wall and the greatest of Roman ruins: the wall of Hadrian.

It seems that this wall was not designed as an impassable barrier so much as a frontier line, since there is inadequate access to its top to make it useful for doing more than fighting off small raiding parties. From certain features, such as the 6-mile aqueduct *north* of the wall, carrying water to the garrison at Chesters, it appears that both sides of the wall were under Roman control. But we will return to its purpose in a moment.

231

Once again, when the Romans withdrew, when they could no longer afford the great cultural mechanism of the wall, it was abandoned. At one wall fort, temple altars were used for cooking, dwellings as granaries, and the wall itself was gradually pulled apart and used to build private fortifications, suitable to a smaller ideology: mere survival. For centuries it acted like a weir, collecting bits of towns, holding on to small markets and farmhouses that drifted into its backwaters. But as a whole it has never been used. There is no use combing it with metal detectors: the wall itself is treasure.

As we saw at Chester, a wall need not only be a barrier of exclusion, a wholly negative thing. Though the wall as an undemocratic device has been a favourite theme in recent architectural thinking, Le Corbusier, one of the most influential of modern architects, said that, 'stones will no longer be used for building — all will be glass . . .' and many other examples, from the German Paul Scheerbart to London's own Cedric Price, could be quoted as advocating this freedom from the heaviness of architecture. It is seen as a restriction on spiritual freedom, and it would not be an exaggeration to connect these frustrated cries for liberation with St Paul's puritanical desire to be free of the flesh, that unpleasant substance which causes us so many problems, with its passions and needs. Yet just as part of being human involves coming to accept and learning to control one's body, so part of architecture is the acceptance and use of walls, strong and heavy, the substance of architecture. The Romans explored with walls, they did not simply hide behind them; that is their positive use, for without establishing borders and giving form to our actions, there can be no growth. The paradox is, that nothing can grow that does not have limitations.

The Romans built solidly, even if in ten years they would have to build a new wall a few miles to the north or south. They could not read the future, and so they put all their energy into building for the present circumstances. In fact Hadrian's Wall was itself rebuilt two or three times, according to changing technical demands. It was obviously felt to be worth the effort, for that effort was a means of cultural survival. As Louis MacNeice has it,

> I must go out tomorrow as the others do
> And build the falling castle;
> Which has never fallen, thanks
> Not to any formula, red tape or institution,
> Not to any creeds or banks,
> But to the human animal's endless courage.
> Spider, spider, spin
> Your register and let me sleep a little,
> Not now in order to end but to begin
> The task begun so often.

The final example in this chapter is London. That London was founded by the Romans is as much as we need to say of its origins. It has not retained a characteristic Roman pattern, having long outgrown the possibilities of such a layout. But a parallel sort of formal continuity can be seen in the reconstruction that took place after the Great Fire, which readopted medieval street patterns in spite of many official proposals recommending more fashionable layouts. But even this applies only to the City. The London we must deal with is a larger thing altogether, including the cities of London and Westminster as well as the vast stretches of industrial and residential development of the last three centuries. The London of this discussion is the head of an empire, the Rome of its age. So we seem, happily enough, to have come a full circle in this chapter.

In more than one respect, London has left the boundaries given to it by older cultures, for it needed to invent new cultural models for a new type of empire. This phase of potent creativity is always brief in any culture, and in that brief period the values must be created by which a society can subsequently live. This is just what happened in Rome, and we have been looking at some of the effects. So it happened in Athens, and at Ur. When these cities show phases of rebuilding after their golden age, this work sits largely on old foundations, following the older designs with modifications, elaborating and exploiting their own past. A city can never be reborn as a newborn child, without a memory; its rebuilding is its memory.

We saw that when the Roman came to Britain, he brought his culture with him, in his patterns and plans. He remembered his way of life, and made buildings that corresponded with that memory. He struggled to play his game in new and difficult circumstances. In this there is nothing miraculously clever. But when in the sixteenth century Pope Sixtus V wanted to recall the glories of that Rome, a Rome he never knew, he could do so by a careful editing of that city's physical remains. His new buildings were not meant to reconstruct the old Rome literally, but to revive its spirit and ideals. The fact that he had but fragmentary knowledge of the old buildings was an advantage rather than a limitation, because he could reinvent at will within the patterns that remained to him. These patterns he did not need to reinvent, only to re-employ.

'The truth of an idea is not a stagnant property inherent in it. Truth *happens* to an idea. It *becomes* true, is *made* true by events. Its verity *is* in fact an event, a process . . . .' Without rushing to embrace the whole philosophy of William James, it should be possible to use his comment to promote a certain way of looking at cities.

The entrance to Liverpool's Albert Docks

To attempt an analysis or even a description of London piece by piece, of its potential utility in imaginative terms, would be an impossibly long task. The proposition, though, is essentially this, that London was, quite recently in years but long ago in the density of modern history, the head of an empire, the world's greatest city, and that it now lies in ruins, as Rome did in the sixteenth century. Still a source of wonder, it is a once great city now less densely populated and almost devoid of purpose. How did this happen?

To take just one example, London's docks were built to meet certain functional requirements of international trade in the early nineteenth century. This was a time when the city was a mechanism for processing 'things': food, cloth, coal, iron, and so on, physical objects. Spaces were required to handle and exchange these things, and we were left with the various docks as physical representations of this necessity and of this achievement. For nothing like this had been seen before, though it was repeated in many of the major cities of Britain: Liverpool, Glasgow, Hull and Bristol among

London in the 1860s, showing the London Docks, then about fifty years old. Why should a place once so powerful with the purpose of empire be cleared away for the construction of bungalows, a move equivalent to the retrogression of Roman villas to sheep pens. If a new cultural use could be found for Portchester and Chester, what might not be possible here?

The Newzealander, by Gustave Doré. The colonial tourist contemplates the melancholy ruins of London, the Rome of its age, and from it draws inspiration to invigorate his culture others. It is not just the fading of an empire that leaves such buildings stranded on the banks of uselessness; Covent Garden is another, domestic, example, and Billingsgate Market too has recently been closed. The fact is that cities are no longer required to perform these mechanical functions, which are all done either in the suburbs or in the countryside. Returning to an earlier theme, here is the motor car, or lorry in this case, eating away the very heart of a city, because all these repositionings of markets and docks depend upon the lorry. That is a separate issue. What we are left with is a London devoid of function, a London in decay. The idea is not a new one. Gustave Doré, having completed his famous series of woodcuts showing the incredible diversity and density of Victorian London, appended a print entitled The Newzealander. It isn't his best composition, but its narrative message is clear, showing a colonial visitor on the banks of the Thames, the ruins of St Paul's in the distance, while at his feet and in the middle distance stretch the vast and melancholy ruins of London's docks and warehouses. He is, one presumes, filling his sketchbook with images to take back with him to New Zealand, much as travellers in the eighteenth century did at Rome. Here is a clue to the use we can get from London, to its power as an idea.

In Le Corbusier's plan for Paris, to which I have referred, he hints at the kind of work that will be done in his clean and noiseless 'city' where, '400,000 clerks of Paris will be able to look out upon a splendid landscape'. It may also be remembered that the intention was to replace the mechanical intricacies of the Covent Garden area with acres of office space, and in fact this is what the modern city is: a place not for physical, but administrative activity. The remains of the 'physical' city are just that, scraps. There seems no reason why these scraps should not be struggled with and assembled into the memory of a glorious city, just as happened at Rome. There, the bits and pieces were assembled into a very powerful work of art, by forcing into relationship things which had appeared merely superfluous.

'Strictly speaking,' wrote the brothers Fowler in their book The King's English, 'metaphor occurs as often as we take a word out of its original sphere and apply it to new circumstances. In this sense almost all words can be shown to be metaphorical when they do not bear a physical meaning; for the original meaning of almost all words can be traced back to something physical . . . Words had to be formed to express mental perceptions, abstract ideas, and complex relations, for which a primitive vocabulary did not provide; and the obvious course was to convey the new idea by means of the nearest physical parallel. The commonest Latin verb for think is a metaphor from vine-pruning . . .' If metaphor in language is the use of the concrete to illuminate and illustrate the abstract, surely that should be possible for us in architecture as well. Looking at the original development of Covent Garden, described earlier in the book, it does seem to have been the method used by Inigo Jones. Now, from this sketch of possible methods, I want to turn to look at how our desire to avoid present difficulties, instead of facing them, simply lands us with new and ever less soluble problems, before returning to the raw material of our urban culture, our dead cities.

The present state of our culture, in respect of the ability to develop towns and cities, is a mess, to put it mildly. We strive to invent The Modern Form for Modern Man, as at Milton Keynes, Cumbernauld or Runcorn New Town, as if some mechanical device will be found to answer our needs, whether these devices are patterns formed by the demands of motor cars or the movement patterns of people. Both are abstractions. But we have seen proof in the examples of Chichester and Chester that there is no value innate in such patterns. There is no prescriptive, mechanical pattern that can answer our needs. Meaning and value lie not in the patterns of mechanics, or in scientific standards of efficiency and cleanliness, but are imposed upon these patterns by the imagination. To repeat James's words, 'truth happens to an idea'.

An illustration of the difficulties to which the mechanical approach can lead may be seen in Runcorn New Town. Cities obviously develop problems in their daily working, and to relieve these we invent mechanical solutions: the autobus is a clear example. When it came to planning Runcorn, however, these devices were no longer seen as palliatives, but as fundamental elements in the make-up of a city. So at Runcorn, desolate and isolated residential quarters have been justified by the provision of a bus service connecting city centre (called Shopping City) with distant dormitory. It would be the same if one were to observe the usefulness of crutches to a lame man, and to compel, as a result, the whole population to use them. It is no way to carry on the building of a city.

Looking at James Stirling's housing at Runcorn, is its sad appearance so surprising? It has no possible connection with anything we could call every-day life, dedicating itself to the motor car as extremely as Chichester has done, but in the opposite direction. For entering the housing quarters at

(opposite) Runcorn New Town. These are the houses that result from a dependence on motor cars and buses. Treat a person like a lame man and he may develop a limp . . . The design is what one would call, I think, uncompromising

Runcorn, one is faced by street after street of garages, the only activity apparent in them being the repair of cars. Stirling has not tried to make an ugly idea pretty, but has exposed its brutality to the full light of day. It should be a lesson to us all, especially to the would-be builders of future 'Shopping Cities'.

A machine of any sort, while it is useful to its ends, is modified as necessary to best meet those ends, with little regard for the effects on its appearance. Only when it no longer has purpose — when it is 'dead' — is it restored to its pristine state, and preserved. This is true of steam engines, of aeroplanes, and it is true of the Central Market building at Covent Garden. But Fleet Street, to take another example, is still a working machine, though for how much longer I wouldn't care to guess. The buildings come and go, and people may care about this or not, but the *street* remains the same, that street which is in physical reality nothing at all, is just an idea. As long as the machinery of Fleet Street exists to keep the idea alive, there is no problem. Once that machinery (and by machinery I mean not just printing presses but the Press as a whole), once it moves away, then the idea of Fleet Street will be in danger. At that point, there will be a tendency to move in and preserve the buildings and restore the street itself, its physical being; to fix its image at death, like a mummy or a death mask. This way we hope to idealise the street, but I would suggest that this is not enough. Besides, where does it end? What about the most functional part of all, the black asphalt that is the literal street? I imagine this is thrown away every four or five years, worn out by use. What is the purpose of conserving all these objects, of banning traffic so that ice-cream eaters can search undisturbed for vanished ghosts? Surely a better proposition would be to send the *idea* of urban life that Fleet Street represents out to where it is needed, to the suburbs and the new towns that are sitting like soulless bodies in the English landscape, waiting for inspiration; or like empty chess-boards, wanting the rules and the pieces to play with.

'What is a man to do out here?' asked Henry Nevinson, a Fleet Street leader writer who had just retired to the suburbs. 'Let's have a look at all these posters displayed in front of the Free Library, where a few poor creatures are still reading last night's news for the warmth. Next week there's a concert of chamber music in the Town Hall. I suppose I might go to that, just to "kill time" as they say. Think of a journalist wanting to kill time! . . . Then there's a boxing competition at the St John's Arms, and a subscription dance in the Nelson Rooms, and a lecture on Dante, with illustrations from contemporary art, for working men and women, at the Institute. Also there's

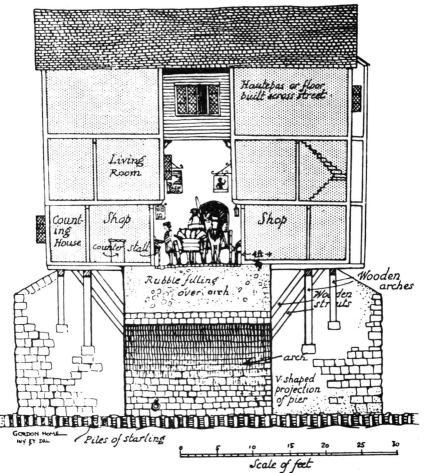

A medieval invention for crossing a river: section through Old London Bridge

something called the Why-be-Lonesome Club for promoting friendly social intercourse among the young and old of all classes. I suppose I might go to that too. It sounds comprehensive.'

And then his mind starts to to reflect upon the Fleet Street he had known for so many years, not a place for killing time, but where people gather to collect the images which form a picture of the whole world. Fleet Street, a focus for the mind, a container of ideas. While he idles in the suburbs, 'the foreign editors are waiting now in their silent room, and the telegrams come to them from the ends of the world. They fold them in packets together by countries or continents — the Indian stuff, the Russian stuff, the Egyptian,

Balkan, Austrian, South African, Persian, Japanese, American, Spanish, and all the rest. They'll have pretty nearly seven columns by this time, and the order will come "Two-and-a-half foreign". Then the piercing and cutting will begin. One of them sits in a telephone box with hands across his head, and repeats a message from our Paris correspondent. Through our Paris man we can talk with Berlin and Rome . . . The voice of all the world is now heard in that silent room.'

So we know that we have the physical material to work with; and we have the inventiveness, the rational ability; surely we don't lack the passion to spend this treasure. Do we? Perhaps a word from the age of reason will help: 'Reason is, and ought only to be, the slave of the passions, and can never pretend to any other office than to serve and obey them.' Those are the words of David Hume.

A game of cricket is not based on the intensity of dramatic incident. It consists of a number of gestures, repeated again and again, with slight variations, none of which is the whole game, or decisive to it. At any one time not a great deal seems to be happening; but after three or four days there is somehow a thing called a game of cricket, with its character. Certain highlights may be remembered, but it is more as a drift that the game is recalled, as a shape. In all this, what a difference circumstances of weather and pitch have made. There is no attempt to neutralise these elements. On the contrary, they are essential to the game. They are written into its history, which after five days, exists where? In the mind. The green patch of earth is only a field of possibility; as too is the city.

Gazetteer

Introduction to the Gazetteer

This book is not concerned mainly with vernacular architecture, but with the grander of British buildings, and these indeed form the major part of the entries in the following gazetteer. It would seem, however, that an introduction to the gazetteer might provide an opportunity to discuss the old methods of construction, which formed and to a certain extent still do form, the background against which that grander architecture appears.

Some time ago, while browsing through a book of Indian cookery, published in Madras, I came across a recipe for lime pickle. It all seemed pretty straightforward until the very end, when one was instructed to, 'put it in a glass jar. You have to keep it in the sun for two months.' At which point, one could only smile. But on reflection it seemed that there was a general lesson to be gleaned from this recipe, studied beneath the cloudy skies of an English summer, and perhaps a particular lesson that would apply to vernacular architecture.

This architecture, like cooking, is concerned with the use of local resources to meet local conditions. The ingredients available to it depend to a large degree upon geology, vegetation, climate and technical sophistication. Brickmaking requires not only clay, but the ability to form and fire that clay, and the famous phrase 'first catch your hare' implies not only the animal's existence in your part of the world, but the ability to bring it to the pot, or in this case jug.

All this is meant to introduce a very brief description of some of the basic principles of building, that once formed the character of regional styles. That they do so no longer is an indication of the progressive industrialization of building components, and their ready distribution throughout the land. This too has its parallel in what is now the food industry.

Vernacular architecture is sometimes regarded as a natural product of the land, a god-given part of the landscape that existed from earliest times until the cruel days of the Industrial Revolution uprooted and destroyed the ancient ways. The truth is that, using materials for the most part locally found, techniques of vernacular architecture developed slowly over the centuries, from the time when people would have considered a house, if they

244

A farm building on the border of Shropshire

had one, to be a lean-to of sticks covered with turf, to the sophisticated levels
seen in the sixteenth and seventeenth centuries. It was in these years that
'common' building enjoyed its golden age, when a large middle-class population found the means to house themselves reasonably well. But the time
was brief; a century later the middle classes had social and aesthetic ambitions that called upon designs and materials from outside the vernacular
tradition, and those traditions were handed down the social scale. Neither
should it be considered that vernacular buildings were put together as

merely practical affairs, and that their aesthetic appeal is happy chance. Many of these buildings were constructed to demonstrate the prosperity and taste of their owners. One should give credit to their success in architecture, rather than ascribe it to naïvety.

When speaking of vernacular architecture, it is usual to distinguish geographically between the Highland zone — to the north and west of an imagined line from Devon and Cornwall, past Wales, through the Pennines and below the North of England, and the Lowland zone, south east of this line. On the whole this is of richer agricultural land and historically at a more advanced stage of economic, social and architectural development. It is here that one finds the softer building stones, such as the oolitic limestones of Oxfordshire, the large oak forests, which are now for the most part incorporated in the many timber-framed houses and barns of Kent, Sussex and East Anglia, and the excellent brick earths of the London basin and the Weald.

In the Highland zone, stone ranges from the granite of Cornwall to the millstone grits of the north-east and Midlands. With this short list — stone, timber and fired clay — we have practically named all the materials of traditional construction, and certainly the chief ones. The beauty and fascination of vernacular architecture derives from the astonishing, almost endless, variety within each type. To describe these many variations is not the purpose of this book, if, indeed, it is to be attempted at all. But a rough idea can be given of how the basic material types are employed.

There are two distinct ways to construct buildings: either a structural frame can be built, to which are attached various materials that keep out the weather, or one can build a solid structure, which acts as support and weather protection at the same time. Frame structures are traditionally of timber, while brick, stone or mud are the materials obviously suited to mass construction. Almost always, though, the roof is a frame structure, made of wood and covered with slates, tiles or thatch, so that in a sense carpentry could be said to be the predominant vernacular craft, while variations in walling systems occur from place to place.

Timber frames are weatherproofed by filling the spaces between framing posts and beams with brick, wattle and daub or mud (these latter producing the well-known, half-timbered buildings). Or they may be sheathed and hidden completely by lath and plaster, weatherboarding or tiles, once again, though it is not uncommon in the Midlands to find timber structures covered by skins of stone and presenting the appearance of solid wall buildings.

Many questions of construction entail jointing. In timber-frame buildings, one member must be joined to another to form a rigid armature of support, and the various types and conditions of jointing exercised the craftsman's skill. With solid construction, strength is gained by the careful joining of much smaller elements, whether bricks, dressed stone, flint, or rubble, which must prevent the wall collapsing under its own weight and that of roof and floors. Solid walls often have a tendency to bulge or lean under these loads, which can push the wall rather than merely sit squarely atop it. For this reason the solid wall is often to some extent framed — laced with timber work to hold it together and tied from one side of a building to the other to keep it true. Obviously the closer the fit between one construction block and its neighbours, the more stable will be the wall, but the fact is that squaring stone is an expensive business, and much of vernacular building technique was concerned with mitigating the defects of materials and resources that were not ideal.

The problems of roofing, on the other hand, were usually associated with trying to cover a space yet not cluttering it with columns or impinging its usefulness with sloping sides; so you didn't bump into things or bang your head. A general difficulty in finding or affording large timbers led to the development of various ingenious systems of spanning wide spaces by employing a number of short timbers. Such is the hammer-beam roof, which itself became a highly decorative feature of house construction.

There are many excellent books available on the subject of vernacular building, both guides and histories, though all writers on the subject agree that guide books have limited value for a building type where no two examples are quite the same, and practically every parish shows some local variation in technique to its neighbours. Both R. W. Brunskill's *Illustrated Handbook of Vernacular Architecture* and J. & J. Penoyres' *Houses in the Landscape* are good analytical accounts of the subject. *The Development of English Building Construction* by C. F. Innocent and Alec Clifton-Taylor's *The Pattern of English Building* are also excellent. Innocent discusses the historical development of building technique, while Clifton-Taylor's book is about the materials of construction. For a well-illustrated account of timber construction, there is Richard Harris's *Discovering Timber Framed Buildings*.

But there is a most important part of the recipe, which the books leave out, thinking it, I suppose, self-evident. Having constructed your building, you must keep it in the rain, for two hundred years; which you couldn't do in Madras.

Christ's Hospital, Abingdon

Christ's Hospital, Abingdon.
Rear view

The Home Counties

BEDFORDSHIRE

Luton Luton Hoo (1764–1903)

Luton Hoo was bought in 1762 by Lord Bute, Prime Minister at the time. Within two years he had Robert Adam designing him a new house and Capability Brown reconstructing the park of 1,500 acres. This garden is one of Brown's finest. The house itself was only partly designed by Adam, though the library was said to have been among his finest interiors. But this was destroyed by fire, and most of the architecture we see today was made in the first years of this century by Mewes and Davis, architects of the Ritz Hotel in London. This remodelling was for Sir Julius Wernher, who had become enormously wealthy in South Africa with gold and diamond mines. But even more than for its architecture and gardens, Luton Hoo is celebrated for one of the finest and most complete collections of art in England with a picture collection extending from the Early Masters through to Dutch and English schools, the Ludlow collection of English porcelain, jewels, silver, tapestries and bronzes.

Bedford Milton Ernest Hall (1853–6)

This is the only complete country house built by William Butterfield. It is built of local stone, and its design illustrates many of the principles of country-house planning at mid-century, and of High Victorian artis-

tic ambition. The plan is irregular, basically an L-shape with a staircase embraced by the angle. This came to be the standard plan for picturesque houses well into the twentieth century, employed by Mackintosh, Voysey and Lutyens. The Gothic style gave licence for formal asymmetry, and this has been used to provide, on one hand, technical advantages which many classical houses were deprived of, such as good daylighting even in servants' rooms, and on the other hand, to present a series of formal inventions. The great delight here is the three-storey bay window on the garden front, which rises past the eaves' level and is transformed into a giant dormer window, complete with pitched roof.

BERKSHIRE

Abingdon Brick Alley Almshouses (1718)

These almshouses were built by a local mason, Samuel Westbrooke, and seem a quite timeless example of arched construction. With their six great arches forming a screen to support a balcony at first-floor level, and the central pediment, they remind one a little of John Soane's stable block at Chelsea, or his Dulwich Picture Gallery. Those, of course, were built a century later.

Abingdon Christ's Hospital (c.1550)

This is the finest of the three ranges of

249

almshouses that surround St Helen's Churchyard. It was founded by Edward VI and built during his reign. It is hard to believe that these are houses for the poor, when we compare them with our modern efforts; but then that's what Pugin was saying a hundred and fifty years ago. There is not really a lot to say about a simple building like this, for the means by which it achieves its ends are obvious to all, in a sense artless. The beauty of the long repetitious cloister is the same as in a brick wall, and results not from mechanical but manual repetition.

Sonning Deanery Gardens (1900)
About ten years into his career, which had been almost entirely concerned with country houses, Edwin Lutyens built Deanery Gardens, which proved to be one of his finest. These are solid references to a solid past, such as Webb used in his Red House at Bexleyheath in 1860. Here, forty years later, and despite what critics say about the old-world substantial nature of this house, it really appears slightly ironic. None of the forms — for example the chimney — has enough detail to be a reference to any specific age or place, it is merely 'chimney'. So with the vaguely Norman entrance door and that generous two-storey bay window: they came from the imagination, not from the past. Some people might call this a modern style, and perhaps it is.

Sutton Courtenay Norman Hall (c.1190–1200)
Sutton Courtenay is anyway a village worth visiting, but this plain little hall standing next to the church is particularly good. The building is simple, and has had not too many changes made to it over the years. There is a little enrichment of the doors and windows, and the roof is decorated by its own construction. Apart from this, it is just a simple stone house.

BUCKINGHAMSHIRE

Mentmore Mentmore Towers (1852–4)
Mentmore is the type of building that gave Victorian architecture a bad name for so long. It is heavy, based on the sixteenth-century Wollaton Hall, but with rather less of the light and inventive decoration that relieves Wollaton. This is almost inevitable in a copy, I suppose, even though the copy is not exact. It was designed by Joseph Paxton in 1852–4 for Baron Meyer Amschel de Rothschild, and because by Paxton, had some of the first hot water heating and ventilation systems in the land. Rothschild's collection of art, for which the house was built, has been dispersed, and the house now serves religious purposes.

Stowe Gothic Temple (c.1741)
This not-so-little temple, once called the Temple of Liberty, was designed by James Gibbs, and is one of the earliest Gothic revival buildings in England. Walpole's famous Strawberry Hill, for example, was not begun until 1749. But then it was a style always more popular among architects than amateurs: Hawksmoor was building All Souls, Oxford in Gothic as early as 1715 (rather than 'new fantasticall, perishable trash'); even Wren had employed it.

The Stowe temple is not in any way historical Gothic, but rather evocatively medieval. To some eyes it is a horror; to some a relief after the custard softness of so many pretty little white temples and bridges, none big enough to be stirring. It is built of ironstone, and seems rather to absorb than reflect light. The plan is delightfully geometrical; where Tresham couldn't solve the problem of how to enter a pure triangular form at his Rushton Lodge, Gibbs managed by making inside and outside meet at the centre of each façade. Then, almost wilfully, he takes one of the pentagonal towers a storey higher than the rest; I wonder how wilful the

whole building really is. We know that Tresham built his lodge full of trinity symbolism. Gibbs too was a Roman Catholic, and it would be interesting if someone were to make a study of this little temple in those terms.

Unlike the Rushton Lodge, this building has an interior of equal refinement to its outside, now a house that may be rented for holidays from the Landmark Trust.

West Wycombe West Wycombe Park
(c.1750–80)
The main body of West Wycombe was built in the early eighteenth century, a plain structure that can still be seen behind Sir Francis Dashwood's remodelling, begun in 1750. Dashwood was founder of the so-called Hell Fire Club, which met at the house for their antics, but he was also a founder of the Society of Dilettanti, a group

West Wycombe Park

interested in the arts. Both Adam and Nicolas Revett supplied designs for reworking the house, but the dilettante in Dashwood made him mix them up and 'adapt' them. The most unusual of the several porticos is that which runs along the south front, connecting two existing wings. A very thin and Palladian design, sitting oddly with all the other porticos, clearly visible, which are tacked on here and there. Perhaps its greatest virtue is that it is made of stone, and avoids that papier maché stage set quality that saturates even some of Palladio's work.

The gardens were laid out c.1780 by Humphrey Repton. The grounds are small, but benefit from the quite hilly countryside round about, and are one of the more delightful places near London to have a picnic.

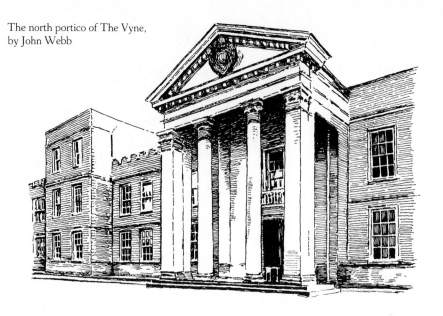

The north portico of The Vyne, by John Webb

HAMPSHIRE

Basingstoke The Vyne (sixteenth–eighteenth centuries)
The Tudor house built by Lord Sandys, Lord Chamberlain to Henry VIII, was much larger than the house that now exists. The main alteration in the seventeeth century was John Webb's addition of a portico to the north front in 1655. It is the first such use in England for domestic work, an idea picked up by Inigo Jones from Palladio, and from Jones by his assistant Webb. So here the house becomes a sacred temple, though the portico is so obviously plugged on that it leaves one wondering about the advisability of rushing into these things. A finer building by Webb is his domed garden pavilion, of brick and tile and good proportion.

Micheldever St Mary's Church (sixteenth century, 1808)
To a plain medieval church, the architect George Dance was asked to add a new nave. The result is so impressive architecturally

as to deserve a mention in spite of the general absence of churches in this gazetteer. The church from outside looks rather swollen, with plain brick additions, but unremarkable. Inside is a display of the

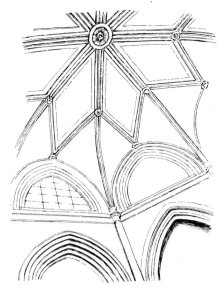

St Mary's, Micheldever

highest architectural skill. Dance's addition between west tower and chancel is octagonal, and really rather secular in feeling; its geometrical execution is difficult to describe and impossible to photograph, but a visit is recommended.

Portchester Portchester Castle (Roman–twelfth century)
The best remaining Roman fort in England forms the outer bailey walls of Portchester Castle, to which it owes its survival; Most of the flint walling and round-ended wall towers are nearly complete, though much of the east wall was rebuilt in medieval times. The inner bailey and keep were built in the twelfth century, and were protected by a moat. The castle has been often used as a prison, particularly during the Napoleonic wars. There is a tale that an officer, having left his horse at the gate while visiting the governor, returned several hours later to find it had been devoured by hungry Frenchmen. There is something about castles that gives people a craving for horsemeat.

Portsmouth Town Defences (seventeenth and eighteenth centuries)
Admittedly, little of the once extensive town defences remain. The Dutch military engineer, Sir Bernard de Gomme, had started the works in 1665 for Charles II, but when Palmerston extended the fortification of Portsmouth in the 1860s–70s, the space-consuming moats and ravelins were replaced by barracks. On the sea front one can still get a feeling of the serious nature of the defensive system, and see the heavy detailing in brick and stone that the job demanded. Some of the original moat still exists, and the brickwork around it is massive. So too are the Long Curtain, and Eighteen Gun Battery. The latter wall contains a simple, squat doorway, through which various naval heroes have left England for their ships; it is still impressive

Stone gate in Portsmouth

to catch a glimpse of some giant warship on the channel, for the sea is, somehow, the last thing one expects to see on the far side of a doorway.

KENT

Canterbury Canterbury Castle (c.1080)
The keep at Canterbury was one of the first stone keeps built by the conqueror, of flint rubble and Caen stone dressings. It is estimated that its original height must have been about 80ft, but this was lost in the early nineteenth century when it was partly demolished for building materials. As the walls grew thicker towards the base, demolitions proved uneconomic and the castle was left as we see it now.

Deal Deal Castle (1538–43)
Deal is one of a series of forts built along the south coast by Henry VIII to repulse any possible invasion of England following the Reformation and the Dissolution of monasteries. (One of these forts, Sandgate, was in fact built with stone from two demolished priories.) It can only just be defined as a castle, not really being a house of any sort, but is nevertheless a remarkable piece of fortification. Part of its elaborate machinery was a device for heating cannon balls, to help

253

them melt through wooden ships. But the fort saw action only in the civil war; its principle of defending from naval attack violated, it proved relatively indefensible from land attack. The battlements were added during the eighteenth century, to satisfy that polite age's desire for the crenellated romance of ancient warfare.

Dover Dover Castle (c.1168–88)
Directly following his victory at Senlac, William the Conqueror marched to take Dover Castle, an indication of the prime importance it then had. This importance was hardly diminished during the long age of castles. (See p256 for plan.)

Henry II completely remodelled the defences, building a new inner bailey with a barbican to its north and south gateways, and raising the great keep. This structure is the largest of its kind in Britain, a massive 100ft cube with walls between 17–21ft thick, of Kentish rag and Caen stone. The Constable Gate was built slightly later, in the early thirteenth century, and became the castle's principal entrance. It consists of a number of curved forms, of differing height, which jut out towards the moat and drawbridge and defend the entry from every possible angle. It also formed the constable's residence and in this sense is another example of a castle within a castle.

Today, far below the stone walls, a nuclear shelter awaits the modern war.

Sevenoaks Ightham Mote (various centuries)
Where else in the world could this house be but in Kent? Ightham still has its wet moat, from which it rises very quietly and keeps its distance. There must be a hundred variations of material here, different bricks set in different mortars, wood painted, stained and weathered, stone carved and plain, glass and metal. The thing that holds them all together appears to be confidence and age.

Igtham Mote

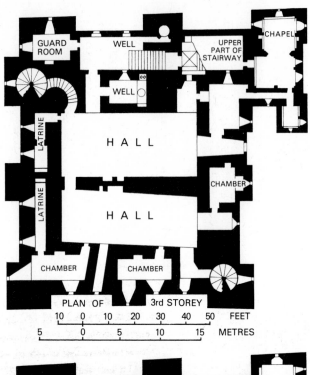

GUARD ROOM
WELL
UPPER PART OF STAIRWAY
CHAPEL
WELL
LATRINE
LATRINE
HALL
HALL
CHAMBER
CHAMBER
CHAMBER

PLAN OF   3rd STOREY

10 0 10 20 30 40 50 FEET

5 0 5 10 15 METRES

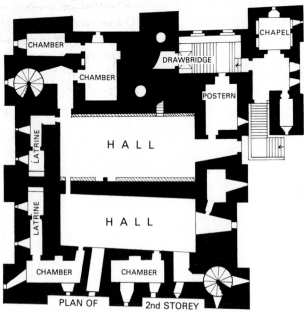

CHAMBER
CHAMBER
CHAPEL
DRAWBRIDGE
POSTERN
LATRINE
HALL
LATRINE
HALL
CHAMBER
CHAMBER

PLAN OF   2nd STOREY

Plans of the keep, Dover Castle

256

Sevenoaks Knole (c.1605)

Knole is said to possess, in its Great Staircase, the first example in England of a staircase treated as an architectural spectacle. To achieve this, the stair well was made open, so that the whole object can be seen standing in space. But there is much more to Knole than the stairs. The shift from Elizabethan to Jacobean architecture is really a change from fantasy to stately dignity. Everything became better ordered, even if more intricate, as for example the marble chimney piece in the ballroom. Classicism has by no means taken over at Knole, but there are hints of it everywhere,

(above) Knole House, Sevenoaks and *(below)* a side view

from the use of a Tuscan order in the Stone Court — an almost correct use — to the gradual abandonment of extraneous decoration on carved wooden pilasters throughout the house. Externally the entrance is an ordered symmetrical façade, but this is only made possible once or twice — the jumble comes bursting out around the corner, and makes the house look, from some angles, like a hill town on some Mediterranean island.

Plaxtol Old Soar Manor House (c.1290)
It is said that the Colepepper family became the largest landowners in Kent and Sussex by their subtle method of capturing and forcibly marrying wealthy heiresses. However that might be, Old Soar seems to have been built by them. It can be clearly seen here just what a medieval manor was, if one remembers that an aisled hall was attached to the solar on the south west, where a modern farm building now stands. None of the details is particularly fine, nor are many preserved, but for a sense of the shape and layout of medieval apartments the building is well worth seeing, not least because of its remote farmyard location.

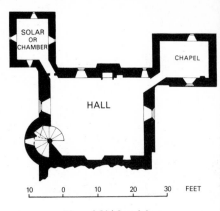

Plan of Old Soar Manor

Sissinghurst Sissinghurst Castle (c.1558)
The brick gate tower is the only monumental part of sixteenth-century Sissinghurst to survive, once a courtyard house where Elizabeth was entertained by its owner, Sir Richard Baker. But the beauty of the house is its re-employment in the twentieth century by Harold Nicolson and Vita Sackville-West. They revived what parts of the house remained around the courtyard, and the tower, and so were left with almost a village-like house, without the trouble of all those village-like people. The gardens, too, which they laid out, remain a model for the semi-wild informal garden, when our present inability to have a gardener behind more than every fifth hedge doesn't so much make a virtue of necessity, as make a lack of virtue respectable.

Sissinghurst

Brunswick Centre, London

LONDON

Tonbridge Tonbridge Castle (c.1080, 1275)

The motte castle at Tonbridge was built by Richard Fitzgilbert on a prehistoric mound, but unfortunately it did not save him from being overpowered and wounded by the forces of William Rufus in 1088. He died three years later. Remains of an oval shell keep that are visible today are of the twelfth century, but it was the de Clare family that c.1275 built the impressive gatehouse-tower. This became the castle's main residence, where for example, Edward I was entertained soon after its completion. It is of five storeys, one below ground, defended by a drawbridge and a pair of portcullises, which could apparently be operated from any one of three storeys. The graciousness of the third-storey hall, contrasted with the narrow toughness of the entry level, gives this building considerable emotional force.

Bloomsbury Brunswick Centre (1968–73)

The story behind this scheme is rather a nightmare. The client was also the builder, and this put the architect in an awkward position in terms of his authority to enforce the proper execution of his ideas. Planning and site acquisition difficulties meant that only two-thirds of it were built: the intention was to create a raised street which would run through to Tavistock Place rather than petering out in the insignificant Handel Street. And originally the scheme was for luxury flats, but the client persuaded the council to fund the housing as council flats. Despite all this the scheme is one of the most successful of post-war complexes, with its shop and cinema as well as housing. (At last the metalwork is no longer Camden Council Orange in colour.) As one walks around the different sides of the building, one sees how each responds slightly differently to its circumstances, and just where the access galleries to the flats

Mary Ward House, London

would be expected to be hidden away, the building opens up dramatically facing Brunswick Square. Its giant supporting pillars remind one of the giant pilasters of the nearby Mecklenburgh Square.

Bloomsbury Mary Ward House, Tavistock Place (1895–8)
Built as the Passmore Edwards Settlement, this building was a community building for social workers, sponsored by the wealthy Edwards. Smith and Brewer, the architects,

won the commission in an open competition judged by Norman Shaw. The brief had asked for provision of a public hall, library, billiard room, dining-room and accommodation, so the building is actually a more complex thing that its simple façade would indicate. Its effects are strong, but simply achieved, for the composition is basically symmetrical. The entrance has been shifted off centre, windows lighting stairs have been made to climb too, and the centre portion of the building has been dropped half a level. It is probably the simplicity of these gestures, and the ordi-

nariness of the materials in which they are made, that makes the building so lively and yet relaxed and unfussy. The white band below the roof was widely copied in the early twentieth century.

Camden Studios, 6–7 Cliff Villas (c.1971) The so-called International Style has come in for so much indiscriminate criticism in the past decade, that an example here might be useful in demonstrating some of its positive qualities. One of its principles was that a certain abstract aloofness was a better respect for the existing urban fabric

Studios, 6-7 Cliff Villas, London

than attempts at copying historical styles. Now, Cliff Villas is not the most inspiring of streets, but these studios don't enter into competition with their neighbours. The straightforward and unpretentious use of glass block and concrete impresses, as does the height of the studios (all too often curbed by density regulations to two storeys in a row of five-storey Victorian houses). The building to the right is by the same architect, Georgie Wolton, built a few years later.

Fleet Road Housing, London

Camden Fleet Road Housing (c.1975)
Camden Council, so it is said, spends more
money per unit of housing accommodation
than any other local authority in London,
and that means in Britain. Here, at least,
they get their money's worth. The layout is
rigidly rectangular, each block of flats stepping back as it rises, but the whole group is
set among a quantity of greenery that
makes this feel much closer to housing set
in the country landscape than does any
tower block I have seen. The appearance of
these blocks depends on a very simple trick
of contrasting heavy black sections of
timber, on handrails, balconies and window
mullions, with the plain white walling. The
black timber then 'reads' on two levels:
robust if thought of in relation to a single
flat, and delicate if taken against the block
as a whole. These are simple tricks in
essence, but of course skill lies in execution.
Everyone knows the magician has a rabbit

concealed about his person; what the
audience doesn't want to see is its lumpy
bulging against his coat.

Camden St Pancras Station Hotel
(1865–77)
There are two distinct parts to this development: the train shed, designed by William
Barlow in 1865, and the hotel, by George
Gilbert Scott, of 1868–77. There was no
single span roof larger than Barlow's at the
time it was built, and it is still the most
impressive structure of its kind in London,
especially if one comes upon it from
Somers Town to the north. But perhaps the
best viewpoint, because it takes in both
shed and hotel, is from the top of Pentonville Road, coming west from the Angel.
Certainly the effect of those spires, climbing up from the strongly horizontal feel of
the whole design, is more romantic than
many genuine Gothic buildings. And when
it is seen close-to the effect does not
diminish: machine-made bricks of several

St Pancras Station Hotel, London

colours, good stone dressings, cast iron, slate — all excellent materials, beautifully combined and detailed.

Chelsea Eaton Square (1840s)

Calling Eaton Square a square is pushing that word to the limits of its definition. Here, the two ends are so far apart as to be invisible to each other through the trees, and so narrow in proportion to the length that the form, even by a modern schoolboy, could not be called an approximation to a square. Right through its middle runs a main road: in fact we almost have a pair of terraces. This odd irresolution is undoubtedly meant to give heroic scale to what was a rather distant new speculative development in the 1840s and '50s when it was built. Thomas Cubitt seems to have built some or most of it.

Dulwich Dulwich Art Gallery (1811–14)

The Dulwich Gallery was built to house a collection, principally of Dutch masters, which had been intended to form the Polish national collection. But King Stanislaus was forced to abdicate and the man commissioned to collect the works, M. Desenfans, eventually left the major part of them to the Dulwich Gallery, founded by Sir Francis Bourgeois. This was built by John Soane in 1811–14, and the fact that little money was available made Soane turn to brick as his main material, with stone used as a plinth and again for details at high level. A curious part of the building, apart from a row of almshouses attracted to it, is the incorporation of Sir Francis Bourgeois' tomb, for which Soane contructed a romantic mausoleum. It has something in common with Vanbrugh's picturesque skyline compositions, and inside is lit by windows at high level glazed with yellow glass. Like sodium light, this has the strange effect of sucking colour out of materials (which in the mausoleum are colourful) while leaving the observer with the knowledge that the colours are nonetheless there. An eerie, poetic place.

Finsbury Finsbury Health Centre (1938)

Following efforts in Peckham to monitor the population's health continuously, as an attempt to improve general health, the architects Lubetkin and Tecton were commissioned to build this, rather smaller, centre in Finsbury. The principle was slightly modified, and this is more a treat-

Dulwich

ment centre than Peckham was, that is, without the social centre facilities. As a building it is more sympathetic. An architect today is frustrated to find bronze and brass fittings, good tiles and woodwork, where he has been reduced to anodized aluminium and formica. The simple splayed H-plan and rounded entrance make it quite a friendly building, too. But then again, it was designed quite logically, in terms of services and planning. Only a few architects in the thirties managed to be as relaxed and unrhetorical with modernism.

Hampstead Annesley Lodge (1895)
Voysey built this L-shaped house for his father, and although rather hidden by trees — or perhaps because of that — it seems the perfect image of a Voysey house. Everything is clear and orderly, but it can never be perceived as a whole; one wants to be able to see more at any one time than is physically possible. Giving up on this, in the end, one relaxes and enjoys the old wooden benches and the foliage, in a place more rural than many an isolated village.

Hampstead 6 Ellerdale Road (1875)
Norman Shaw built this vast house for himself, and as is usual with architects' own houses, it is full of things Shaw himself liked, but must have been constrained from putting into houses for his clients. It is built on a sloping site, using this for dramatic effects a little like those of Mackintosh's School of Art in Glasgow (q.v.). The tall attenuated window facing Ellerdale Road, as much as the castle-like skyline, adds to this feeling, in spite of the fact that the building is all red bricks and tiles.

Hampstead Flats, Lawn Road (1934)
These flats were designed as 'minimal dwellings' by Wells Coates, a Canadian designer who was one of the most stylish and inventive on the English scene in the

1930s. The building was an intellectual's stronghold, where such figures as Walter Gropius, Marcel Breuer, Moholy-Nagy and Agatha Christie lived. (Apparently she wrote the never ending Mousetrap there.) The point of the design was to demonstrate the possibility of providing, by good design, adequate living accommodation in very little space. It is successful, but raises the kind of question scientists have to answer about their experiments: who uses the results? This sort of model was later put forward by local authorities to justify the construction of miserably small flats for their tenants. This block is now badly neglected by the council, who bought it some years ago.

Holborn Kodak Building (1911)
Another odd man out in London architecture, John Burnet in some curious way managed to be both a successful and a fine architect, without ever being avant-garde. The care he took over his buildings is evident in all the detailing, here in bronze and stone. Strips of baroque panels, with ventilators, and windows, run up from floors between columns of stone. There is no attempt at classicism, just a plain treatment of the façade in terms of its elements, and some decoration. There is a faintly Egyptian coved bronze cornice at the top, but since the building itself makes no effort in the same direction it seems to work very well.

Holborn Sir John Soane's Museum (1812)
Private museums were, in the eighteenth century, the only kind there were. Owners of large houses in town and country regularly opened their collections to the public, and some, like Thomas Hope and John Soane, built their houses expressly to display works of art. Over the years, Soane

(overleaf left) Annesley Lodge, London
(overleaf right) 6 Ellerdale Road, London

bought three houses in Lincoln's Inn and remodelled or rebuilt them at various times. No 13, the house now open to the public, was built in 1812, and takes the terrace house practically to its limits of development. Narrow corridors open into colonnaded rooms with domes and wells, walls fold back to reveal a basement grotto, light filters into the rooms just where you would expect wall and ceiling to join one another; and everywhere are mirrors, tiny or great, convex or flat, using light that comes from who knows where to contradict the existence of walls, which seem so hard to locate.

Kew Kew Gardens, Lodge (1867)
Eden Nesfield once worked together with Norman Shaw, and though Shaw later became the more famous of the two, many of the more interesting architectural ideas of the 1860s and '70s were Nesfield's. At Kew, in 1867, he produced this little three-bedroomed lodge, and with it produced one of the most perfect of Queen Anne buildings. It is of a warm orangey-red brick, with a steep roof in red tile. Out of this project four dormer windows (to light bedrooms), and connecting roof to wall is a pargetted plaster coving. An exaggeratedly large chimney climbs through all this and emerges through the centre of the pyramidal roof. Virtually every element of what was to become the Queen Anne style was laid out here, and nowhere more successfully.

North Kensington Trellick Tower,
Golborne Road (1973)
A fair amount of criticism has been aimed at this building, but perhaps that is because the same architect, Erno Goldfinger, made such a disaster of the Elephant and Castle development some years earlier. All his work has been regarded with suspicion since that time. I can't help thinking that this tower of public housing, standing

ankle-deep in the squalor surrounding the Portobello, railway, motorway, etc, will soon be regarded in a better light. Apart from designing a splendid tower composition — which is perhaps the easiest part — Goldfinger managed the difficult part with a good deal of skill, and success. That is, he solved the problem of what happens when these towers meet the ground. Usually we have a couple of grubby swing doors on a windy concrete terrace, but here a well-detailed series of platforms leads gradually and formally towards the tower. It is that combination which usually eludes designers: objects to look at and objects to enter.

Pimlico Churchill Gardens (1946–50)
Westminster Council, left after the war with this partly ruined site, decided to hold a competition for the area's reconstruction as an estate of public housing. This was won by two young architects who established their reputations with the scheme. It is a very reasonable project, and on the ground is almost acceptable: certainly well detailed, which is a thing all architects value. There was considerable effort to tie the scheme in with the surrounding areas by building shops in the main street frontages and so on. At the time no one could have done a better job. The question that seems most obvious now, is why did the construction of a few flats and houses demand this acute change in the formal development of the city? It was a formal development not only unprecedented in England — in fact the idea was based on French theory — but also a proposition more suited to the extension of a city than its renewal. Despite the refined nature of the parts, the concept as a whole seems somewhat oversimplified. Again we have an escape into detail in the face of issues too large too handle. For all the talk of modern theory, the post-war period was dismally short of intellectual fuel. In the end

schemes like this one are described as 'nice', 'pleasant', and 'tidy'. This may not amount to damning with faint praise; but it isn't quite praise, either.

Poyle McKay Trading Estate (1978)
'"Listen, Mr. Mead. I know the temptations which a grocer has to a too cosmopolitan philosophy. I can imagine what it must be to sit all day as you do surrounded by wares from all the ends of the earth, from strange seas that we have never sailed and strange forests that we could not even picture. No Eastern king ever had such argosies or such cargoes coming from the sunrise and the sunset, and Solomon in all his glory was not enriched like one of you. India is at your elbow," he cried, lifting his voice and pointing his stick at a drawer of rice, the grocer

McKay Trading Estate

making a movement of some alarm, "China is before you, Demerara is behind you. America is above your head, and at this very moment, like some old Spanish admiral, you hold Tunis in your hands." Mr. Mead dropped the box of dates which he was just lifting, and then picked it up again vaguely.' G. K. Chesterton, *The Napoleon of Notting Hill*, 1904

The usual modern warehouse, with its corrugated version of tile hanging at its top, cheap brick below, and arbitrary windows and doors puncturing its flanks, is a sad sight. It seems to represent a mere acceptance of the fact of warehousing, without any attempt to find a cultural meaning in the activity. Storing boxes of tin beans is

269

banal — but all activity will be banal until we give it importance by understanding, influencing its part in the cultural chain. These warehouses with offices attached, completed in 1978 by John Outram, are almost alone in their attempt to saturate the building fabric with the importance of its role. The resulting building is one of the most impressive of the decade.

Primrose Hill Flats, 10 Regent's Park Road (1955)
When a gap occurs in a London terrace, there is always the great issue to be decided: should it be filled in to match the neighbours, or should it be occupied by a quite independent building? The conversation can fill more space than many terrace houses, but this building by Erno Goldfinger seems a good argument for the second point of view. This results, I think, from the finesse of the object itself, so that the break in the terrace is a pleasant interruption, not an irritating one. Again, it is not a rhetorical building; its materials and shapes are unfussy, and it does make a formal gesture to the street it stands in by projecting flat balcony fronts at the plane of the terrace on its west, while its main wall lines up with the house to its east.

Roehampton Roehampton Estates (1952–62)
The London County Council was responsible for this estate, called by one critic 'the finest low-cost housing development in the world'. The scheme was built in two halves, Alton East (begun 1952) and Alton West (begun 1955) which are of different character. The intention was to house 9,500 people on a site of some 130 acres, reclaimed from the large Georgian mansions that had spread out by Richmond Park. These 9,500 were mainly ex-Londoners, being shifted out when planning policy demanded this after the war. In concept, the development mixes high- and low-rise buildings, towers

and terraces, in an attempt to create housing in a parkland. This, it is always hoped, will be more or less like a nice house for everyone in an eighteenth-century landscaped garden. Such a bizzare idea ought to produce surreal results, but never has. One can criticise the ideas and execution in one of two ways: the ideas can be accepted as good intentions, and we can compare the reality to the ideals; or we can criticise the very notions. In the first we would begin by criticising the road system, which is indecisive, neither rural lane, nor urban efficiency. It hovers and fails. To take the second way of criticism, we could say that the only reason the scheme succeeds is that it exploits in a most arrogant way the rural nature of its location, using historic houses as quaint remainders, locating itself high on the back of a tradition it sets out to destroy.

Westminster All Saints' Church, Margaret Street (1850–9)
To step into All Saints after visiting, say, a Georgian church, with its pale blues and whites, its evenness and intentionally bland qualities, is, to say the least, a contrast. William Butterfield built the church between 1850 and 1859 as the model church of the Ecclesiological Society. It was meant to show others how to build for the new ritual and glamour of high-church ceremony. Outside, the walls are an exhibition of strenuous labour, for the patterning and layering of coloured bricks seem almost to ask one to follow the slow construction of the wall by the bricklayer. Inside, colour is everywhere jumping out of the darkness at you. Detail is laid on detail, and because there is a certain continuity of form and approach to detailing, the whole affair hangs together. The windows now contain stained glass, but originally were clear, which would have made a great deal more sense: multi-coloured lights on multi-coloured objects is merely excessive and confusing.

Westminster Westminster Hall
(1097–9, 1394)

The first Westminster Hall, built by William Rufus in 1097–9, had the same dimensions as the present hall: 240ft x 70ft but its roof would have been supported, like that of a church, on two rows of columns. Some of the stone capitals from these columns can still be seen in the Jewel Tower in College Mews. In 1394 Richard II had that roof taken off and an enormous single-span, hammer-beam roof built to replace it, considered by those who are supposed to know, to be among the finest timber roofs in Europe. Impressive it certainly is.

When the Norman kings shifted residence from Winchester to London, they built this as a national version of the domestic Hall type. In it were handled the political affairs of state.

Whitehall The Banqueting House
(1619–22)

Though the Queen's House at Greenwich was begun in 1616, the Banqueting House was the first major public building to be built in England in the pure Italian manner. It was designed to replace an earlier structure destroyed by fire, and shows in one building all the refinement of architecture that Jones had learned studying Palladio's works in Vicenza. Because the entrance is not in the main façade but at the side, Jones rejected the use of a pediment over the central section. Instead he gave it emphasis with a slight projection. Strictly speaking (and why not speak strictly about such an academic as Jones?) the notion of windows on two storeys to light a single volume space within would have been unacceptable in classical terms; it is neither expressive of the interior nor paradoxical, and appears, as a result, to be merely an easy compromise.

Westminster Hall

Whitehall Horse Guards (c.1751–8)
London's chief example of Lord Burlington's Palladianism, the Horse Guards' Building was designed by William Kent and built c.1751–8, after his death, by John Vardy. It shows the slightly academic 'catalogue' method of design, where a number of separate volumes of stone are linked together and decorated with as wide a variety of architectural detail as possible. There must be a dozen different window types on the west façade, but when compared with Vanbrugh's work, showing a certain literary restraint. The picturesque qualities of the building are again very polite: those twin towers with their square windows seem to rise up only to yawn, and the clock tower is scarcely sufficient to wake the building up. The middle band of the building is its most rhythmic part, and Portland stone helps any building.

OXFORDSHIRE

Woodstock Blenheim Palace (1705–25)
After the Duke of Marlborough had defeated the French army at Blenheim in 1704, thus halting the progressive domination of Europe by Louis XIV, Queen Anne marked the victory by offering to build him a house in Woodstock Park. Marlborough chose Vanbrugh as his architect after seeing designs for Castle Howard, and to Vanbrugh as well as to 'all people and all parties I conversed with' the house was to be a national monument as well as a residence. There is, simply, nothing else like it in England; no royal palace comes near to it for grandeur or force of composition. George III, upon seeing Blenheim for the first time, admitted: 'We have nothing to equal this.'

It is a classical building in some ways, medieval in others, and reaches closer to the realms of what might be called 'pure architecture' than any other substantial

building in modern times. Detail is everywhere secondary to effect; the massive finials are visible for miles around, intended to anchor the house to all parts of the grounds. Seen from close quarters they produce the effect of disbelief experienced by the artist in Fuseli's print of 1777, 'the artist in despair confronted by the scale of the ruins of antiquity'.

When the Duke became ill, Sarah, his wife, took over the supervision of works. 'I mortally hate', she said, 'all gardens and architecture.' Everything was too expensive for her, or too big. What it is to be an architect! Poor Vanbrugh struggled on, with the political and architectural assistance of Nicholas Hawksmoor, until he resigned in 1716, fees unpaid. When in the year before his death he tried to visit the completed palace in the company of the Earl of Carlisle, he was refused admission even to the grounds. Strange to say, there are still clients of this philistine and spiteful nature to be met with.

Great Coxwell Tithe Barn (thirteenth century)
The Great Barn was built by the Cistercian Abbey of Beaulieu, shortly after it was granted the Manor of Faringdon in 1204. The excellent condition of the whole structure probably owes something to the fact that it is founded on the natural stone that is near ground level. The roof is of course the main interest here, a wholly timber structure of immense scale. It is an exercise in shortening the length that any particular member is required to span, and the top of each post bristles with struts to an almost comical degree. The nicest piece of structure seems to be the horizontal tie beams across the aisles, which take the roof thrust off the wall (which a sloping roof naturally tends to overbalance), back on to the main posts. This arrangement, however, would appear to make those curved wall brackets superfluous. The result of all

Blenheim Palace

this effort externally is a mountainous roof of great beauty.

Minster Lovell Minster Lovell Hall (fifteenth century)
By the River Windrush stand the fragmentary stone walls that are Oxfordshire's loveliest ruin. In the fifteenth century, they were part of one of the country's grandest aristocratic houses. It was built for the most part in 1431–42 by the seventh Lord Lovell, but was forfeited to the Crown by the Yorkist ninth Earl after Bosworth Field. The Earl of Leicester was responsible for taking it to pieces in 1747.

Though a substantial part of the building

(opposite and above) Tithe Barn at Great Coxwell

remains, the main attraction of Minster Lovell is its setting, found at the end of a quiet road, not high up, but set down by the river among trees and rushes.

Moreton-in-Marsh Chastleton House (1603–12)
The estate was bought in 1602 by Walter Jones, a Witney wool merchant, from the unfortunate Robert Catesby, of Gunpowder Plot notoriety. He built this large but not palatial house, which remains practically unaltered. Despite the formal symmetry,

the house is not entered on the central axis, but by the side of a projecting bay. For a house so rectilinear, the Long Gallery is a strange surprise, its ceiling a tunnel vault richly decorated with plasterwork.

Oxford Ashmolean Museum and Taylorian Institution (1841–5)
Charles Robert Cockerell, who designed the Ashmolean when in his early fifties, had been determined to bring the vigorous qualities of classical Greek architecture back into modern work. He saw the works of Wilkins and Smirke as being pale and lifeless, stylistic copying without any real understanding of Greek culture. In this building one can see how he attempted to create this vigorous style. Possibly because he was so well read in classical culture, he was aware that within the rules one was not only free, but obliged, to be inventive. The Ashmolean owes something to Soane's work, with its projecting columns on the east end supporting statues of France, Italy, Spain and Germany. He himself called it a 'tribute to the memory of Nicholas

Chastleton House

Hawksmoor', and the south front of each projecting wing make the reference clear. But beyond that, the way Cockerell assembles the pieces, especially difficult with the many various themes he has to sustain in the design, is his own.

By the late 1840s he was isolated, quite uninterested in the Gothic revival and arguments about style. 'Our architects never will [understand] that the Requirements, the Construction, and the Materials of a building are the essential things, not the superficial application of a "Style".' The only work he admired wholeheartedly in later years was the Crystal Palace.

Oxford Florey Building (1966–71)
Between 1966 and 1971, James Stirling built the last of his Leicester Engineering Laboratory derivations, and it makes a curious sight. As one critic said: 'The forms . . . remind one more of those which clothed the heroic functions of post-revolutionary Russia, than they connote musings of Oxford undergraduate life.' (Jencks) This is so, and one wonders why such effort has

Radcliffe Camera, Oxford

277

Garden Building, St Hilda's College, Oxford

gone into an attempt to overthrow, in a far from revolutionary time despite what people may think of '68, an architectural tradition as successful as that in Oxford.

Oxford Radcliffe Camera (1737–49)
Both Hawksmoor and Gibbs produced designs for this building, and though the latter eventually built the present structure, his designs were influenced by Hawksmoor's initial proposals for a rotunda. (It was Hawksmoor who built the circular mausoleum at Castle Howard.) Circular buildings cannot be built just anywhere; they need either to be seen from a long way away in open landscape, or to inhabit a space well enclosed by buildings, as here at Oxford. Gibbs has provided as a landmark

to the city's skyline a very Italian building, and very mannerist at that.

The principle seems to have been the use of massive gestures and at the same time the achievement of a certain weightlessness to the building. For part of mannerist art is its use of paradox. Here a heavy dome has heavy supports — but beside and not under it; these in turn are supported by the 'light' Corinthian order, in pairs of columns — again, beside and not under; below all this is a heavily rusticated ground floor, intractable, primitive stone, but handled with the delicacy and refinement of the upper levels. Of modern additions, the little concrete channels for holding the front wheel of a bicycle were the most enjoyable, little classical brackets adding to the mannerism by holding up the whole building. But these have now been moved away from the wall and are free standing.

Oxford Garden Building, St Hilda's College (1968–70)

As the demands for residential space increased at St Hilda's, the architects, A. & P. Smithson, were called in to establish the best use that could be made of the limited resources available, whether this was to mean alterations of old or construction of new buildings. Any sensible architect builds something new, and here the Smithsons built their most successful work since Hunstanton of nearly twenty years earlier. The plan is simple, a square building sitting symmetrically between two older structures, with a covered walkway linking all three. The building has a clean 'back', but of good stock brick, nothing cheap. The front is glass and concrete, with a heavy timber trellis system spread across it. This works well on the outside, in conjunction with the concrete (the two materials, one the negative image of the other, in which it has been poured to set) which seem to belong together. It is perhaps a bit insistently used indoors, however.

SURREY

Guildford Sutton Place (c.1523)

The builder of Sutton Place, Sir Richard Weston, was an assistant to both Cardinal Wolsey and Thomas Cromwell. Instead of the customary stone dressings and quoins, windows and parapets, the building employs nothing but terracotta. The material's use was recently imported from Italy, and though used gingerly on Hampton Court, became the dominating feature of this house. It means, of course, that the whole building is made of burnt clay, like a large pot. The wall no longer supports special pieces of natural material, with its texture of sediment and the operations of nature. With terracotta it becomes necessary to do that by hand, to provide

decoration on every surface. A very pretty effect. The third Sir Richard Weston was also an innovator; he brought, apparently, both turnips and clover to English agriculture.

Ham Common, Richmond Flats at Ham Common (1955–8)

These blocks by Stirling & Gowan, built in 1955–8, have become famous in some quarters as 'the ultimate repudiation, not only of all historical stylism and sentiment, but of any suspicion of romantic charm . . .' with 'complete aesthetic dependence upon proportional ratios, and upon nothing else' (Furneaux Jordan). Well. It must be, rationally, difficult to justify all those different and awkward windows, without reference to romance. One flat owner who decided to demolish a partition found herself with 3 different windows in one room. And since some of the style comes from some houses built in France shortly before by Le Corbusier, it is only recent historical reference, not none. The building remains famous, but the reasons change.

Hog's Back Julian Sturgis House (1896)

Voysey always denied his role as a father of modern architecture, and although he has been regarded constantly as such, his repudiation is understandable. His architecture is not sufficiently strident to sit comfortably beside the later puritanical works. And above all, one senses that he was a craftsman architect, of a breed quite different from those who succeeded him. His house for the American, Julian Sturgis, shows the very clear understanding he had of what architecture should be in England. Those slender and tall chimneys, that stand as well against the grey sky as against the dark roof and the right-angle roof pitch, are examples of the heavy modelling he used in a country that has too little sunshine to cast shadows. The drainage is very pleasing, too.

Sutton Place

SUSSEX

Bexhill De la Warr Pavilion (1933–6)
Erich Mendelsohn had been in England only a few months when he won the competition, in collaboration with Serge Chermayeff, to build this recreation pavilion. It carries on the style of work he had been doing in Germany, but is unique in this country. If it is compared to the laborious modernism of say Conell, Ward & Lucas, the difference becomes apparent: the plan is not only clear, but delightful, with nicely considered junctions between terraces, lawn, main hall and so on. And no one else would have had, nor did have, the confidence he had to deal with the staircase that projects out from the entrance front. Unfortunately both architects left England shortly afterwards for the United States, and the Bexhill pavilion remains a more or less isolated example of their work here.

bulb; put all these, pretty promiscuously, but pretty thickly, on the top of the box. Then stand off and look at your architecture.' Wm. Cobbett on the Royal Pavilion.

The specific aesthetic effects of this rambling Indian-esque construction are far less important than its association with the high society that built and played in it. The whole place was designed as scenery, a place to see and be seen. In the first Pavilion of 1787, the Prince's bedroom was 'so designed that he could recline at his ease and by means of mirrors watch everything that was happening on his favourite promenade'.

One tends to think of this as a large folly, but, considering that only one other building in the Indian style was constructed (at Sezincote, for a retired Indian merchant), it might be said that it was architecture so perfectly suited to its purpose, and there being but one such purpose in England, there could be but one such

Brighton Royal Pavilion (1815–22)
'Take a square box, the sides of which are three feet and a half, and the height a foot and a half. Take a large Norfolk turnip, cut off the green of the leaves, leave the stalks nine inches long, tie these round with a string three inches from the top, and put the turnip on the middle of the top of the box. Then take four turnips of half the size, treat them in the same way, and put them on the corners of the box. Then take a considerable number of bulbs of the crown-imperial, the narcissus, the hyacinth, the tulip, the crocus, and others; let the leaves of each have sprouted to about an inch, more or less according to the size of the

building. It was erected, as everyone knows, by John Nash, the Prince of Wales' favourite architect.

Brighton St Wilfrid Church (1933–4)
A very remarkable building by a remarkable figure. Goodhart-Rendell was almost alone amongst English architects of the time in using materials openly and simply. Rather than stopping there and declaring architecture to be all material, he used that belief as a technical theory, which could support architectural ideas. He had trained with a church architect, and during his life compiled the immense *Index of Victorian Churches,* so it seems clear that his prin-

281

Pevensey Castle

ciples derive from the High Victorian era. Here, instead of mosaic and marble, he has to work with concrete, bricks and roof tiles to shape his building tightly around a ritual.

Pevensey Pevensey Castle (c.1100)
The Romans were the first to build a fort here, in the third century, which was unusual for Roman work, in that it wasn't rectilinear. The substantial remains of this fort were employed by William the Conqueror as a shelter when he first reached England, and it formed the basis for one of his first stone keeps. It appears that the Norman builders may have filled in the hollow Roman bastion adjoining their keep for use as a siege engine platform.

As the port began to silt up, Pevensey lost much of its strategic importance, but it remained defendable and was in fact laid siege to frequently until the seventeenth century.

The West Country

AVON

Bath King's Bath (c.1597)

Before the famous Beau Nash arrived in the mid-eighteenth century to teach society how to enjoy itself politely, the King's Bath was an open air swimming bath, men and women together, and apparently as brimming with exuberance as with water. The element that seems so absent from all these Bath baths is water in any quantity, but the joy of this old structure is that it was a species of flooded architecture, a post-diluvian scheme, where the civilized past is up to its ankles in water; cleaned and refreshed, it can emerge to a new life.

CORNWALL

Launceston Launceston Castle (twelfth and thirteenth centuries)

It appears that Launceston was a stronghold for a post-Roman Cornish lord. The Conqueror's brother, Robert de Mortain, improved and held the castle, a bailey constructed in the twelfth century, and within that, a shell keep added in the thirteenth. The tower rose 35ft above the wall of the outer shell, at the base of which was a battlemented walk. Thus there were three concentric defensive rings, at differing heights, which could form fighting platforms. What Sydney Toy called 'a most formidable structure'.

Restormel Restormel Castle (c.1200)

Restormel is a shell keep castle, built around 1200 on a motte that dates from the previous century. It is founded on the natural soil of a hill, the mound being formed with the earth cast up against the wall during excavation of the surrounding ditch, once a moat. What had been wooden buildings within were replaced by stone structures in the thirteenth century, concentric around an internal courtyard. In 1354 and 1362, the Black Prince held his court at Restormel. These were times, naturally, for elaborate preparations and extensive repairs, though from quite early times water was brought into the castle by lead pipes, discovered in recent excavations. Built originally by Baldwin Fitz Turstin, it went to the Lord of Cardinham in 1100, whose grandson built the keep walls.

St Germans Moyle Almshouses (seventeenth century)

The most simple of buildings benefit from the most simple of architectural devices. Rather than seek to cover the building in classical detail, which could not have been afforded, the unknown builder has chosen to control the necessary forms of building and to turn them into architecture. The result is a very picturesque row, though not in the eighteenth-century sense. Notice also the two different points of access, one for the first-floor balcony, another for the ground floor, which adds to the idea that each access level is a street in its own right.

Moyle almshouses

Tintagel The Old Post Office (fifteenth century)
The origins of this house are obscure, as well they might be. Essentially it is little different to many small manor houses, being of stone walls with a cruck frame roof. What is rather surprising is its survival, and its extraordinary picturesqueness. It is all local stone — slates and walls — and resembles a little craggy mountain, hollowed out for habitation.

DEVON

Barnstaple Penrose Almshouses (c.1627)
With its bridge and its wide River Taw, Barnstaple has a generous feeling to it. It has been fragmented, of course, but some of the pieces are well worth seeing, none more so than the almshouses founded by the will of 'John Penrose sometime Maior

of this towne Ano. Dni. 1627'. Twenty houses surround a courtyard, entered through a central opening of the façade. The street front has three two-storey gabled sections containing trustees' boardroom, entrance and chapel. Between these runs a single-storey colonnade, granite columns resting on a low stone wall. The rhythm and movement of all this are lovely. Bullet holes from a Roundhead attack during recovery of the town decorate the boardroom door.

Luscombe Castle Luscombe Castle (c.1800)
Between the years 1796 and 1802, the landscape architect Humphrey Repton was in partnership with John Nash. In 1800 they combined to produce, for Charles Hoare the banker, this asymmetrical villa-castle-mansion, with Gothic tower and porch. Around it roll soft hills, and suddenly the pressure of formality is off the *nouveau riche*.

DORSET

Athelhampton Athelhampton Hall
(c.1500, c.1550)

As a one time Lord of Mayor of London, Sir William Martyn could afford to build his house to the highest standards of the day. His work at Athelhampton remains largely undisturbed in itself, though the mid-sixteenth century added a range of buildings, the parlour range, of a quite different character. The original hall is battlemented, with windows in the perpendicular style and a heavy gateway. Less than half a century later, the accepted idea of a decent house had changed considerably, for here is a building with gables jutting high out of its roof, the eaves of which project over the wall; windows of much greater size; and something approaching a unified design. One of the subtle pleasures of this group is the colour change between building stone in the different periods.

Corfe Corfe Castle (c.1200–5)

Beginning, as usual, as a motte castle in the late eleventh century, Corfe eventually grew to be one of the finest and strongest castles in the country. When it finally fell to a siege by the Parliamentarians in 1646, this was a result of treachery rather than military weakness. It was subsequently slighted with such violence that only about a third of the great tower remains. This all adds, however, to the pathetic romance.

Melbury Sampford Melbury House
(c.1530–40 and later)

A strange house built by Mr Giles Strangeways. In its original form the house was entirely Gothic in detail, though square in plan and with four symmetrical façades. Much of this has disappeared under later additions and restructurings. Yet its most delicate detail remains, the hexagonal prospect tower, rising clear above the surrounding roofs to give views of the countryside on five of its six sides.

Most important of later remodellings to the house were carried out by Anthony Salvin for fifth Earl of Ilchester in 1872, and twelve years later by George Devey, who together added a library and stable court, complete with battlemented tower, which make up the impressively piecemeal house as we see it.

Grevel House, Chipping Campden (see p287)

GLOUCESTERSHIRE

Bibury Arlington Row (c.1380)

It is thought that this row of cottages was built originally as a sheep-house, serving the monastery. During the seventeenth century it was converted to dwellings for people, weavers who supplied cloth to

Arlington Mill. They are all of stone — roof and walls — with timber cruck structures, which gives them a strongly geometrical effect against the landscape. One thing they don't do is blend in with it, which is the popular conception of vernacular architecture. Although pretty, so are many of the nearby villages and buildings; and considering the vast popularity of this particular row, perhaps it would be advisable to give it a bit of a rest.

Chipping Campden Grevel House
(late fourteenth century)
Domestic architecture in the fourteenth century was not habitually given features as distinguished as the bay window to be seen here. William Grevel died in 1401. He had been a merchant and presumably a rich one, for this type of carving was not usually to be afforded by individuals. It is worth pointing out how useful the Gothic style was in terms of piecemeal building. Here, as indeed on any church, it was possible to construct one fine detail, when that was all you could afford, and keep the background simple. The homogeneity felt necessary to later classical styles often forced builders to

Arlington Row, Bibury

add so much water to the wine as to make it lose all vigour.

Tewkesbury Houses in Church Street
(fifteenth century)
The confined nature of Tewkesbury, between rivers, estates and abbey, no doubt contributed to the town's early adoption of planned development. The main block of houses in Church Street, nos. 34–50, are perhaps the earliest example of this. They did not originally form part of the abbey precinct, but were developed by the monks on a speculative basis and let out to citizens in the town. The church was in an ideal position to accomplish this, with its enormous capital. Such were the simple beginnings of the church's speculation, which culminated in nineteenth-century developments like Paddington in London.

SOMERSET

Barrington, Nr Ilminster Barrington
Court (c.1514–20)
Lord Danberry, a military commander who served in France with Henry VIII and was present at the Field of the Cloth of Gold, built Barrington shortly after his marriage

in 1514. The odd feature of the house is its near perfect symmetry at such an early date, but with all the traditional features of a medieval manor house. It is conjectured that a French mason or designer had a hand in the affair. The stone is from Ham Hill, and has been used with a good deal of restraint. Even the spiral finials fall short of being frantic.

Glastonbury The Tribunal House
(fifteenth century)
This little building, built as a court house by the Abbey in the fifteenth century, is one of the most rational houses in England. It is a house for the city, extending back into a deep site, and so exploits what frontage it has to the full. The upper front room, with its exquisite wind-braced ceiling exposed to view, is unfortunately occupied by cases full of historical odds and ends, so that the openness of the space is somewhat lost. Still, the series of stone-mullioned, leaded windows that run across the room, give it a sense of lightness seldom encountered. The little staircase winding from floor to floor is somehow, too, just what it should be and no more. The rationality lies in this, that each part is delightful not because it pleases in itself as a separate object, but in its

harmonic relation to the rest, and the comfortable relation of the whole to the town around it.

Mere Fish House (early fourteenth century)
The Somerset Levels is a low-lying area between the Mendip and Quantock hills, so low-lying that for much of its history it has been partly submerged, by fresh or salt water. In medieval times the area was salt marshes, but Mere and Glastonbury stood above these marshes on a small area of raised ground. It is said that this building was a fisherman's house, where he not only lived, on the upper floor, but also dried and cured his catch. The thought of it alone is disheartening. This fisherman would have been employed by the Abbey monks, to whom his fish would have been sent. The house is ruined inside, but the fireplace on the ground floor indicates smoking of fish, and the external staircase would have led to living apartments.

Montacute Montacute House (c.1590)
Montacute was built by Edward Phelips, a lawyer who clearly spared no effort on behalf of his clients, for he built one of the largest houses of his age. His plan, typical

Nunney Castle

of the Elizabethans, seems to have been to build a wall of little incident in a rather loose overall framework. The warm colour of the stone he used, from Ham Hill, is ideally suited to this, precisely because of its winning charm. One doesn't regard what is done with it as too important; just to have it there seems enough. But in fact the incidents that make up the façade are in themselves nicely designed and made, with less of the fanatical surface decoration than often accompanies these sixteenth-century limestone mansions. The completeness of the house, and its reconstructed Elizabethan gardens, make Montacute a rare house, and a fine one.

Nunney Nunney Castle (c.1370)
As so many buildings of the fourteenth century, Nunney hovers between the reality of being a house and the desire to be a castle. It has been described as a very French building, with its neatness, four equal height towers, and lacey battlements. Certainly there is little of the picturesque about it, and even the large hole in its north tower fails to inspire awe. But what it lacks in the sublime it makes up for in delicacy, and sitting in its moat, surrounded in turn by lush green fields, it is a fine thing to see. Cromwell captured it in only two days.

Wells Wells Cathedral (c.1230–1260)
'It is easy to see such a work as no framework of merely architectural designing, but as a whole piece of sculpture, and to recognise its object as not of aesthetic composition but of religious presentation.' (Prior)

This fact of religious representation is indeed the importance of the west front of Wells. It is architecture brought into the service of mythology and legend quite explicitly, where architecture must become representational, figurative, to say what is required. There is no abstract contemplation provided for: here are actual figures to whom stories attach, the equivalent popula-

tion of a small village in stone. You don't need television, with its two-dimensional figures, when you have real stone people such as these.

Wells Vicars' Close (mid-fourteenth century)
These forty-two houses were built to house the many vicars who were roughly equivalent to a board of directors, each being the representative responsible for a certain church landholding. The idea of building a terraced street to house them is a happy one, and one quite striking for its date. The street tapers slightly towards its north end, which gives it an appearance of great length, and this is helped by the high chimneys that rise from the front of each house, forming an immense colonnade. Within this very strong framework, which at first sight makes one think the building is all of one period, one sees that façades have been replaced (and, I suppose, interiors) at various dates. Brick, pebbledash and bay windows have insinuated themselves into the scheme of things, and that, one might think, is the beauty of strong formal gestures.

WILTSHIRE

Great Chalfield Manor House (c.1480)
The builder was a certain Thomas Tropenell, who 'prudently prospered during the Wars of the Roses' as Christopher Hussey has it. Here we have a perfect fifteenth-century example of a house being constructed all at one time to represent the owner's idea of country life. All the elements are here: oriel window, weighty porch, kitchen and guest wings, all asymmetrically composed, but set to balance one another.

(opposite above) Vicars' Close, Wells
(opposite below) Great Chalfield Manor

11 Church Street, Lacock

Lacock No 11 Church Street (eighteenth century)

Lacock must be among the best preserved villages in England. It belongs to the National Trust (who paint the call boxes grey to match the stonework, which must make them difficult to find on a foggy morning) and they have kept the scale, and more surprisingly, the workings of the village in a very believable way. There is of course Lacock Abbey, one of the earliest houses touched by Renaissance influence, and there is also Fox Talbot's dark room, a barn that now contains a photographic museum. But there is also No 11 Church Street, with its very odd frieze of capitals.

Where they come from is a mystery; someone obviously bought a job lot, and would have used them all, had there been five or fifty — waste not, want not, even in classicism.

Stourhead Stourhead (c.1720, c.1800)

The estate of Stourhead was acquired in 1720 by Henry Hoare, son of the famous banker and Lord Mayor of London, Sir Richard Hoare. This was the man who, having bought the estate 'immediately bought Mr Campbell's books'. Colen Campbell, spokesman for the neo-Palladian movement, subsequently provided designs for the house. Initially this consisted only of the central block, and the two wings were added about 1800 by Hoare's great-grandson. It was Henry Hoare II who, from 1740 on, built the 'Claude Lorraine' landscape garden, set around an irregular lake so that one is always looking into the view rather than out from the centre. Everything remains beyond the water, unreachable, which is as it should be. These monuments, buildings and temples are too small to impress from close quarters. From a distance they evoke imagined possibilities; near to, they are just a little silly.

Stourhead

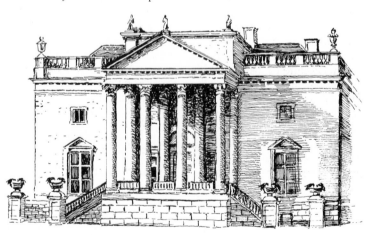

Warminster Longleat (1570s)

Designed by John Thynne in the 1570s, Longleat has been said to represent 'the momentary High Renaissance of Tudor architecture.' Thynne had also designed, or at least superintended, a house in London for his employer, Protector Somerset, between 1547–52. Somerset House was demolished in 1777, but it is known to have been a courtyard house; in other words, the main façades were spread around a court-yard, as at Kirby Hall, and generally typical of English architecture of the time. This probably has something to do with the notion of a grand 'house' being a small village; for town squares were to re-adopt this form about the time Somerset House was demolished. Longleat, however, turned this form inside out, presenting the absolutely symmetrical façades outwards. The implication is that this is one man's enormous house, and the trick works; it is one of the most powerful houses in the land.

Westwood Manor. Garden

Longleat was the first of the great country houses to go commercial after the last war, and while one appreciates the difficulties involved in converting a private house into a tourist attraction, many of the developments, particularly the car parking arrangements, are not the happiest con-tribution to the architectural landscape. The plea that these additions are necessary carries some weight, but one may care to remember that in the philosophy of the day, when Longleat was built, reality was divided into three realms. These corres-ponded to heaven, the world, and the under-world, or hell; the last of which was simply the kingdom of necessity.

Westwood Westwood Manor
(c. 1400–1640)

In a way, Westwood Manor is the represen-tative type of English house, combining an overall asymmetry and organic feeling with

Wilton House

precision and clarity in the pieces that make up the whole. The house was built in four main periods; it was begun around 1400, extended by Thomas Culverhouse in the 1480s, again by Thomas Horton, a rich clothier, between 1515–30, and finally in the early 1600s by the last of the Hortons and his brother-in-law, John Farewell. Each owner seems to have added quite distinctive items to the building — Thomas Horton's tall bay window on the north wing, John Farewell's extraordinary King's Room with its plaster wildlife, Thomas Culverhouse's Hall. The relationships between these pieces is informal — in fact only a relationship of use and character rather than architectural theory. The outside of this group hardly suggests such delights as the Great Parlour, with its plasterwork ceiling and coat of arms, but on the other hand it offers a group of extraordinarily peaceful and unfussy gardens, each one a little room with a pool of lily ponds and gold fishes in the middle of its floor.

Wilton Wilton House (sixteenth and seventeenth centuries)
Although Wilton is famous for the remains of a mid-sixteenth-century house, including the so-called Holbein Porch, now a garden pavilion, it is yet more famous for the south front, added by Inigo Jones and Isaac de Caus in the 1630s. This was built for the fourth Earl of Pembroke who succeeded his brother in 1630. The two were 'the incomparable pair of brethren' to whom the first Folio of Shakespeare's plays is dedicated. *As You Like It* was first performed here, incidentally, giving some idea of the artistic patronage they sponsored. To return to the south front, it was apparently intended as one of two wings flanking a central portico. This plan was interrupted by the Civil War and never taken up again. Yet the single wing built is no mean design, far more relaxed and to the point than Jones's Queen's House at Greenwich. The interiors were destroyed by a fire in 1647, and restored by Jones and his pupil and assistant, John Webb. The cube and double cube rooms are theirs in decoration, rich with white and gold.

East Anglia

CAMBRIDGESHIRE

Cambridge Cripps Building, St John's College (1963–7)
This building, an extension to the college housing about two hundred undergraduates, must represent the best of mainstream modern English architecture. Where other buildings set out to *make* space, as Churchill College or the History Faculty, the Cripps Building seems to accept the charms of the space it finds. In a very unforceful way, it wanders along, meeting other buildings, rivers and so on, responding to each in the politest of ways. The design works very well, but is as frustrating to critics as it is pleasing to those who use it: its reasonableness makes it impossible to get over excited about.

Ely Ely Cathedral (octagon-lantern 1322–c.1350) (see p296)
Such an enormous and complex building as Ely can't be properly described in an entry of this size, but one element of it may be examined, the famous octagon. When the Norman crossing tower collapsed on 22 February 1322, it fell into and damaged the chancel, so that whatever replaced the tower would have to start from scratch. From transept chancel and nave aisle, one bay was removed, so that the octagon could cover the full width of the nave and transept crossing. Constructionally, the octagon is a marvel, employing the largest oaks available in England at the time, and using them to build a type of polygonal hammer-beam roof. But more intriguing than the construction is its form: eight is, in medieval terms, a number representing the world, not soaring spirituality, and the octagon, approaching the circle, is its corresponding form. Chapter houses, for example, where secular matters were dealt with, are typically octagonal. Indeed, one's sensation upon entering under the crossing is likely to be restful rather than exhilarating, a result of the generosity of the widened space. Wren used the same trick in St Paul's, that monument to English humanism. So it seems that here at Ely we have, in some way, a Gothic dome and a humanist architecture.

ESSEX

Audley End Audley End (1603–16)
The daughter of Lord Chancellor Audley married the Duke of Norfolk, and their son, as Earl of Suffolk, built Audley End. The house was once much larger, and what is now the front was only the side of an enclosing courtyard. Although everywhere seeking symmetry, the forms here are more medieval than classical. It seems that the intention was to build a series of planes each one taller than the one in front of it, and so create a perspective of turrets, roofs and chimneys. Even in the entrance front, just one of these 'layers', one can feel the advance and recession of masses. Vanbrugh made alterations here in the 1720s, and he would obviously have enjoyed the place

Ely Cathedral

Audley End

immensely. For my part, I think the great cedar hedge is rather superior to the building itself.

Colchester Colchester Castle (c.1075–80)

The largest great tower in England, Colchester was also one of the first. It was built mainly of Roman bricks excavated from nearby ruins and Kentish rag. Once a storey taller, the tower was partly demolished c.1683 for materials. The similarity between this and London's White Tower suggests the same designer. Inside are some spectacular stone fireplaces and an excellent museum.

Great Coggeshall Paycocke's House (c.1500)

Thomas Paycocke was, apparently, the town's main cloth merchant, and his business must have prospered. It is almost a cloth-like house, in the way its structure, close studding, is on one plane with brick infill, making solid materials into a flat surface varied only in colour and texture. Some studs are carved into the frieze which is embroidered with pattern and even the initials 'TP', for Thomas Paycocke. It is this refinement of a quite simple idea that makes this one of the most appealing buildings in the country.

Hedingham Hedingham Castle (c.1100)

A house of some substance this, with a good deal of style. There is nothing meagre about the chevron moulding around the entrance door, or on the doorways surrounding the Great Hall on the second floor. On all levels but this, a wall divides the interior in two, but here a huge arch passes across the space, which is double height, and suddenly there is a volume four times that of the others. The castle is built as two buildings, one within the other, and a passage at each level runs between them.

Layer Marney Layer Marney Towers (c.1520)

Layer Marney is in a sense the culmination of a lunacy for tower buildings. The house to which this was meant to be the entrance was never even begun, and even this tower, exceeding those of Oxburgh and Hampton

Hedingham Castle

Layer Marney Tower

297

St Osyth's Priory, Gatehouse

Court by volumes, was only hastily completed before its builder died. The beauty of it is all external, apart from some interesting alterations made in the entrance early this century, and not least of these beauties is the use of terracotta. Rather than the usual battlements, Layer Marney uses angle turrets to complete its skyline, each of which is capped by a semi-circular terracotta gable, with a pair of dolphins on them. This, with Hampton Court, is one of the earliest uses of that material in England.

Loughton Loughton Hall (1878)
Loughton Hall was built by Eden Nesfield, the less well-known but intellectually more advanced contemporary and friend of Norman Shaw. It is built in that style of near, but not quite perfect, symmetry (c.f. Ockwells Manor House, c.1450) which can sometimes seem an affectation. The details and forms, particularly the 45 degree pitched gables, are crisply made. These gables play a strange trick, advancing out over the bay windows to protect them, but then receding in the middle to stress once more the independence of the tall bays.

St Osyth St Osyth's Priory, Gatehouse (late fifteenth century)
That there is a clear preference in the flat East Anglian countryside for vertical stripes on buildings is demonstrated by the flint and stone designs, known as flush-work, of which this gatehouse is an example. In timber framing, such as at Lavenham and Great Coggeshall (qq.v.) there could ostensibly be a technical argument for vertical patterning. But here there is none, only the display of severed flint, lying in the same plane with ribbons of ashlar. The gatehouse is the most rewarding remnant of St Osyth's Priory, a twelfth-century foundation, pulled down shortly after its dissolution in 1539.

LINCOLNSHIRE

Boothby Pagnell Manor House (c.1180)
The Manor House is the most complete example of Norman domestic architecture that remains to us. In other words, it is a house and not a castle. It was built c.1180, in the time of Henry II, and in common with earlier houses, living accommodation is on the first floor. Access to this floor was by an external stair, though the one that now exists is modern, as is the roof. The slender windows are what is called 'transitional' in the sense that they are no longer simple round headed openings, but have been split by a central shaft, and yet they are not quite Gothic because each half remains round-headed, under a single half round moulding. The square window on the east front was added in the fifteenth century, and the small window it replaced was shifted around to the south front. Think how much use we could get out of windows if we were to make them of stone today. The hall has a hooded fireplace, that is, it projects from the wall and tapers back into it, carried on two corbels, and is, perhaps, the best existing part of this house.

Lincoln The Jew's House (twelfth century)
Clearly a stone house of this size would not have been typical of late twelfth-century towns, but the fact that it is of very much the same plan as rural manor houses is an indication that particular town house types had not yet developed. This appears to have been a merchant's house, and he would have used the ground floor as warehousing and the upper rooms for living. This in itself is a simple conversion of rural practice. The entrance is particularly elaborate, and though difficult to pick out, chain links are carved into its arch. Above the door the chimney breast is extended like a slightly threatening welcome.

Louth The Turk's Head (nineteenth century) (see p300)
There is a simple gesture in this building that makes it worth illustrating, and worth seeing. Louth has a series of streets that widen occasionally into long squares, and this pub closes one end of such a space. And yet, they are not proper squares — they don't require that formality and do demand that the street carries on, checked but not stopped. The lower two stories of the Turk's Head — the Turk's body as it were — flow around the corner to continue the street, but perched above is the gable end, white and assertive, acting like a pediment at the end of the square.

NORFOLK

Caister Caister Castle (1432–46)
Caister was built by Sir John Fastolf, a distinguished veteran of the battles of Agincourt and Rouen. It is built of locally made brick, a factor perhaps not favourable to its survival, since later generations found it an easy quarry, and have left it just a fragment. The most interesting aspect of the castle is its use of water. Not only did the River Bure serve to feed a defensive moat, but during

The Turk's Head, Louth

the building's construction, materials were brought right up to the inner island in this way, not an insignificant advantage in a time when roads were primitive and few.

Castle Acre Castle Acre (c. eleventh century)

This is a pretty village, built for the most part, as it happens, with stones prised from the castle walls. Little of the keep therefore remains. It was originally built by William de Warenne, Earl of Surrey, who also founded the Priory. A stone gate still stands at the top of Bailey Street in the village. It seems that in the twelfth century, the bailey was surrounded by a stone wall, the keep strengthened, and the hall within made considerably more substantial. Excavations are still being carried out on the site and no fast conclusions have yet been drawn about the work. A visit should be made to the priory, which apart from its impressive late

Norman west front, intact amidst the porridge-like ruins of flint walling, has a little prior's house, remodelled in Tudor times. This stands out, with its wood and tiles, like a colour picture appearing in a black and white film, so strong is the difference between habitable and desolate building.

Castle Rising Castle Rising (c.1130–40)
It makes a curious sight, this not insignificant keep, when looked down upon from the high banks that surround it. It looks like a child's model of a castle, or a toy, and quite incapable of defence. It appears that these earthworks, though in substance pre-dating the keep of c.1138–40, were hurriedly raised during some crisis, and thus deprived the keep of the commanding aspect undoubtedly desired by the Norman builders. For this keep is not a tower, like Rochester, but in its squatness and decoration is an elaborately defended hall-house. It was built by William d'Albini, second Earl of Sussex, immediately after his mar-riage to Henry I's widow, Alice. The status conferred by such a marriage demanded a rather special dwelling, and Castle Rising was the result.

As well as the castle, the town claims a wonderful set of almshouses, the Trinity Hospital. These were rebuilt in 1870, of fiery red brick and tiles, but the hospital was founded in the early seventeenth century by the Earl of Northampton, Henry Howard.

Holkham Holkham Hall (1734–61)
In a sense this was a dream house, for its builder, Thomas Coke, found the land a virtual desert and began its reclamation to form a suitable site for a classical palace. Here indeed was the Whig idealist shaping up nature. As a young man Coke had met Lord Burlington and William Kent, the house's architect, in Rome while on his Grand Tour. The influence of Palladio is obvious at Holkham, where the house is

Trinity Hospital, Castle Rising

formed by five pavilions: one central and four as wings. This idea of detached objects is carried right through the exterior, for not only have we got these five discreet pavilions, but the windows don't form rhythmic patterns in the usual classical way. As Sir John Summerson has said, there is hardly a single case where two adjacent openings in the same plane are of the same design.

The most monumental interior space in Holkham, in fact of the whole of the 'Burlington circle's' work is the entrance hall. Sources of its design are various but the effect is one of pure classical drama. With its long flight of steps widening down from a narrow door, it makes a perfect setting for the Roman antiquities in Coke's collection.

A descendant of this Coke was the famous Coke of Norfolk, a Whig agricultural reformer who made great efforts to turn Norfolk from sheep grazing country into good arable land.

Norwich University of East Anglia (1962–72)

Denys Lasdun got the commission for this project in 1962, and made it the first compact layout to be seen among the new universities. On this very pleasant site, he chose to bank up the students' residential accommodation with views towards the river, and to lay the teaching space close alongside, providing access to both by a central service road. The architect himself looked forward to 'the backyard mess of undergraduates' activities, games rooms, laundries, cars, and bicycles'. This conception is a good one, that there should be the 'urban' and the 'rural' sides to a building. But somehow that access road is less successful than it might have been. Perhaps Lasdun was hoping that the activities he described made a consideration of the architecture unimportant, but just because a thing is informal doesn't mean it should not be carefully put together. Instead we have here a space more left over than

302

purposefully made. Still, it is the most intelligent of the new university schemes.

Norwich University of East Anglia
Sainsbury Centre for Visual Arts (1974)
High technology, jogging, and the healthy life; sleek fast cars and no pollution; the future; progress; hope eternal. The Sainsbury Centre is our century's version of the country house full of art, since we feel that either it is wrong to keep it all to oneself, or wrong to let strangers walk around one's house. In 1974, Foster Associates dropped this building in the path of Denys Lasdun's masterplan for UEA (q.v.). It seems like a large toy, a nicely made toy, with all its moving parts and busy servicing; it is a child's reaction when confronted with contemplation: do something else, keep busy, get out the meccano set, but don't just look at the paintings.

Oxburgh Oxburgh Hall (c.1482, c.1835)
Sir Edward Bedingfeld, given a licence to crenellate in 1482, built at Oxburgh this square courtyard house set in a water-filled moat. In fact, not exactly this house, for in the late eighteenth century the hall opposite the gatehouse was demolished, and only 'reconstructed' in the 1830s. The gatehouse-tower is certainly the most impressive piece, rising seven storeys in brick and dominating the building from the outside to the extent that variations in the façade are forgotten. Inside, the hall which sits at the north-west corner is one of the finest rooms, original though restored. If

Technology as a moral doctrine. The disappointing truth for many architects is that the demands made on buildings are not very different now from what they were two or three hundred years ago, and can still be satisfied with the same means, of bricks and tiles. This proves disappointing to architects like Norman Foster, who would rather believe that we need buildings as sophisticated as aeroplanes. At the Greenwich Observatory the telescopes were highly sophisticated, the building which sheltered it simple. Here at the Sainsbury Centre for Visual Arts the reverse is true: bits of canvas and stone are sheltered by a building that hopes to convince us that opening our eyes demands all the resources of modern science

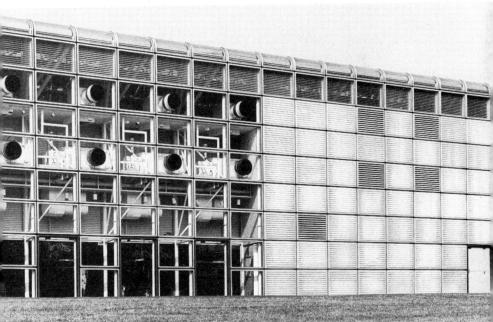

Oxburgh Hall

one visits on a sunny afternoon, the sunshine will be found to bounce off the water and ripple across the ceilings.

SUFFOLK

Bury St Edmunds Abbey Ruins
Once one of England's most powerful monasteries, St Edmundsbury is now reduced to a landscape of fragments. But now, among fragments, they are some of England's most powerful.

That there is a straight road against which the gates and several buildings finish, unifies the precinct. A building like the Charnel House (late thirteenth century), which would be impressive anywhere, or the Norman Gate, are made rather more impressive by their proximity to the vast chunks and outlines of the abbey. This was a building 505ft long, with a west front of 246ft wide (Lincoln, for example, is 175ft wide). It was mainly built during the late eleventh and early twelfth centuries. The odd part of the west front is that it has been taken over by houses of various dates and sizes. One of these, externally, consists simply of sash windows and a door, set among the undulating rubble, which long ago was stripped of its stone facing. Not only does this give an immediate sense of scale to the ruin, but it also says something about how quickly one identifies a Georgian house even when reduced to two elements and a set of proportions.

Heveningham Heveningham Hall
(c.1778–84)
Heveningham is a lesson in the successful application of stucco to brick. It was built for a Dutch merchant, Sir Gerard van Neck, and is a good model of what the neo-Palladian architects, in this case Sir Robert Taylor (exterior) and James Wyatt (interiors) were called upon to deliver. The

house was wanted complete in a short space of time, so that brick and stucco was the only speedy answer. Then, too, the immense classical façade needed no medieval pretensions since it linked straight in to the classical world. Finally, the gardens were laid out by Capability Brown in the early 1780s, to complete the businessman's absorption into the natural order of things, in the space of five or six years. The hall, designed by Wyatt, is practically the perfect English interior, with its soft lighting, broad proportions and peacefulness. The ceiling, too, is half classical but half reminiscent of the famous English fan vaulting of the Gothic age.

Ipswich Sparrowe's House (c.1670)
The rich plasterwork and sensuous bay windows that decorate this house are unequalled elsewhere in England at the time. Most of what we see was built in the seventeenth century as additions to a fifteenth-century hall; that room's hammer-beam roof can still be seen on the first floor. The pargetting and plasterwork that decorate the exterior seem to represent a tour of the Continents (except Australia, discovered seventy years earlier, but waiting a further century for Captain Cook's exploration). Inside there are stucco ceilings of the same date, and others of the eighteenth century which represent Architecture, Music, Painting, Geometry and Sculpture.

The house gained extra significance in the 1870s when it became a source for the work of Norman Shaw, and subsequently others.

Ipswich Wills Faber Building (1975–6)
There are strange poetics in this building, designed in 1975–6 by Foster Associates. Its roof is covered with grass, and with its thin wall following an irregular path around the site, it appears like a piece of the urban jigsaw which has been lifted up and had a

building cleverly inserted. But as to how this poetic quality developed, it may be instructive to observe that in Italy a building's floor area for rental purposes is measured by the outside of the wall, whereas in Britain the measure is internal. It does not take long to see that the thinner the wall, the better becomes the ratio of lettable to gross floor area. Here at Wills Faber, not only has the wall oozed its way to the very limits of the site, but it has attenuated itself almost painfully on the way down to ½in thick. Architecture becomes subject to the practical difficulties of constructing a sheer wall with minimal fixings. If one were to express a reservation about the building, it would be that in setting oneself a difficult question and then finding its answer one does not necessarily prove the question to have been worthwhile.

Lavenham The Guildhall (fifteenth century)
To get an idea of the type and methods of timber-frame construction in East Anglia, Lavenham is the town to visit, and a particularly precise example of the art is the Guildhall. Unlike the square patterns found in the north west, here we have vertical close studding, a technique demanding a certain wealth and precision. Diagonal bracing was always necessary, but was often cut into the post from inside the wall so as not to spoil the vertical striped appearance. Here only the corner bracing is visible. The pity is that so many of these wooden buildings warp and twist, and many examples can be seen in Lavenham of buildings that appear to be falling into the street. I know that for many people this is the charm of the style, but I can't help thinking that there is greater value in the vigorous refinement of materials than in their droopy senescence.

Little Wenham Little Wenham Hall (c.1270–80)
This hall is one of the earliest houses, as opposed to castle keeps, in England. Living quarters are raised up, above a brick-vaulted undercroft, and the house is fortified. It was built for Sir John de Vallibus, and has the further interest of being one of the earliest uses of purpose-made brick, in contrast, for example, to Roman brick quarried from ruins and reused.

Orford Orford Castle (c.1165–73)
All that remains at Orford is the keep, but that in itself is one of the most unusual structures in the country. It was built by Henry II, and held by him during the period of his son's revolt. Circular inside, the tower externally is an irregular polygon with three large buttress towers attached. One of these is larger than the others, acting as a forebuilding and stair tower. The other two buttresses are also hollowed out to provide chambers, accessible through passages from the central circular space. There are floors on five levels, the tower rising to a height of 90ft.

Little Wenham Hall

Sparrowe's House, Ipswich

The Midlands

DERBYSHIRE

Bakewell Kedleston Hall (1757–65)
Spreading out like a great animal skin stretched in front of a fire, the plan of Kedleston, by James Paine, aims to cover the largest area possible. It set out as four pavilions surrounding the main house and connected to it by quadrants. By designing in this way, the architect gives himself a certain freedom to vary the scale and design of differing parts of a very large building. In comparison to some of Vanbrugh's designs it may seem rather tame; but that was the age. Robert Adam took over from Paine in 1760, and built the south front, in an heroic Arch of Constantine style, and the incredibly rich hall. This room, 40ft high and 67ft by 37ft in plan, is lined with a series of sixteen columns in pink alabaster. The hall is still at this time the largest room of the house by a long way, still its centre: but what a difference in feel — to make a sobering comparison — to Penshurst.

Bolsover Bolsover Castle (1612–21)
Bolsover was built on the site of a twelfth-century keep that had been left slowly to decay. It is another piece of medievalism, but on a scale that exceeds anything else of the century. That is not surprising: it was built by Sir Charles Cavendish, whose mother was Bess of Hardwick. The architect was again Robert Smythson. Having the castle theme ready to hand was obviously an advantage, since it made sense

Bolsover Castle

of whatever Smythson and Cavendish could cook up in the way of crenellated construction in a dramatic setting. It provided a context for the work. Inside, this is harder to justify and some of the chimney pieces are . . . indescribable. The whole building has an extremely fleshy quality which is Elizabethan architecture at its most violent.

Bakewell Chatsworth House (1687–1707)
The first, south, front of Chatsworth was built between 1687–89, to designs by William Talman. His client, the fourth Earl of Devonshire, had been made the first Duke for his role in promoting William of Orange in the Revolution of 1688. Because the house was built piece-meal, the duke deciding every few years to expand his intentions, the house is slightly wayward, but the south façade is very remarkable. Compared to other country houses of the time, it is palatial, in its severe forms and extravagant detailing. Those massive keystones over each window, and large columns not in the centre but at each end of the house — these are very strong. They could have been merely weak design, but the serious nature of the form, its flat roofline and heavy cornice, somehow convince one that the whole effort is serious.

The gardens of Chatsworth are one of its chief attractions, the main designs also being executed by the first Duke, and his immense cascade garden still exists. Since his time, every fashion in garden design has had its day in Chatsworth. Paxton was head gardener here and built the giant glass houses, direct antecedents of the Crystal Palace.

309

Chesterfield Hardwick Hall (1590–7)

'Mal di pietra' is the Italian expression for those gripped with the passion to build and never stop building. It was indeed the passion of Bess of Hardwick, but she fortunately had the wealth to satisfy it. Medieval features are rapidly disappearing here (as is the wall itself, into sheets of glass) with the hall being turned 90 degrees and acting as entrance to the house rather than a traditional hall. There was, of course, no need for a traditional hall in a house like this. The only decoration of this plain house is the use of Bess's initials atop the towers (ES — Elizabeth Shrewsbury). It is said she even had the front lawn cut so that her initials were legible in the lay of the nap. The famous large windows are oddly handled, seeming to be just ordinary windows as a result of indeterminate scale. It is in the end quite a surprise to see a window-sized window, opening out of one of these enormous sheets. The only indication of scale otherwise is the innumerable diamonds of glass that go to make up each sheet.

Matlock Bath Arkwright's Masson Mill (c.1783–twentieth century)

Coming across a building the size of Masson Mill, a huge water mill that dominates the river valley, one is struck by the immensity of eighteenth-century ambition, and its hard character. But that can only be a first impression, because most of the mill was built in the early years of this century. It is not infrequent that we forget how small, comparatively, and rural, were the buildings of the Industrial Revolution.

Arkwright's Masson Mill, Matlock Bath

310

The staircase, Hardwick Hall

HEREFORDSHIRE

The original building still exists, a strange layer cake of venetian windows, bracketed between the larger subsequent wings of red brick. It was built by the notorious Richard Arkwright, who, having seen both Kay and Hargreaves go unrewarded for their inventions in the industry, went to great lengths to protect the patents on his spinning machine. He fought with practically everyone, especially his partners, and when in the late 1770s the mob burnt his factories, he prepared to fight with them as well. In the mill at nearby Cromford he assembled, 'Fifteen hundred stand of small Arms . . . and a great battery of canon . . . (and) upwards of 500 spears . . . fixed in poles of between 2 and 3 yards long'. In the end, these weapons were not needed, though Arkwright seems to have thereafter avoided putting windows on the ground floor of his buildings where possible.

Brockhampton-by-Ross All Saints'
Church (1901–2)
The architect of this little church was William Lethaby, biographer of Philip Webb and first principal of the Central School of Arts and Crafts in London, founded in 1894. He trained with Norman Shaw, and became one of the leaders in the arts and crafts movement with his book, *Architecture, Mysticism and Myth*. All of that was meant to be based on strict rationality, combined with honest construction and so on, and is here expressed in a rather nice chancel, vaulted in concrete supported on stone arches. Curious, though, how rationality always drew designs towards a medieval appearance, like nails to a magnet. If one wants to feel arts and crafts at its most earthy, this thatched concrete church is the place to visit. The outside is unforgivable, but inside one or two details are worth looking at, particularly the nave windows.

312

LEICESTERSHIRE

All Saints' Church, Brockhampton-by-Ross

Ashby de la Zouch Ashby de la Zouch
Castle (tower 1474–1483)
From the twelfth until the fifteenth centuries, Ashby was not a castle but a manor
house. Only after the Wars of the Roses,
when Edward IV granted Ashby to his
Lord Chamberlain, William, Lord Hastings, was the great tower added. Only half
of this Hastings tower remains standing,
but it is an impressive sight. In a sense it
represents the renewed importance of
towers, increasing the available accommodation within the bailey, and as private
fortifications within the bailey for the lord,
surrounded as he was by mercenaries. The
fact that it was sited at the edge of existing
defences rather than in the middle also
made for easier supervision of the enclosure, and possibly, for easier escape.

During the civil war, Ashby was of
central importance in the areas of Notting-
hamshire, Derbyshire, Staffordshire, and

Leicestershire, and extensive improve-
ments were made to it. But the inevitable
starvation and disease forced its capitula-
tion to the Parliamentarians in 1646, and
the castle was subsequently slighted, as we
see it today.

Kirby Muxloe Kirby Muxloe Castle
(c.1480–3)
Kirby Muxloe was begun on the site of an
older manor house by William, Lord
Hastings, but was never completed. Hast-
ings, who had been very close to Edward
IV, was summarily executed by the Duke of
Gloucester in 1483.

The best-preserved parts of the castle,
apart from the moat, are the gatehouse and
west tower, and this second building is
perhaps the more impressive. All the bricks
were made locally for the building, and it is
a strange sight to see so much cooked earth
all in one place. The formality of the

313

Kirby Muxloe Castle

Leicester Engineering building

design, too, is striking in these fifteenth-century castles, especially those like Kirby which were not their builders' main residence (Hastings owned the nearby Ashby). The contrast is evident between the old manor-house plan, unearthed at the beginning of this century and built only a few years before the castle made its demolition necessary, and the castle itself.

Leicester Leicester Engineering Building (1959–63)
This could be seen as the first building in England since the 1920s to repossess the spirit of English architecture, based as it is on a very practical approach to aesthetic problems. Each piece is crafted in an individual style, with different materials and structural systems. All is held together by the character of the architects, James Stirling and James Gowan. The building is more fully discussed in Chapter 5.

Lyddington Bede House (late fifteenth century)
Bede, a medieval word for prayer, was often used in connection with almshouses, since it was usual for a benefactor to stipulate that those who enjoyed his generosity should pray for his soul. This building was not

erected as almshouses, however, but as a house for the Bishop of Lincoln. Only in 1602 did Thomas, Lord Burghley turn it into almshouses. The best part of the building is the timber ceiling in the hall, panelled and carved with tracery.

Melton Mowbray Stapleford Park (c.1500, 1633)

Here at Stapleford, Lord and Lady Sherard made extensive repairs in the 1630s, to what was essentially a house of about 1500. There is a wing called Lady Abigail's Range which forms a strangely Gothic composition. It seems that even as late (or as early) as 1663 there was a strong taste for medieval effect. Into the existing wall were inserted rows of reliefs taken from various churches, and half a dozen statuettes of Lady Abigail's ancestors. Above all this, a trio of voluted gables dance along the roofline. It appears that the 1500 wall was virtually plain, treated as a flat sheet to be written upon. It has what a guide book should call charm.

NORTHAMPTONSHIRE

Higham Ferrers Bede House (c.1428)

This bede house, or almshouse, was built by Archbishop Chicheler, a native of Higham Ferrers who also founded a college and school in the town. Little remains of these other foundations, but the Bede House stands as an example of the beautiful stonework of this region. It is built in bands of ironstone and whiteish limestone, colours that go particularly well with the grass of the churchyard. Inside, the building was divided into cubicles for a dozen men, and a chapel set at the extreme east end.

Rushden Lyveden New Build (c.1605)

Looking at the buildings put up by or for Sir Thomas Tresham, William Blake's phrase comes to mind, that 'Art can never exist without Naked Beauty displayed. The Gods of Greece and Egypt were Mathematical Diagrams.' For Tresham's buildings are almost pure geometry in stone, and they are overtly religious in character. He

Stapleford Park

316

Bede House, Higham Ferrers

Lyveden New Build

appears to have employed architects, in this case Robert Stickells, but must have directed much of the design himself. While the Triangular Lodge at Rushton was built on the theme of the Trinity, Lyveden (called 'New Build' to distinguish it from an older house nearby) was symbolic of the Passion. The house is not a ruin, but was simply never completed after Tresham's death. Its plan is a Greek cross, with bays at the end of each arm. One of these serves as the entrance, making a far better job of it than the Triangular Lodge, where the door was slapped in one side, off centre, when it was thought no reasonable solution could be found. The only thing to do in such cases is to multiply and exaggerate things. Palladio, given the same problem of geometrical impenetrability at the Villa Rotunda, put four entrance fronts on the thing, one on each side. It isn't perfect — it never can be, setting up Platonic geometry and then putting doors in it — but it works well enough to fool you for a while. At any rate, Lyveden uses that same principle and gets half way there.

One of the most delicate details here is the quoining, done in a stone only a shade different in colour to the walls, and in the same plane, which is only distinguishable from the rest of the wall for this reason. Usually, of course, quoining is done in a different material, stone in a brick wall, or at a different plane to the wall. The Lyveden detail is very subtle.

Stamford Burghley House
The amateur architect in the sixteenth century was, for domestic building, the only kind there was. If a man wanted a splendid house he more or less had to work it out for himself, and this is what William Cecil, Lord Burghley, did here between the 1550s and 1580s. This, and the long period

Brewhouse, Burghley House

318

over which the house was built, explain its somewhat piecemeal character. Compared to Longleat, the house is of an older fashion. It has a clear entrance front to the west, guarded still by twin towers, and a courtyard. Within the courtyard is a monumental tower, each stage and item carefully culled from books. They occasionally got their levels wrong, and one façade has a string course which threatens to plough into the earth, but is checked just in time, and at least the roof line is straight. Some of the most illuminating aspects of Elizabethan life are found by studying the brewhouse, and the kitchen, full as it is of giant turtle shells.

NOTTINGHAMSHIRE

Southwell Southwell Cathedral
(c.1100–1260)
Until 1884, Southwell was a minster, not a cathedral. It remains one of the few buildings that can still give a reasonable image of what the west front of a large Romanesque church looked like. For they neither had flat tops nor sliver-sharp spires, but vaguely pyramidal roofs (though these at Southwell are nineteenth-century restorations). The symbolic value of Romanesque design is seen clearly here: gate-like towers guarding the corners, very like the towers of a castle wall and a central 'keep' rising high above the rest; the western towers acting together to form a gateway (though this effect is lost in Southwell where a fifteenth-century window was inserted in the west front). The whole is a kind of city of god.

Nottingham Wollaton Hall (1580–88)
The architect of Wollaton was Robert Smythson, who later went on to build Hardwick Hall, though a certain amount of the planning seems to have been done by the owner, Sir Francis Willoughby. He was a man made rich by coal, but with, as they

say, good connections, and he could afford to back those up by building Wollaton. Its plan represents a half-way stage in placement of the hall. Early Elizabethan designers placed the entrance centrally, as at Kirby (q.v.) and let the hall run off to one side of the house; at Hardwick (q.v.) the hall is placed axially and is entered from its short side; here it is entered in the traditional way, but placed centrally, and an L-shaped corridor is needed from the central entrance to reach it. It is altogether a transitional house, in the sense that its innovations were not repeated. So too, the large corner towers are right on the corners, whereas it later became more usual for towers to be set in towards the entrance and to let the corner go its own way. These towers are very static, heavy things, pinning the building firmly to the ground. Perhaps this is what appealed so much to the Victorians, who used Wollaton as a model for their country houses. The house now is a public museum, full of stuffed animals of the largest varieties, which seem to suit it well. A very much more friendly house today than its appearance would make it seem.

SHROPSHIRE

Acton Burnell Acton Burnell Castle
(c.1284–93)
This is the earliest example of what is in effect, as at Stokesay, a fortified house, but unlike that building retaining the outward form of a castle. Nunney in Somerset is a fourteenth-century example of a castle built in an undefendable position, and here is one without even a moat. The builder was Robert Burnell, chaplain to Edward I when still Prince Edward, Chancellor and Bishop of Bath and Wells when he built Acton Burnell. Perhaps because its defensive function is secondary, the forms are quite plain and give an impression of incisiveness

with shape rather than scale. The west façade consists of two vertical towers flanking a central projection, the recesses between being deep. That sharp clarity is in contrast with the friable red sandstone of which the castle is built, hollowed and grooved by the rain. The building was turned into a barn in the eighteenth century.

Ludlow Ludlow Castle (c.1100–1500)
Ludlow was originally the main castle in a chain of thirty-two that guarded the Welsh Marches, and was first built in timber at the time of Domesday by Roger de Lacy. The castle's earliest stone building is also its most unusual, being a small circular chapel, thought to be an intended reconstruction of the Church of the Holy Sepulchre in Jerusalem. It was built about 1140. Over the centuries the castle was much altered and extended, and the ruins of its fourteenth-century hall range give an indication of its former palatial standards of comfort. It was here that, between 1472 and 1483, the Prince of Wales and his brother lived, before their eventual removal to the Tower of London and infamous disappearance. When Edward IV founded his Court of the Marches, for the administration of justice

in Wales, he made Ludlow its centre and the castle prospered. Milton's *Comus* was first performed here, in 1634, but in 1689 the Court of the Marches was abolished, the castle's importance was diminished and its physical decline began.

Shrewsbury Howard Street Warehouse (1835)
Hard by the railway, but in fact serving the Shropshire Union Canal, stands the impressive neo-Classical warehouse. It was designed by Birmingham architects Fellows & Hart, and behind its truly antique grandeur of scale is a quite different construction. The warehouse proper uses iron columns with iron arches, and a timber roof structure. The terminal of a canal was a very different proposition to that of a railway, because it dealt in goods and not people: there weren't all those concessions and compromises to be made. But then, railway warehousing often has this quality of unsociability, too.

Stokesay Stokesay Castle (c.1240–90)
The manor house is really a house with defences rather than a military building. At its centre was the hall, used until the sixteenth century for meals in common and

Howard Street warehouse

Stokesay Castle

manorial court meetings. Here at Stokesay the hall is unaltered since the thirteenth century. Its windows are unglazed, closed only by wooden shutters, and there is still a smoke-hole in the roof. Fires were lit on a hearth in the middle of the floor, also still visible here.

To the north of the hall is part of a tower-house built during the reign of Henry II, to which some overhanging timberwork was later added. The dominant south tower was added in 1290 by the then owner, Lawrence of Ludlow, the son of a wool merchant and financier of Edward I. The half-timbered gatehouse was added about 1570 in a style characteristic of this region, of which more can be found in the town of Ludlow itself.

Stokesay was garrisoned during the Civil War but the defences, consisting mostly of a moat, were such that the garrison surrendered without struggle, saving not only their lives, but the buildings as well. Un-occupied for generations, it is one of the few manor houses to have escaped modernization or extensive alterations which, though they made other manor houses habitable, make it difficult for us to imagine their original state.

WARWICKSHIRE

Tysoe Compton Wynyates (early sixteenth century)
Compton Wynyates is a courtyard house in the traditional medieval style, but treated in an entirely picturesque way. One of the artistic achievements of the English has been the development of techniques for expressing their disdain for intellectual clarity, and here it is, Sir William Compton's version of that attitude. The plan is quite straightforward, and would be capable of practically any elevational treatment. It isn't bristling with lumpy projections, for example. Yet the elevations are all

up in the air, dozens of different windows, chimneys and gables here, there and everywhere — a shambles. But it takes the sting out of that plan, and must be easier to live with, for some, than a house like Longleat.

Kenilworth Kenilworth Castle (c.1120–1250)
In 1266, when Simon de Montfort was holding Kenilworth, the castle came under heavy siege by Henry III. Although de Montfort eventually had to surrender, it was disease and starvation that was the cause; his defences remained impenetrable. As well as having very substantial tower and building defences, the castle gained further and unusual defence by a diversion of the two streams which flow past the castle mound, to form a lake of about 100 acres. To the east the land was marshy, and so the besiegers could find no point near

enough to the castle to sink a mine. It was during this siege that two stone cannon balls, launched by either side towards the other, were said to have collided in mid-air.

The castle was converted from a fortress to palace in the 1320s by John of Gaunt, and in the sixteenth century it belonged to the Earl of Leicester, who further adapted and modified the building.

Warwick Warwick Castle
The shell keep of Warwick was heavily remodelled in the late seventeenth century, and presents a curious picture of historical inaccuracy. In the fourteenth century, a range of buildings was added to the east wall of the bailey, and later the massive tower was built on to the west wall. But the most individual element of the castle is Caesar's Tower, built by Thomas Beauchamp, Earl of Warwick, in the early fifteenth century. It occupies a strategic position at the castle's north-east corner, rising 147ft from its plinth. Its six storeys contained prison (below ground), living chambers, ammunition store and guardroom. Its plan form must be described as bulbous — where did they develop these strange shapes?

WEST MIDLANDS

Birmingham Aston Hall (1618–35)
How right it seems, this heavily fabricated building, sitting among the industrial suburbs. It, like its industrial neighbours, is mostly of red brick, with strong patterning in darker brick. Only the corners and windows have stone dressing.

The plan finally resolves the contradictory requirements of hall and symmetrical plan, by abandoning any pretence of a traditional hall. Here it is central, and clearly an entrance lobby. As for the elevations, there seems to be a conflict between the desire to give the house a horizontal

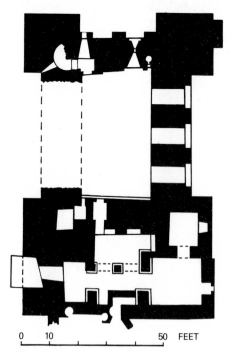

0   10   50   FEET

Plan of Kenilworth Castle

322

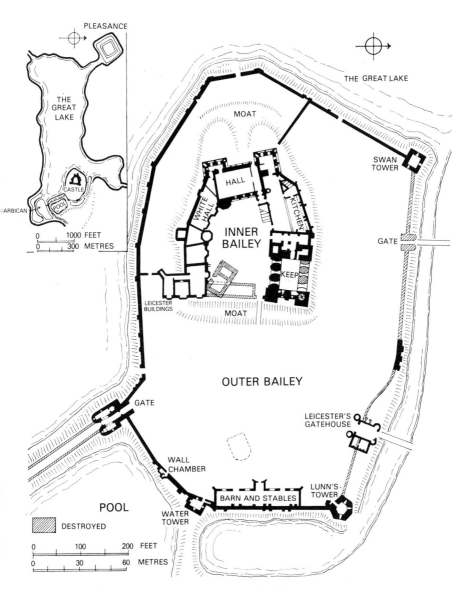

PLEASANCE

THE GREAT LAKE

MOAT

SWAN TOWER

THE
GREAT
LAKE

CASTLE

POOL

ARBICAN

0   1000 FEET
0   300 METRES

HALL

WHITE HALL

KITCHEN

INNER
BAILEY

GATE

KEEP

LEICESTER
BUILDINGS

MOAT

OUTER BAILEY

GATE

LEICESTER'S
GATEHOUSE

WALL
CHAMBER

LUNN'S
TOWER

POOL

BARN AND STABLES

DESTROYED

WATER
TOWER

0   100   200 FEET
0   30   60 METRES

Kenilworth Castle

emphasis, with heavy projecting string courses at each level and broad strips of glazing, and the wish to cover the building with pointy towers and turrets. The east front in particular seems to lose itself in the confusion: the strong parapet over the central block seems to make nonsense of the tower that rises immediately behind it, and vice versa.

The house was built by Sir Thomas Holte, though he wanted thirteen years of building before moving in, and another four to see its completion. Its architect was John Thorpe.

Birmingham Bull Ring (c.1960–5)

Birmingham, alone among major English cities, has continued to grow in population since the last war. This means that programmes of inner city renewal, and the road and redevelopment projects these have involved, have had to be carried through without that use of redundant land that other cities enjoyed.

The Bull Ring development stands on what was, in the seventeenth century, the

Curzon Street Goods Station

village green. By the time the present development was built, the area was the dense market centre of Birmingham. Having decided to build an inner ring road, and needing somewhere to put it, the city clearly saw that this miscellany of buildings could easily be demolished, the road constructed, and the market rebuilt in the odd spaces left over. The major change was in ownership of the land, which passed from many hands to few, and the architecture reflects this domination. The wheelings and dealings carried on as they had done at Centre Point in London, and to much the same effect. The Rotunda building, standing at the centre, is the best piece of architecture available, a mixture of offices, shops and banks. But in the end, a city depends more on the connection between its pieces of architecture than upon the pieces themselves, and here those connections were left to chance.

Birmingham Curzon Street Goods Station (1838)

This is, or rather was, the other end of Euston Station in London; or the other way around, I suppose, since Euston lost its glorious arch. Philip Hardwick designed both, giant doors to a newly invented mobile room. The Greek Ionic architecture has been translated from temple to booking hall. One doesn't know how seriously to take these things because, although undoubtedly beautiful, the idea of building monuments and then using them practically, as if being monumental were somehow not enough, is too prosaic altogether. At Euston the arch was just an arch; but then, they pulled that down, no doubt just because it did serve no purpose . . . I suppose one can't win.

Birmingham Town Hall (1832–49)

Birmingham's Town Hall was put out to competition, and the winner of that was Joseph Hansom. The Hansom cab is a later

Birmingham Town Hall

and better-known of his inventions. He was bankrupted by this building, because part of the conditions was that he should indemnify the builder, who in turn found himself in trouble with money. At any rate, it was taken over and completed slowly by Charles Edge. The tightly packed group around Chamberlain Place is now destroyed, and the building is a little on its own; but compared with the work of Smirke or Wilkins farther south, it has a less pompous, more detached feel to it. This has got something to do with the heavy rusticated plinth that the columns stand on.

WORCESTERSHIRE

Worcester Railway Bridge (nineteenth century)
The canal had been in existence for many years when the railway built the bridge across it, climbing its way up to the highly decorated Shrub Hill Station. The bridge seems typical of the practical skill of Victorian designers, sharing the same

technology as the canal structures it was built to make obsolete. All is brickwork, and the bridge has three gestures to make. Twice it rises in great arches, once to clear the canal, second a road; then, to save the cost and weight of extra brickwork, a large hole is punched through the bridge above the narrow road arch. The care about detail and material, and the simplicity of approach, are again the equal of those in the canal structure below the bridge, which seems to have been a tradition worth extending.

Railway bridge over the canal at Worcester

325

The North

CHESHIRE

Congleton Bradbury's Works (twentieth century)
Not an especially ancient building, Mr Bradbury's, but remarkably evocative. The river helps, as does the bridge in the foreground, dating from the early nineteenth century, and the result is a strange reminiscence of Paxton's Great Exhibition building. Those long unbroken runs of glazing contribute to this, with the three-storey corner tower at one end, but so does the curious rainwater system, for some reason starting not at the roof but one floor down, leaving the glazing above it unobstructed. Congleton offers other surprises, of brick and stone. It was a silk weaving town in the eighteenth and nineteenth centuries, and several of the older mills can still be seen, and a good bit of warehousing as well.

Congleton Little Moreton Hall (fifteenth and sixteenth centuries)
Pevsner's description of this black-and-white timber extravaganza as 'at first unbelievable, and then a huge joke' is not far off the mark. But then, the English take their jokes seriously: this is one of the country's most popular and well-loved buildings. If you don't laugh, you call it picturesque in the sentimental sense. In fact the building, hanging out on all sides and

presenting gables to the onlooker at every turn on the south side, is rather aggressive. It depends upon the observer whether he finds effusive affection an endearing or repellent quality.

Jodrell Bank Jodrell Bank Radio Telescopes (1949–65)
These are more awe inspiring when seen illicitly across fields rather than from the official entrance. The largest was the first built, in 1952–7, and is 250ft in diameter. None of these telescopes is optical — all are designed to receive radio waves. The complex belongs to the University of Manchester.

Knutsford The King's Coffee House, King Street (1907–8)
If you have a taste for the bizarre, the town of Knutsford will be a dream come true. Apparently, this Coffee House, and the series of villas in Legh Road, were built for a glovemaker called Watt, who forced a number of more or less willing architects to build him these improbable things. But the Coffee House is exceptional even amongst such company, and beyond being simply strange, many of its architectural ideas are very good: its staircase, the tower with its battlements, those heavy slab cornices. Everything has simply got out of hand, which for a glovemaker I suppose is not good enough. The saving grace here is the narrowness of the High Street, which makes the onlooker unable to see more than a small section at a time.

Little Moreton Hall

Factory at Congleton

King's Coffee House, Knutsford

Radio Telescope, Jodrell Bank

Adlington Hall

CLEVELAND

Macclesfield Adlington Hall (fifteenth, sixteenth and eighteenth centuries)
The family of Legh has been at Adlington since about 1310, and it was a Thomas Legh who, around 1500, rebuilt the hall, with a hammer-beam roof, and the other buildings around a courtyard. This and additions of eighty years later were generally of oak and plaster. But it was the eighteenth century, in the shape of Charles Legh, which added the south front that gives the house its exceptional character. It has a thirteen-bay classical design with a four-column portico rising through three storeys. The portico has remarkably little to do with what is behind it, and for that reason, rather than being bad design, becomes just another pleasing element in the general mêlée.

Middlesbrough Bell Brothers' Offices (1883)
The Bells were among the more prosperous of iron founders in Middlesbrough. Philip Webb, architect of these offices, was employed by the family to build several houses at various times (mostly now demolished), and this was in fact the only commercial building he designed. It is always difficult to understand where Webb found the odd pieces he used to assemble a building, or just how he succeeds in tying them all together. The bottom two storeys are stone, and strongly horizontal, with the three ground-floor arches being quite squat in proportion, and a deeply projecting cornice at the top of the second storey.

Bell Brothers' Offices, Middlesbrough

330

Above this is a white stucco, vaguely Dutch, third floor, with great wavy gables. Having passed from Bell Bros to Dorman Long to British Steel, the offices are, at the time of writing, empty, and in a very dilapidated state.

COUNTY DURHAM

Durham Durham Cathedral
(1091–c.1130)
Durham is a remarkable building for several reasons, not least of which is the short space of time in which it was built. From 1091, when William of St Corileph returned from exile to become bishop and laid out the new abbey church, it took only some forty years to complete. The rib-vaulted roof, first of its kind in existence, appears to have been part of the original design and not a last minute change as is often thought. But despite the delicacy of that vault, Durham is the most masculine of English cathedrals. Half an hour spent in

Lorton Hall, pele tower and range

the Galilee is an exploration of Romanesque design at its most vigorous, comparable, say, to the mosque at Cordova in Spain. This Galilee, incidentally, was built as a Lady Chapel, placed here rather than next to the Presbytery after several attempts to build it there had ended in disaster. This was felt to be a continuation after death of St Cuthbert's aversion to women; his shrine stood next to the originally intended site.

CUMBERLAND

Lorton Lorton Hall (c.1663)
The original part of Lorton Hall is much earlier than the date above, and consists of a pele tower of uncertain age. The pele tower was a simple fortification built extensively in Cumberland and Northumberland in the fourteenth century and after. Shooting out from the side of this tower is a range of buildings of a very surprising classicism. A two-storey building, it has seven bays on each floor (though they don't quite line up). First-floor windows have simple chevron

332

pediments above a continuous string course, so giving a mannered indication of classical architecture without the necessity for pedantic proportional accuracy. One suspects that in any case this would have been out of the question here. The ground floor has the same pediment detail over the door only.

Lowther Lowther Village (c.1765–75)
This remote and half completed village was begun by Sir James Lowther, a carpet manufacturer, to the designs of James Adam. The notion of one- and two-storey buildings for labourers forming the kind of layout found at Bath or Edinburgh, is curious to say the least. But for all the 'fantastic incongruity of its plan, which exhibits the grandest features of city architecture . . . upon the mean scale of a peasant's cottage', the idea is correct. The village must in some way represent the city, as much as cities need parks and trees.

HUMBERSIDE

Burton Agnes Burton Agnes Hall (1601–10)
This is a large house, but by no means of the same order as Burghley or the other palatial buildings of the Elizabethan and Jacobean age. There is, in fact, a curious and pleasing contrast between the simple forms and materials of the house, and the extreme elaboration of some of its interiors. In particular, the south front, with its bow windows rising through three storeys, is a design unusually relaxed and tranquil. The entrance steps, so often an awkward part of these seventeenth-century houses, seem to me one of the best features here. But from the peaceful red brick of the outside, one soon encounters a hall screen of indescribable frenzy. So one does not try to describe it. Strange to think that the same mind could have chosen both this, and the house design.

LANCASHIRE

Cartmel Fell Broadley's, Lake Windermere (1898–1900)
When Voysey built Broadley's, facing Lake Windermere to the west, he was at the height of his career. Never again did he have as a much work as he then enjoyed, or execute it with such skill. Though one may prefer the slender whiteness of houses like that at Hog's Back, Surrey, of two years earlier, this house is more relaxed, and has

333

that quality of belonging to a place, a quality that eludes the critics' grasp. He has made, on the outside, a strongly formal façade, and then within that strong form has modified details to suit circumstances, as where the central bay window reflects the double-height room behind it, or on the drawing-room chimney carried through the roof to one side of the house. But the un-revolutionary nature of the architecture is evident from the fact that it does not need a lot of explanation; the language is a dis-ciplined version of one which we under-stand.

Chorley Astley Hall (c.1655)

This house, which Nikolaus Pevsner refers to as being 'bizarre', contrives in some way to be both modern and old fashioned at the same time. The property belonged to the Channock family from the fifteenth cen-tury, but was only made their main house in the 1570s and the principal part was only built after the last of the Channocks had died, around the mid-seventeenth century.

That is the odd part, for although the house would in many ways have been daring in the 1930s, with its walls of glass and clean geometry, it seems quite primi-tive and unrefined in comparison to seven-teenth-century architecture. Its brickwork has unfortunately been rendered over,

making the façade bleaker than it need be. But there are few other houses that can equal the first-floor band of windows. These light a single gallery, and seem to a modern eye to be structurally a very daring feature. What holds up the wall and roof above?

Hoghton, Nr Preston Hoghton Tower (c.1565)

For its date, Hoghton Tower seems an old-fashioned building, and by all accounts the family were a conservative lot. Since the twelfth century they had perched up on the hill, and when they did decide to rebuild, the forms were the asymmetrical ones of the fifteenth-century manor house. But conser-vative may only mean, in this context, unfashionable, and by extension, durable. It is a house at least as readily understood by a twentieth-century architect as those nearby spiders' webs of black and white. The inner courtyard is the finest part, with stone paving, flat stone walls and a large semi-circular stair flowing down from the entrance porch. A single statue stands on a pedestal in the courtyard, his feet roughly at a level with the floor inside the building.

Astley Hall, Chorley

334

Rufford Rufford Old Hall (late fifteenth century)

The 'black and white' part of this house, that is, the oldest part, was modified in 1662 when a brick wing was added to it. In a way, this is not a bad thing, because the brick provides the quiet foil that a building like Little Moreton Hall could benefit from. What they did with wood in those days is remarkable, and remarkably difficult to understand. There is the part-octagon bay window, to light the high table, which on the ouside is a design of great simplicity. Yet once these people got out the carving knife, the simplicity vanished, as that great moveable screen in the hall proves. The whole interior is like this. A tour of the garden is recommended.

Samlesbury Samlesbury Hall (c.1545)
This property belonged to the Southworth family from the early fourteenth century until 1679. What is seen now is generally from the mid-sixteenth century, externally

(previous page) Rufford Old Hall

Hoghton Tower (see p334)

very heavily restored, or even redesigned, in the nineteenth. The sight of the long range facing the courtyard, with the hall emerging from it near the west end, is nonetheless a powerful thing. Heavy patterning seems not so much to prettify the building as to remove it from the normal architectural expression and turn the building into a number of clear, self-contained forms, on which the roofs sit like paper hats. It doesn't look as if you could live in it, in a way, because it seems so much closer to the world of ideas than the world of things. Inside, the hall has a bizarre moveable screen, and a massive fireplace, well worth a look.

LIVERPOOL

Merseyside St George's Hall (1841–56)
Competitions were held for two buildings, one for a public hall in 1839, the other in 1840 for the city's Assize Courts, both of

338

which were won by a young London architect, Harvey Lonsdale Elmes. The city corporation therefore decided to combine these two buildings, and added a concert hall to the programme, in order to get a really impressive civic building. This they certainly got, though Elmes died in 1847, aged thirty-three and C. R. Cockerell took over the work. To the latter is due the change in style from Elmes's severe neo-classicism outside to the altogether richer, fruitier style of the interior.

St George's Hall stands at the height of British neo-classicism, and possesses all the dramatic, restless grandeur which was the great achievement of this style. Although each part of the building — assize courts, public hall and concert hall — is made subordinate to the massive order of columns and entablature which circle the building, each part is also seeking to express its presence as a separate identity. This Corinthian order has been stretched like ribbon around the very individual massing of the building's parts. On the south end the assize court is approached end-on at the top of a long flight of steps under a portico with pediment. This could almost be a separate building except that what should be its side turns into a huge portico of sixteen columns, which marks the entrance to the public hall on the east. The wall continues and on the north a semi-circular end reflects the shape of the concert hall within. As the columns circle the building they change. Sometimes they are round columns, sometimes square pillars half-embedded in the building below, at other times as pilasters stuck to the wall itself. The sense of conflicting order and individuality is played at just the right level with the result that this very large building not only avoids monotony, but becomes a positive element forming the city.

The interior is completely the work of Cockerell, and the rich luscious detailing uses the severity of the exterior as a foil to its splendour. There is just that difference between early and high Victorian.

Liverpool Speke Hall (sixteenth century)
Speke Hall is one of the great houses of its kind, the black-and-white houses of the north west. The buildings were erected over a period of about a hundred and twenty years, around a courtyard, and are

Speke Hall

of a consistent style. The most dazzling part of a house designed to dazzle, is the hall, which contains a large Elizabethan chimney piece, Flemish panelling with carved reliefs, and a lovely flat ceiling. All this wood seems to glow and shine slightly.

NORTH YORKSHIRE

Coxwold Shandy Hall (eighteenth century)
If we include buildings of a humble character as being worthy of attention, then Shandy Hall has the added attraction of having been the house of Laurence Sterne, author of the wonderful *Tristram Shandy,* 'written in a bye-corner of the kingdom, and in a retired thatched house, where I live in a constant endeavour to fence against the infirmities of life, by mirth . . .'. Red brick, big chimney stack — these needing attention — and set in among this, the white windows seem curiously bold and geometrical. The thatch has been replaced by slates.

Fylingdales Moor Fylingdales Early Warning Station (1961–2)
These three Radomes have received a certain amount of critical attention since they were built by the Air Ministry Works Department, in the lonely and bleak moors. More than being lessons in the purity of form, they seem to raise more fundamental

Shandy Hall

questions about architecture. One of the purposes of a building is to let some things in or out while keeping others out or in, and the elaboration of the points of entry become architecture. Doors, windows, chimneys — these operate in most obvious ways; piped services slightly less so, either appearing only within the building (water) or trying to hide outside it (rainwater). But everything that went in or out of a building had a physical entry. What happens to architecture when what passes through isn't

Fylingdales

340

visible, as here, with radio waves? You may call the architecture beautiful in its purity, but that purity is only a result of our inability to sense the building's purpose.

Helmsley Rievaulx Abbey (c.1135–1250)
Though strictly speaking a church building and therefore outside the scope of this gazetteer (see Introduction), Rievaulx was also once a community of some six hundred souls. Of necessity it would have provided agricultural labour, cooks, physicians, builders and indeed all the skills required in community life. If this alone is not sufficient to qualify it for inclusion, it could be mentioned that it hasn't been a church for over four hundred years, is now a ruin, and is owned by the DOE. Not a church, then, but an ancient monument.

I don't intend to talk about the church architecture of Rievaulx, but rather to point out that it is an example of medieval town planning at a practical level.

Monasteries had to be self-reliant, and the degree of material organisation necessary to make them so led to technical advances unheard of in towns and cities for a further two hundred years. Water power was thoroughly exploited, grinding corn, providing water (for making beer as well as for cooking and washing), operating machinery for cloth manufacture and used in the tanning of leather. When it had done all this it would carry away waste. This organisation of the power of one river — or spring in this case — was superior to anything in towns. As late as the nineteenth century, London tipped its waste into the Thames upstream of the draw-off point for drinking water, a health hazard never tolerated in monasteries.

Each monastery of a particular order (Rievaulx was Cistercian) was based on an ideal, adapted only as necessary to meet extraordinary conditions. Both the purpose of the communities and their social organization were understood and ritualized, or in current speech, standardized. It is interesting to compare this monastery, where the place and the buildings were of secondary importance to the ideals they expressed, with modern planned towns, where place and buildings are considered most important and where the only ideal principles are economic.

Richmond, North Yorkshire Richmond Castle (c.1080–1170)
Richmond Castle has a very pretty relationship to both the River Swale and the town to its north. Its bailey is triangular, with the keys on an apex toward the town, and a long curtain wall standing against the steep cliffs above the river. The curtain, in places 10 feet thick, was built in the 1080s by Alan the Red, together with Scolland's Hall, one of the earliest of English stone halls. Scolland was, apparently, the name of Alan's steward. The great keep tower, once reaching a height of some 100 feet, was built on top of the original gateway.

Ripon Fountains Abbey (c.1150–1250)
It is a strange sensation to see such vastness of human effort staying in a place quite silent of men. At its best, Fountains must have been the equal of a town in population and industry, and was certainly better laid out and serviced than any contemporary towns. I daresay the high level of discipline had something to do with that: perhaps cleanliness really is next to godliness. The abbey was attached to the estate of Studley Royal in 1768, by William Aislabie. His efforts at creating a garden of architectural images, a catalogue of emotional and intellectual stimuli, were better rewarded than most, for he has as the centrepiece the majestic ruins of Fountains Abbey, which is no mere folly.

Ripon Ripon Cathedral (mid-twelfth century)
Ripon is a relatively small cathedral, and

(above) Richmond Castle
(right) Ripon Cathedral

a relatively new one. Until 1836, it was only a parish church, and that probably explains the unified design of its west front. In form, it keeps the twin towers of Norman cathedral design — city watch-towers complete with battlements — only the symbolic nature of the architecture seems to have gone. If it is compared with Lincoln, Ripon does not evoke anything like a city gate, and the palace arcading is missing. Only in its forms does it remain the bulky symbol of authority, and this is especially evident around the south and north sides, where the robustness of construction suggests a fortification.

Whitby Church of St Mary (various centuries)

Up the long and winding steps from the old town, so long that there are benches to rest upon on the way, brings you at last to St Mary's, a type of domestic church on a cliff top. The basis of the building was constructed in the twelfth century, and has subsequently been tinkered with by every

Town Hall, Whitby

Whitby Town Hall (1788)
An unusual building, this hall, illustrating that the past often lies lurking in the most obscure of places, waiting to show that it has anticipated the future. Many town halls were jacked up on columns, to provide covered market space below, but rarely was the staircase arrangement as beautifully thought out as this, a simple cylinder completely free of the building's edges. Early this century people got quite agitated by Le Corbusier's Villa Savoy, which does much the same thing (though for reasons of view rather than urban economy). But in many ways the older building is more surreal, by jacking pure classicism up in the air: what could be more bizarre in classical terms?

NORTHUMBERLAND

Bamburgh Bamburgh Castle (twelfth century)
Bamburgh stands on a precipitous finger of basalt, some 130ft above the sea. The site has been fortified in one way or another since prehistoric times, but since William II took the site in 1095, it remained a royal castle until the sixteenth century. Who built the castle we see today is in doubt; the keep would appear to be twelfth century, a strong square tower with a rather good

age, most of all the Georgian. It was the eighteenth century that domesticated the building with its sash windows and external staircases, that lead in fact to internal galleries. Of these, the church is full. Even the crisply white rainwater pipes give this neat civic air to the building, which must have been a wonderful sight when the 2,000 people it accommodated were milling and bustling about it.

Bamburgh Castle

plan. It was during the Wars of the Roses that the castle was badly damaged, being in fact the first castle in this country to succumb to the force of gunpowder, Warwick 'the Kingmaker' taking it in 1464.

It was bought in 1704 by Lord Crewe, and restored and rebuilt during the following centuries. It is said to accommodate more people than any other English castle save Windsor, and judging from all the television aerials, this may be so.

Corbridge Vicar's Pele (early fourteenth century)

Life in the vicinity of the Roman Wall was not easy in the Middle Ages, with the constant threat and frequent occurrence of raids from Scotland. Hexham Abbey has a north wall substantially thicker than the other three, which says something about these realities. During the fourteenth century and after, this border country saw the development of peculiar defensive towers, generally rectangular, of three or four storeys, and with embattled parapets. This pele tower, as they became known, at Corbridge, was the dour residence of the parish priest. Its walls are 4ft thick, of four storeys, stone faced and contain a vaulted lower floor. The second storey was the living room — the piano nobile of fourteenth-century Northumberland — and above that, on a timber floor, the bedroom. The Vicar's Pele remains about the best example of this type of fortified house, peculiar to the border region.

Seaton Delaval Seaton Delaval (1718–29)

Built by Sir John Vanbrugh for Admiral George Delaval. Neither of these men lived to see its completion, Vanbrugh's greatest building and a project for which Delaval was unstinting of money and effort.

Baroque architecture is more or less defined as distortion of the classical architectural elements, and with less room to manœuvre than at Blenheim, Vanbrugh

Vicar's Pele, Corbridge

has here made every element and distortion look as if it is bursting out of the cubic villa which forms the basis of the house. Medieval turrets thrust forward at every corner, pairs of coupled columns, together with their massive cornices, have detached themselves from the building, coming forward toward you, a staircase spills out between them and the pediment has lifted off the house in apparent surprise.

Traditionally in classical architecture rustication is used on the lowest floor or semi-basement of a building because it is meant to imply mass and weight. To Vanbrugh it was another means to distort our impression of what had weight and what didn't. The heaviest rustication is therefore reserved for the chimney stack, the building's loftiest part.

More restrained than the north is the south façade, where less of this rustication is employed and where a delicate Ionic portico sits atop the staircase. The skyline remains extremely dramatic.

As at Blenheim two wings project to form a Grand Court of low arcades with stable and kitchen courts behind. This enclosure helps pull one's attention towards the building and helps give the impression of great scale.

Warkworth Warkworth Castle (1200–50; keep c.1440)

Art followed slowly the needs of protection in castle design, for obvious reasons. Although admirable as objects, these castles are not considered to have been designed to please the eye. Yet it would be foolish to dismiss the psychological force of such a building on its would-be attackers. Aesthetics isn't merely a question of delight. Burke recognised this when he spoke of the sublime nature of much aesthetic experience. Certainly before the rudiments of castle building could be ascertained by science, a wall would be strong enough when it *looked* strong enough, and this certainly has aesthetic meaning.

At Warkworth a twelfth-century curtain wall and gatehouse enclose a courtyard of about an acre, in which the foundation of a collegiate church and a kitchen can be seen, dating from the reign of Henry VIII. The gatehouse illustrates the improved fortification techniques picked up during the crusades. A portcullis and machicolations, together with two protruding polygonal towers, make the defence of the curtain wall very secure.

The keep, as a last stronghold of defence, was outdated by the fourteenth century and became the Northumbrian equivalent of the manor house, developing at the same time in the south of England. The plan itself is remarkable for a keep of this date since it was built more for comfort than protection. Generally, comfortable buildings at this time became slightly rambling

346

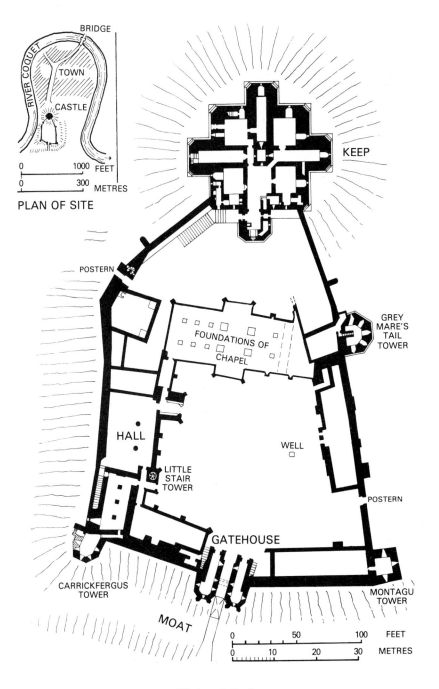

BRIDGE

RIVER COQUET

TOWN

CASTLE

0   1000   FEET

0   300   METRES

KEEP

POSTERN

FOUNDATIONS OF
CHAPEL

GREY
MARE'S
TAIL
TOWER

HALL

WELL

LITTLE
STAIR
TOWER

POSTERN

GATEHOUSE

CARRICKFERGUS
TOWER

MONTAGU
TOWER

MOAT

0   50   100   FEET

0   10   20   30   METRES

Warkworth Castle

347

and asymmetrical. But all the force of formal design makes this plan look in a way very modern. Proportions of spaces are rectangular or square, their organisation in the house is very compact and geometrical. The relationship of room to room is reminiscent of some of Frank Lloyd Wright's house plans.

Warkworth is one of Britain's most splendid castles, partly because of its siting, high on a peninsula in a loop of the Coquet River, where it dominates the town below. Also, its severely cubic form, in honey coloured stone, stands alone, not crowded by overfriendly additions.

Warkworth Castle, The Grey Mare's Tower

(below) Conisbrough Castle

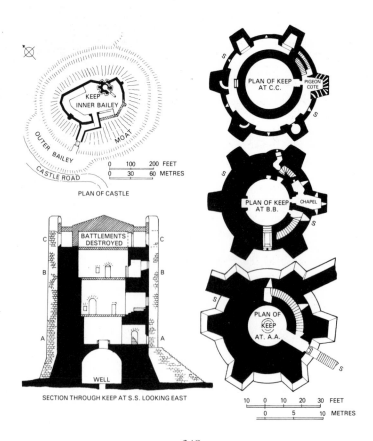

KEEP
INNER BAILEY

OUTER BAILEY

MOAT

CASTLE ROAD

0   100   200 FEET
0   30   60 METRES

PLAN OF CASTLE

BATTLEMENTS DESTROYED

WELL

SECTION THROUGH KEEP AT S.S. LOOKING EAST

PLAN OF KEEP AT C.C.   PIGEON COTE

PLAN OF KEEP AT B.B.   CHAPEL

PLAN OF KEEP AT A.A.

10   0   10   20   30 FEET
0   5   10 METRES

SOUTH YORKSHIRE

Conisbrough Conisbrough Castle
(c.1174–90)
Conisbrough sits on a natural mound, and
consists of a bailey and keep. It is the keep
that provides the castle's main interest, a
round tower supported by six massive buttresses. The lower wall is battered —
inclined — all around the keep, including
these buttresses, and above this stage the
walls rise 15ft thick. There are three levels
to the keep, and on the second accommodation for a chapel is dug out of one of the
buttresses; on the third, stairs, dovecote,
oven and guardrooms occupy all these
positions. In England, the keep is unique,
though similar structures can be found in
France.

Sheffield, South Yorkshire Park Hill
Housing (1958–61)
Of the many attempts to find a new type of
housing pattern to replace the terrace
house, this group is undoubtedly among
the most successful. Whether the terrace
house as a type was really in need of replacing, or whether a refinement of the
type would have been more desirable, are
matters that only received consideration
after a good deal of demolition had taken
place, and a good many tower blocks constructed. This scheme attempts to build a
number of 'streets in the air' — access
galleries of sufficient width to act as meeting and play spaces rather than simply
corridors. To some extent this works in
practice. The scheme is more fully
described in Chapter 5.

Thorpe Salvin Thorpe Salvin Manor
House (c.1570)
Like the Cheshire Cat, only the smile
remains; that is, only the south wall of this
house is standing, but a lovely façade it is.
The shapes that survive — two corner
towers, a rectangular entrance bay and two

Conisbrough Castle

high projecting chimney breast bays —
stand so well without a house behind, that
the ideal would surely be to live in the
gatehouse and look at that useless façade.
Firmness and delight — two out of three is
not bad.

TYNE & WEAR

Newcastle-upon-Tyne (c.1168–1178)
The site of Newcastle was fortified in
Roman times, and was first defended after
the Conquest around 1080. Henry II began
the present keep, using the same mason

Park Hill Housing, Sheffield

Thorpe Salvin Manor

Castle Keep, Newcastle

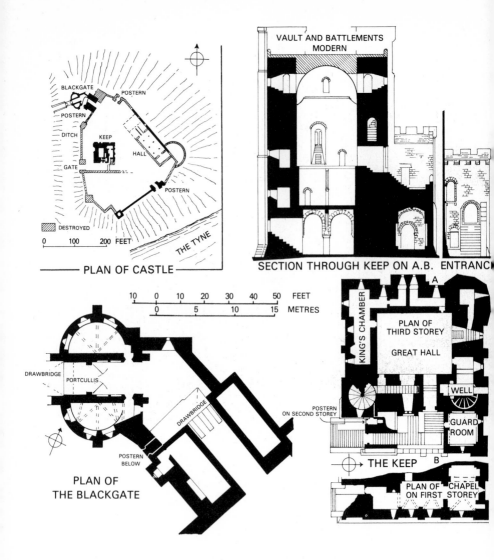

VAULT AND BATTLEMENTS
MODERN

PLAN OF CASTLE

SECTION THROUGH KEEP ON A.B. ENTRANC

BLACKGATE
POSTERN
POSTERN
DITCH
KEEP
HALL
GATE
POSTERN
DESTROYED
0   100   200 FEET
THE TYNE

10   0   10   20   30   40   50   FEET
0   5   10   15   METRES

DRAWBRIDGE
PORTCULLIS
DRAWBRIDGE
POSTERN
BELOW
PLAN OF
THE BLACKGATE

POSTERN
ON SECOND STOREY

A
KING'S CHAMBER
PLAN OF
THIRD STOREY
GREAT HALL
WELL
GUARD
ROOM
THE KEEP   B
PLAN OF   CHAPEL
ON FIRST   STOREY

Newcastle, plans of the castle

who was later to build Dover for him. Most of the bailey defences have been destroyed. The keep is of sandstone, three storeys tall, and buttressed at corners and on its sides. A chapel on the first storey was accessible originally only from the outside, for use by the garrison in general. The main staircase leads directly to the great hall, from which a staircase leads down to the second level.

The walls are thick, and contain a number of intricate staircase arrangements, chambers and posterns, allowing various escapes and manœuvres to those defending the castle.

Black Gate, built around 1247, was the main entrance to the bailey, and still exists, jutting out like a crooked finger from the bailey walls. It really consisted of two gates, separated by a ditch, which could operate together to defend each other.

352

Central Station, Newcastle

Newcastle-upon-Tyne Central Station
(1846–50)
The great advantage of a railway station as
opposed to a terminus is that it gives, in a
major city anyway, a great length of façade.
Here John Dobson, the architect who col-
laborated with Stephenson on building the
High Level Bridge, made the most of the
possibilities, with a classical design set out
along a series of curved platforms, some of
these over 1,300ft long. The design is
immensely solid; with the light ironwork on
the platforms, it seems even more so. They
liked speed, the Victorians, but didn't confuse railway trains with buildings: they
knew that architecture is heavy and doesn't
move.

Newcastle-upon-Tyne Surtees House
(seventeenth century)
This house in Sandhill is one of a last little
group huddling near the castle hill for protection, whereas the rest of Newcastle has
practically disappeared to make way for a
Bold Vision of the North. The less said
about that the better. Compare the delicate
effect of this façade, which apart from six
classical carved pilasters on each storey, is
wholly of glass, with modern all-glass
buildings. A parallel could be drawn between this and a brick wall, where the
assembly of many small elements is as a
map of the human care and effort that went
into its construction. How will we re-
achieve this?

353

WEST YORKSHIRE

Halifax Piece Hall, The Square (c.1775)
This building deserves a place mainly because it is of a type one doesn't associate with British architecture; I can't think of another example of a large, colonnaded market square. Here, the buildings are of two and three storeys. The purpose of the building was to house a cloth market, individual merchants having rooms in the colonnade sections where they could display their 'pieces' of cloth. Of these, there were over 300. With Covent Garden in London it is one of the few monumental and dignified market buildings. The architect was one Thomas Bradley, of whom little else is known.

Piece Hall, Halifax

Scotland

AYRSHIRE

Maybole Culzean Castle (1772–92)
Before Pugin came along, and gave to
Gothic architecture the same moral back-
bone that had long supported the serious
pursuit of classical architecture, the style
was as much a mine for imaginative exploitation as Renaissance work had been to the
early Elizabethans.

So, in a sense, Robert Adam's work at
Culzean is not accurate or scholarly at all,
but like Vanbrugh's work, depends wholly
on its evocative and emotional force. In
fact, much of the medieval detailing here
was picked up by Adam on his early Italian
tour, and the forms he hangs them on are
fairly classical. But the building was very
influential, and appears to have helped
keep a certain muscularity in Scottish
architecture, which threatened to submit to
an over-refinement of classicism.

DUMFRIES AND GALLOWAY

Caerlaverock Caerlaverock Castle
(c.1280–1300)
Though it is unclear just who built this
castle, Scots or English, it was at different
times held by each. Edward I laid siege and
took it in 1300, but a dozen years later his
constable changed sides and Robert Bruce
took possession. Caerlaverock has been
partly demolished and rebuilt, several

times, and it seems a piece of fortune that it
survives so well today. In plan, it is triangular, a tower at each apex and two at its
entrance corner. In 1634 the castle's owner,
Lord Nithsdale, built himself a three-
storeyed house against the east wall,
employing those pronouncedly triangular
window pediments so common to Scotland. Here they are equilateral triangles
with a flattened upper apex — just as the
castle's plan.

FIFE

Falkland Falkland Palace (c.1540)
Traditional Scottish ties with France, as
well as the marriage of James V to Mary of
Lorraine, provided an obvious route for the
importation of Renaissance design to Scotland. Remodelling work at Falkland Palace
was carried out in the 1540s which shows
the early use of classical elements, and is
interesting, apart from its rather isolated
delicacy, for another reason. That is, that
when styles move from one country to
another, it tends at first to be because of
some individual's importation of compatriot craftsmen — in this case Mary of Lorraine's. These craftsmen build only details,
and it seems to take a later, perhaps more
detached, generation to consider the
theoretical aspects of a style, rather than its
incidental detail, and use it to produce
whole buildings.

Culzean Castle

Caerlaverock Castle

Falkland Palace

St Andrews Castle

St Andrews St Andrews Castle
(c. 1200–1600)

Most of what is visible today at St Andrews is the product of two building phases. The first, of about 1390, saw the construction of a gatehouse and screen wall on much the same lines as the work at Tantallon, and for very much the same reasons. The natural defences, while not equally good here, are of the same type. During the second building phase, around 1570, the gateway was blocked up, the building remodelled, and a new entrance made through the screen wall.

The most interesting feature of St Andrews is its surviving mine and countermine tunnels. In a siege of 1546–7, when Protestants were defending the castle against Catholics under Mary of Guise, a mine was begun by the besiegers. This was discovered by those defending the castle, who sank their countermine and success-

St Andrews, mine and countermine

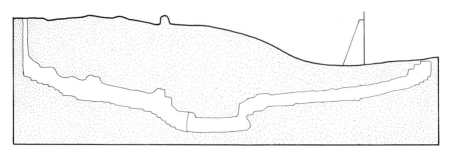

fully interrupted the offending shaft. The castle did eventually fall, one result being that a certain John Knox, who had been inside it, spent two years chained to the oar of a French warship.

St Andrews St Andrews University Residence (1964–9)
This residence was planned as the first of four, but for some reason the other three blocks are unbuilt, and this one unit remains, rather isolated. Several of the visual tricks used here, such as casting each separate room at a slight angle, giving a saw-tooth profile, come from the post-revolutionary work of the Russian Constructivists, like Melnikov. The nautical imagery so beloved of the building's architect is evident here, with access to the rooms being off a large deck-like corridor, complete with porthole windows. The use to which such devices are put is to make the block stand alone, an independent object in the landscape like a ship at sea, and to give each room of the residence more visual importance than a simple flat row of windows would. I imagine the problems of detailing all those corners and angles so that they don't leak must have caused headaches. This must certainly count among Stirling's best buildings.

HIGHLAND

Ardersier Fort George (c.1745–63)
Col William Skinner, Chief Engineer of North Britain, was the designer of this fortress, though his efforts were never put to the test. Perhaps that is just as well, considering that the earlier fort of Augustus was defeated by a single shot in 1746. Fort George was built to house a garrison of some 2,000 men following the 'forty-five, and its main defences are against artillery attack. With its heavy walls towards the Moray Firth, and deep angular ditching to

landward, the plan covers about 16 acres. The way it has all been made to work, with the prosaic language of domestic Georgian architecture, is a strange achievement. It is a pure, and very peaceful architecture. One can imagine the Hanoverians just itching to make the whole of London look like this.

Borthwick Borthwick Castle (1430–2)
There are few buildings as impressive architecturally as Borthwick. Its curtain wall is wedge-shaped in plan, and within it stands the tower, a U-shaped plan, that rises to a height of 100ft. This tower is built as a house, each floor having a main room served by two smaller ones in the projecting wings. But with walls that vary between 10–14ft thick, it is clearly a house to be defended. Unfortunately, its only military action was brief and unsuccessful. While holding out for the Royalists in 1650, the castle was bombarded by Cromwell, and yielded after the first volley had carried away a good chunk of walling. This damage can still be seen today.

Edinburgh Greyfriars Church (1612–20)
The most interesting post-Reformation church in Scotland, from the point of planning for the new services, was built in 1592 at Burntisland in Fife. That church has a square plan, pyramidal roof and central tower. The church of Greyfriars was Edinburgh's first reformed church, and in its plan remained a traditional nave and aisles building. But although many of its features are traditional, the composition of the façade seems worth special mention. The great ogee curves which form the aisle parapets are the reverse of normal practice, swelling up first and then in as they reach the nave roof. But here they meet two heavy buttresses, which one is convinced in this case are structural but nonetheless seem strongly mannerist. Not on those buttresses but behind, on the wall, is set a thin pediment, punctured by a circular

window and topped by three obelisks. Though all these elements are more or less standard of their time, I can't recall another building which uses them to make such a vivid architecture.

Edinburgh Holyroodhouse (1670s)

At the Restoration, the Palace of Holyroodhouse was rather badly in need of reconstruction. The Surveyor General at the time was William Bruce, and he seems to have been the architect most thoroughly acquainted with the pure classicism. His courtyard buildings in Holyrood became a main source of inspiration to later Scottish architects, and have one or two rather special features. First, the windows are of a very large size indeed, which gives the building a light appearance, completely apart from the defensive house tradition with its small openings. Second, the detail is all very flat, for he used pilasters applied to the building's face rather than columns. The product is an architecture which is quite unflamboyant, a kind of plain statement of architecture.

Greyfriars Church

North Berwick Tantallon Castle (fourteenth century)

The remains of Tantallon castle, and its siting on a promontory high above the North Sea, are among the most impressive in Britain. Three of its sides fall sharply away to the sea, while on the fourth a series of wide ditches effectively isolates the buildings. It was built by the Douglas family, who held it against various sieges, including one laid by James V in the early sixteenth century.

The beauty of the building is in the exploitation of its natural defensive position. The human works consist of a single 50ft high wall, some 12ft thick, with a tower at each end and gatehouse in the middle. The other sides of the castle could be left open (though one was in fact built in). The main fortification was the gatehouse, built on principles similar to those in England at the time, which was the main residential part of the castle.

360

Holyrood Palace

(above) Tantallon Castle
(left) Hopetoun House

South Queensferry Hopetoun House (c.1720–60)

The dates given here are for works by William Adam, and subsequently his two sons John and Robert, for the remodelling of a house built by William Bruce around 1700. The plan of these remodellings, with its curved arcades joining the main house to subsidiary pavilions, is clearly based on the work of Vanbrugh, but the elevations seem of another order altogether. While each pavilion has an elegant little lantern — something that Wren might have built — the main house has none of the massive turretry of Vanbrugh's work, nor even a pediment. It is as if they got half way there and gave up, but possibly this is a result of the long building period; too much thought may have eliminated imaginative design.

STRATHCLYDE

Glasgow Lion Chambers, Hope Street (1906)

This building was the last major work of its architect, James Salmon, who had built many strange and wonderful things in Glasgow. Building so far north presents certain practical problems, such as how to get light into deep rooms, that perhaps force architects to experiment with new forms and materials earlier than elsewhere. The north front of Lion Chambers, with its three sets of bay windows carrying glazing over the face of the whole building, is a remarkable piece of logic. The building is of reinforced concrete, and this helps it over another difficulty: conventional walls would have been so thick as to make the rooms legally uninhabitable. These walls though, are of 4in thick reinforced concrete. All this, and a lovely baronial roofscape.

Lion Chambers, Glasgow

Glasgow McGeoch's Building, West
Campbell Street (1905)

J. J. Burnet, the most successful Glasgow
architect of his time, is best known for his
later work, like the Kodak Building in
London; but that was six years in the future
when he put up this large warehouse for
McGeoch's. Here there are signs still of his
French training — the two pedimented
windows impossibly far apart, tied together
with a balcony and creating a piano nobile
of massive size. There does seem to be
more pleasure in geometrical form and
plain material, than in reworking classical

elements. The corner tower, especially at
third-floor level, is a lovely junction of
square and circular forms, and this kind of
interest runs right through the design. It
seems a very sensible way of building up or
composing a façade, as compared with subsequent techniques which treated the
façade equally, at top, bottom, middle or
sides.

Glasgow Moray Place (1859)

Alexander Thomson built Moray Terrace
in 1859, though he probably designed it
somewhat earlier, and in its two-storey
compactness somehow manages to squeeze
more out of classicism than someone like
Nash contrived to in the whole of Regent's
Park.

There is something Egyptian, or of the
Stoa, in this building. It is a simple colonnade atop a podium, running between two
porticos. But the thinness of the decoration
is very severe — you almost need to squint
to see it and the stonework is cut sharp as
knives. There is no compromise of the kind
Nash loved making, in terms of window or
door spacing, and we are left with a glass
box within a stone one.

Glasgow Glasgow School of Art
(1897–1909)

Here is a modernism which springs directly
out of traditional Scottish building,
designed by a man who, despite the efforts
of historians, evades classification and
stands alone as a modern master of architecture. His work hints at Art Nouveau,
associations with Voysey, Scottish castles
and many other influences, but when you
try to pin them down, they slip away.

The north façade presents a series of
broad studio windows and areas of perfectly smooth masonry. This is a very
severe front, which being on the north side
is hardly ever sunlit. The openings are cut

Library, Glasgow School of Art

Claypotts Castle

TAYSIDE

square and unmoulded. But relief from any feeling of oppressiveness is gained by the use of light metal balls and stalks which form a transparent screen in front of the solid masonry. These bits of metal also have a curious use, being designed to aid window cleaners in their task.

The west front, added in 1907, has a quite different character to the north front and is probably the best work Mackintosh ever did. Three great oriel windows rise 65ft above a steep slope, continuing the use of large volumes infilled with small scale units. The effect of lightness is astonishing considering the large masses involved. This effect is reinforced by the strong vertical composition which gives a dramatic upward movement to the narrow façade. Behind this window is the library, one of Mackintosh's most famous interiors. The galleries give it a fine delicacy, with their wooden beams reaching out like hands to grasp their timber supporting columns.

Dundee Claypotts Castle (c.1569–88)
It has been remarked that although the tower-house as a form of dwelling was very common throughout Europe, and perhaps seems exceptional to the English only because of its unique rarity in that country, the surprise in Scotland was its great popularity with the upper classes. But in a country of always precarious political

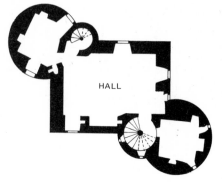

Plan of Claypotts Castle

366

Linlithgow Palace

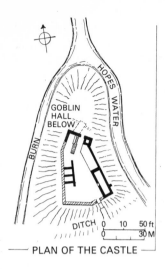

PLAN OF THE CASTLE

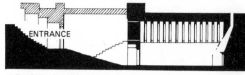

LONGITUDINAL SECTION THROUGH GOBLIN HALL

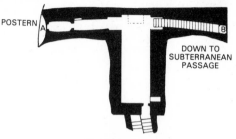

PLAN OF GOBLIN HALL

SECTION THROUGH GOBLIN HALL AT A.B.

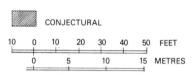

CONJECTURAL

Yester Castle

stability, it obviously became necessary to turn a defensive house into a house that was also magnificent, and eventually this led to seventeenth-century houses like Craigievor and Crathes in Grampian.

Houses like Claypotts were steps on the way, and this house shows a spreading out sideways, with its Z-plan, to provide not only better defensive cover but much better accommodation. Because flat roofs were no longer necessary as fighting platforms, the top level was roofed in to provide more rooms, and the result is a building with an extraordinary amount of space inside it.

LOTHIAN

Linlithgow Linlithgow Palace (1618–21) James V during his reign (1513–42) had rebuilt the castle of Linlithgow very much as a domestic rather than defensive structure. The large windows at low level are one indication of this. But in the early seventeenth century, the North Quarter was remodelled by William Wallace in a way slightly reminiscent of the work Jones did at Kirby Hall in England. Though Wallace rebuilt a whole façade, it is plain masonry except for very heavily pronounced pediments that float above each window. The effect is far more classical than most people give it credit for. There is a general assumption that this naïve phase of classicism was always weak, but the character of this façade is anything but that, with its steeply etched triangular pediments. This pronounced triangularity is characteristic of Scottish classical detail.

Yester Castle (thirteenth century)
The north curtain is Yester Castle's most substantial remains above ground. This wall still stands in some parts to a height of 70ft, cutting off and defending the tip of a high promontory at the junction of two rivers. The castle's most unusual feature is an under-croft, 37ft x 13ft, cut into the rock of this promontory. It is known as the Goblin Hall, and was clearly intended as a refuge or headquarters in time of attack, with its access from the castle keep, its postern gate and its well.

Wales

CLWYD

Flint Flint Castle (1277–86)

The outstanding feature of Flint that still survives is also an unusual one: its Great Tower. It was one of four towers on the corners of a rectangular enclosing wall, but where the other three were joined to the wall, the tower here stands clear of a wall that curves inwards to allow the tower its own moat. Accommodation was not in the centre, which remained a hollow light well and ventilation shaft, but in a circular mural passage. Flint was the first castle built by Edward I in Wales in his campaign of 1277, and its natural defences are good. The tidal waters of the Dee estuary filled the moat, and allowed the castle to be provisioned from the river.

Attached to the castle, but never completed and now obliterated, was a planned town, a favourite hobby horse of Edward's.

DYFED

Kidwelly Kidwelly Castle (c.1270–1320)

Although there was a timber castle here of Norman construction from around 1100, this was apparently burnt by the Welsh in 1215. The present castle was begun in c.1270: the square curtain whose lower walls are still visible, and its four corner towers of which rather more remains. The outer D-shaped wall with its defensive residential gate was put up in the fourteenth century. It was clearly felt that attack from the river would have been unsustain-able as a serious proposition, so that the east wall could be left without this second ring of defence.

Pembroke Pembroke Castle (c.1200–50)

The most ancient part of Pembroke Castle is its imposing great tower, a huge 50ft diameter cylinder standing 80ft tall on the summit of precipitous cliffs. At the highest of its four levels is a stone dome. It is here that Henry VII is said to have been born, and certainly it later was thought of by him

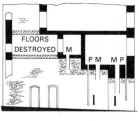

SECTION

FLOORS DESTROYED M

P M   M P

```
0      10      20   FEET
0      3       6    METRES
```

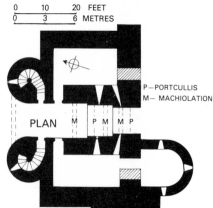

PLAN   M   P M   M P

P – PORTCULLIS
M – MACHIOLATION

The gatehouse, Pembroke Castle

Rubber factory, Bryn Mawr

as his house. Much of the inner bailey curtain has been destroyed, and the gateway to it, but the general state of the castle is impressive.

GWENT

Chepstow Chepstow Castle (eleventh-thirteenth centuries)
Begun as one of the first stone castles in Britain, Chepstow occupies a commanding position next to the river Wye. It was begun by William FitzOsborn, first Earl of Hereford, and the tower he built still stands. William Marshall, Earl of Pembroke, was responsible for the next phase of work during the thirteenth century, consisting of a curtain wall with its circular towers, barbican, and heightening of the great tower. During the Civil War, Chepstow was held briefly for the king, but fell when the curtain was breached near what was later called Marten's Tower. For it was in this tower that Henry Marten, one of those held responsible for the execution of Charles I, was imprisoned for twenty years following the Restoration.

Skenfrith Skenfrith Castle (c.1220–40)
The keep at Skenfrith is a round tower, built on an eleventh-century artificial mound of rubble and sand in c. 1220–40, a rather early example of the circular plan keep. Its quadrilateral bailey is enclosed by a stout wall, in turn protected by round towers at each corner, though one of these has been destroyed, along with gateway.

While the River Monnow gave water defence to the north-east wall, a moat surrounded the other three.

GWYNEDD

Caernarvon Caernarvon Castle (1283–93, 1296–1323)
With Conwy, Caernarvon is the best-preserved fortified town in Britain, and the most complete. Somerset Fry compares it with the striped wall built by Theodosius II in the fifth century to guard Constantinople. Edward I picked up so many ideas from his crusades that this seems entirely likely, and shows that castles were built for aesthetic as well as military power. This castle was immensely expensive, but remained unfinished despite the efforts of hundreds of conscripted labourers who unwillingly went to work on the project. In effect, the castle acted as the 'keep' of a fortified town, built by Edward at the same time, for that king was a great one for planning towns (cf. Flint, Kingston-upon-Hull). The castle is clearly a weapon of attack as well as of defence, and seems to sit by the water's edge like a ship at harbour. It gives a definite sensation that not only is it not to be attacked, but that if not treated carefully it will move on to the offensive itself.

POWYS

Brynmawr Rubber Factory (c.1950)
Like the Boots Factory in Nottingham, this is a purely industrial building whose programme has been abstracted and turned

371

into architecture. The brief was not for a building which could be extended, but one within which changes could be made according to different production demands. The architects (Architects' Co-Partnership) managed to use the requirements for a high level of natural lighting to play rather pretty architectural games on the roof, with the concrete domes punctured by skylights, their spandrels glazed. When outside this discipline, the same architects become very mannered, as at their St Paul's Choir School in London.

Everywhere GPO Telephone Kiosk (from 1926)

There are more little kiosk buildings about than most of us notice, from the mysterious Temple of Gas, shown in Chapter 8, to the red and white striped shelters erected by GPO repair men while they work on the infinity of wires below the streets. The telephone call box is one of the most enjoyable. It exists only to put one in touch with other places, not really for its own sake. It acts like a railway station, airport, or even temple: the physical end of a service network. Service and kiosk are of course mutually dependant, neither being of any use without the other. As Flan O'Brien said, 'The gift of flight without the sister-art of land-ing, that is always in doubt . . .'. So we have these delightful and slightly mysterious containers (and Doctor Who has only reinforced the mystery) dotted about the countryside, each connected to all the rest. Doctor Who is not far off the mark: it must be considered as some kind of transportation, that can take you right across the world, if you are quick with your shillings.

The designs in production until recently were made by Giles Gilbert Scott, and appear to be based on a design by Sir John Soane for a tomb in Chiswick Churchyard. Certainly the slightly domed roof is a Soane device, and the reference to disembodied communication would not be inappropriate.

Further Reading

One introduction to a subject is all anyone needs; since this book serves that function, this bibliography contains books of more particular interest and detailed study.

Of writers of history, the most intelligent and informative is still Sir John Summerson, among whose works are *Georgian London* (Penguin, 1962), *Heavenly Mansions* (a collection of essays) (Penguin, 1970), and *Architecture in Britain 1530–1830* (Penguin, 1970). A good technical history is C. F. Innocent's *Development of English Building Construction* (David & Charles, 1971), which concerns itself with traditional methods of building, but also provides an insight into the nature of all building processes. Other histories, relating to specific periods, are J. Alfred Gotch, *Early Renaissance Architecture in England,* and *Architecture of the Renaissance in England* (Batsford, 1894); Christopher Hussey's beautifully illustrated series *The English Country House,* Early, Mid-, and Late Georgian (Country Life, 1955, 1956, 1958); Mark Girouard, *Life in the English Country House* (Yale, 1978), and *The Victorian Country House* (Yale, 1979); Rudolf Wittkower's *Palladio and English Palladianism* (Thames and Hudson, 1974); Dyos & Wolffs' *The Victorian City, Images and Realities* (RKP, 1973); and finally Henry-Russell Hitchcock's *Architecture in the 19th and 20th Centuries* (Penguin, 1971), which covers architecture throughout the world. For the development of social architecture in the last century, there is Peter Davey's *Arts and Crafts Architecture: A Search for Earthly Paradise.* Two books of a slightly different character, and two of my favourites, are Hugh Phillips' *Mid-Georgian London* (Collins, 1964) and Leigh Hunt's *The Town* (OUP, 1848). Each is full of anecdote and expresses a richness of city life extending well beyond traditional notions of architecture. This is also true of Frances Yates's books, *Theatre of the World* (RKP, 1969) and *The Art of Memory* (Penguin, 1970).

For those who want more information about particular architects, there are fine books on Wren, Vanbrugh and Hawksmoor by Kerry Downs; Arthur Bolton wrote well illustrated books about the Adam brothers and about John Soane; Sir John Summerson felt sufficiently inspired to have written two books on John Nash; the lives and works of Capability Brown,

Soane, George Dance, Humphrey Repton, and Henry Holland have been written by Dorothy Stroud; those of Thomas Hope and C. R. Cockerell by David Watkin. Hermione Hobhouse gives a wonderful account of the Victorian building world in her biography, *Thomas Cubitt, Master Builder* (Macmillan, 1971). Philip Webb's life was written by his pupil William Lethaby; that of Richard Norman Shaw by Andrew Saint and of William Butterfield by Paul Thompson. Edwin Lutyens' strange career has recently been recorded by his grand-daughter, Mary Lutyens. The work of Charles Rennie Mackintosh has been covered by Thomas Howarth, and that of his English contemporary C. F. A. Voysey by D. Gebhard.

Acknowledgements

I owe a special debt of thanks to Derek Weber, without whose confidence the book would not have been written at all. Toby Buchan was more than generous with his expert practical advice in the early stages, and equally, Barbara Wace has given me not only the benefit of professional advice to a beginner, but constant support throughout the project. Carolyn Sansbury was patient in listening, and often brought the discussions back from remoteness to intelligibility. Many of the ideas in this book have been discussed with James Gowan, who also read two or three chapters in manuscript and gave comments that were frank enough to be useful, but always encouraging. John Outram too gave a good deal of help to unformed ideas.

Several people read parts of the book in manuscript, not an enviable or an easy task, and provided help in other ways. My thanks to Bianca Bottero, Gillian Darley, Andrew and Maria Garnett, Laura Grandini, and Tony and Margaret Richardson. Anthony Lambert has given a great deal of help, and I thank him for bearing with me.

I would like to thank the following publishers for permission to use the material mentioned: Basil Blackwell, Philosophical Investigations by Ludwig Wittgenstein; Faber & Faber, Autumn Journal II from The Collected Poems of Louis MacNeice; Methuen London, Character and Comedy by E. V. Lucas; Oxford University Press, The King's English (3rd edition, 1931) by H. W. & F. G. Fowler; and Thames & Hudson, Dialogues With Marcel Duchamp.

Photographs are my own, except the following: Glasgow School of Art, which belong to that institution, and other Scottish photographs, which are by the Scottish Tourist Board. The Boots Company provided photographs of their Nottingham factory.

Index

Page numbers in italics refer to illustrations; those in bold type to gazetteer entries

378

383